Zdenek, Jessica

Detoxing God

ISBN-13: 978-1541001695

ISBN-10: 1541001699

1. Memoir 2. American Christianity 3. Childhood Sexual Abuse
4. Women's Spirituality 5. Native American History 6. Conspiracy

Copyright ©2017 by Jessica Zdenek
All rights reserved

All quotes used with the intention of sharing humanity's collective wisdom with the common good in the author's understanding of "fair use" and our unalienable rights to life, liberty and the pursuit of happiness.

TARALOMA Earth Temple Publications
Moorhead, MN

Photos: Cover by Grant Swenson © 2016
Author Photo by Anna Marie Photography © 2014

For our collective healing

AUTHOR'S NOTE

I have done my best to recreate these pivotal experiences in my life with the inspiration of the dear muses who grace me. I am not attempting to retell the historical past in linear time. I am re-imagining it and making an artistic expression of it based on years of reflecting on major themes in my life (which I also did in therapy for 10 years) in order to heal and grow. In re-writing my story, I am also creating alternative timelines and opening up future probable realities that I might not repeat the same mistakes of my past, but truly shake off the chains that have bound me. This book is based on real people and real events. In this work, I give voice to my intuition, symbols, and dreams as an offering and honoring of my divine feminine nature.

Memories are strange in that we often remember the same event much differently, sometimes less historically and more archetypally in line with our own personal and collective psychology. I am not offering a telling of "The Truth" but simply *my truth* with the hope that my words may carry the resonance of a much larger truth that is emerging in our collective consciousness. There are, of course, many ways to the center of things and my path is just one of millions of spokes in the grand cosmic wheel to which we all belong. If I have any keys or healing codes that are helpful to you, please take and drink deep. If this is not your field to tend and mend, then kindly find your own way home. (That's *fuck off* in Minnesota Nice.)

For the sake of the narrative, I have combined some events, characters, and reimagined the details of conversations and situations to capture the tone and feel of my memories, creative re-interpretations, and re-expressions of the past in an artistic way. This is a therapeutic key that I am using to open doors for healing. Many important people and events I have left out of this telling in order to condense the major arching narrative themes into a storybook form. I have also changed various names and descriptions in order to protect the privacy of others. I would ask the reader to keep in mind that I stepped back into the voice of my teenage self when I wrote of my early family life and her perspective leaves out many others, as teens typically do in the work of making a self to survive in the world.

Though I do not go into it much in this book, I want to add this filter to the big picture: it is possible that my family—along with others in the general population—have been exposed to various types of military technology that does not serve our greatest good. My father did top secret work in the Air Force and as a mystical intuitive girl growing up I could see into some of the darkness behind the veils of authority around me. Often there was too much suffering from my own trauma to make sense of it all until much later in life. From what I have seen, this technology is designed to bring out our baser natures and keep us from expanding our consciousness. However, the power of human choice is everything and it will be the reclaiming of our sovereignty and dignity that leads to our inevitable freedom.

Ultimately this is a story about me, my experience, my perception and my journey of healing. It is my hope that my story will serve as a girl guide for others who've had to navigate their way through similarly gnarly stuff. This book is also intended for those souls who have faced the challenge of detangling themselves from fundamentalist and evangelical Christianity when it threatened their inner most dignity.

At times the reader may feel this achy kid reaching out through the pages for love. But you do not have to love her. Only I do. This book is about my search for eternal love. I know it lives in each of us; it's been so easy to fall in love with the light in others. Falling in love with myself has been the challenge and the spiritual work I write of in this book.

I do not intend to speak on behalf of the Native Americans. They have many greater story tellers than I. As I heard their stories growing up, it helped me find healing and hope for my own. I feel akin to them in some deep way that I cannot explain. I know how much work I have done, and continue to do every day to heal the trauma of my past which comes from a place of white privilege. I imagine multiplying that through many generations and I can't even conceive of the collective trauma that the Native American's have experienced. What's even more astonishing to me, as a witness at Standing Rock, is this people's continued devotion to relatives, to the land, and to love for all of creation. And I desperately long to be a part of a community like that for I see how a stone that the builders rejected can indeed become the cornerstone of a renewed creation. I am acting as a bridge and a priestess on behalf of my ancestors, weaving together things once seen as opposite and evil; now we can see our cultural polarizations as the other side of human wounds that need mending now. I trust we all have a vital piece of the cosmic puzzle. Let us make the sacred connections.

I ask the reader for grace (especially those super detailed-oriented ones) as you hold the first edition of my self-published memoir which is sure to have a few more frisky typos. I decided to self-publish after a few interested publishing houses expressed concern over my passionate spirituality and there was just no way I could tone it down. I realized I would have to own and birth my story; this was my baby. This is a very human work of art, and by the grace of the muses, may it still serve as a doorway to the divine realms.

This book would not have seen the light of day without someone caring to see the light in me when I could not see it in myself. I wish for all beings to experience this wondrous presence that seeks out the lost and loves us back together.

Jessica Jean Zdenek
April 9, Palm Sunday, 2017
Moorhead, Minnesota

DETOXING GOD

Contents

Transcendence

Part I
The Tree of Knowledge of Good and Evil

Whore
Daughter
Puella Aeterna

Part II
The Tree Cut Down

New Girl
Cheerleader
High Priestess

Part III
The Tree of Life

Padawan
Virgin
Mother

Part IV
Healing Leaves

Incarnation
Afterward
Post Script
Gratitude
End Notes
Select Bibliography

In the beginning darkness covers everything.
Not light, but sound first breaks the void—Shhh. Leave it alone.

There is a voice of one crying in the wilderness,
"Prepare the way of the Lord!"
If all are silent rocks will cry,
"Prepare the way of the Lord!"

Rocks that sit at the edge of the cliff,
Rocks that kiss the great abyss,
"Prepare the way of the Lord!"
Rocks that live in the pit of my stomach?
Be Quiet. Leave it alone.

Silent night, holy night,
The little Lord Jesus no crying he makes.
Silent night?
Yeah right.
No crying?
That baby's dying!
Shut up and leave it alone!

In the beginning darkness covers everything.
Until I speak,
And then—

There is light.

> *Our lives begin to end the day we become silent about things that matter.*
>
> -Martin Luther King, Jr.

Transcendence

When I am five, my mother puts her hands on each of my shoulders, her face inches from mine.

"Jessica, Jessica! Jesus is coming back soon! Do you understand me? Jesus is coming back very soon!" Maybe that wasn't my mother. That thought occurs to me now as I recall how my mother swore this never happened. So now I wonder—was it an angel that looked like my mother? My mother looks just like an angel, so it would be difficult to tell.

Tears fall from this beautiful woman's large eyes which look like two blue planets. She seems as if she has been crying for a long time, maybe eons. Maybe she is me at 40 (but she looks 29!) I too have been crying for a long time. Maybe I am the angel that visited myself that day to give that little girl the hope that she needed to get through all those desperate years.

It's odd how time has shifted my perception in this memory; I am outside of my body looking down upon myself. A lot of my early memories are this way, like I am floating around in the air, in a sort of liminal space or in a dream. My dreams are so vivid; sometimes I mistake them for reality. Maybe I'm still deciding whether or not to incarnate my own skin. Maybe I have heard these stories or cut and glued them together from the dangling confusion of my childhood. Maybe they have been inserted by other intelligences. Maybe I have had MKUltra trauma inducing experiments enacted on me as a child and I flew to other dimensions of the cosmos to compensate for the pain. How do we know what we know? I feel this is most true: if we doubt the worth of our souls, then we know only illusions.

"Okay mommy," I say, willing to do anything to make her pain go away. But her hands weigh on me. They are so heavy. Even when she lifts them, I feel her pushing me down into the earth.

Pat Robertson's face is so big on the television. He talks about the end of the world, of sinners that make God want to destroy the earth by fire. He says the Devil is using feminists and AIDS to ruin our world and that Halloween is a satanic holiday. My mother bans us from dressing up and going trick or treating for most of my childhood. No masks. No costumes. No fun. Thanks, Pat. (Years later I happened to meet his daughter and granddaughter and I told them my sad tale. They admitted they didn't listen to him and they celebrated Halloween anyways.)

Pat Robertson's voice echoes in our home like an Illuminati mind control script. Images of flames and scary faces haunt our living room. His fear and hatred are palpable. I'm not sure he knows the same God who talks to me, the God I feel is so lovingly gentle. As early as I can remember, I watch the sky wondering if the world is about to end, wondering if the angel was right. I watch the sky looking for light and Jesus' white robes. I think if Jesus comes again, at long last the suffering will be over, and that sounded like a good thing to me, not the scary nightmare that Pat always talked about.

~

"That guy is a nut job and I don't want to be associated with him!"

"This is just what I remember, Mom. These are my first memories. Besides everyone watched him in the 80s right? I mean, he ran for president."

"But we grew out of all that! It was hardly a part of our life at all. Why do you have to write about this? It embarrasses me."

~

I don't want to embarrass my mother. I don't want to embarrass anyone. I want us to find healing. I want us to wake up. I want humanity to ascend. I want to teach my children how to live in peace. I want to heal the traumas done to our innocence so that we will be a wise people who do not so easily give away our power to those who do not have all beings' highest good in mind or at heart. I want to warn people to be wise because there are many wolves in sheep clothing (and some sheep in wolves' clothing). I want to create a world where even the wolves and the demons can come out of the closet because they are turning towards the light for healing and reconciliation now, in this lifetime. I want to live in a world where the wild truth runs deeper into freedom and joy, where the blame game finally ends, where all beings are treated with dignity and respect, where cooperation and care and commitment to one another and the sacred balance returns Earth to Eden. It sounds Pollyanna. Stupid hippy shit. I know. I recall one time my father, told me world peace was joke and I was an idiot to even think it was possible—we had bad guys out in the world that needed to be killed. I never understood how he held that belief in tension with Jesus' teachings on loving your enemies.

I know my vision offends the status quo. That's sort of my mission. May my word dissolve blockages in the sacred hologram and may the sound of my voice cause the desert to bloom.

~

Many who have suffered childhood sexual abuse struggle between keeping silent and speaking themselves into their own rightful being. History's harsh flames flicker in all of our eyes and many of us feel the grave risk of physical, emotional or social death when we stand in the unconscious gaze of the crowd or stare into the bloodthirsty mouths of our jailers. We have all witnessed the annals of persecutions. We have all seen the changing masks of authority and glimpsed the vacant drivers behind them. We have all felt the insecure attempts to please at all costs in order to survive, to deny the self that is hidden behind seamless uniforms and costumes of power. We have all witnessed those who work tirelessly to rid themselves of their unwanted shadows that they have refused to behold or love. I am directing all of these shadows back to the light now. Sometimes a simple compassionate witness is all that is needed to change the world.

Before I say more, let me make one thing clear: this telling is for healing. It is for love.

~

God visits me, not in the light, but in the shadows of an old movie theater in upstate Rome, New York where our church meets for worship on Sunday mornings. I have my stuffed animals with me and some crayons. My mother plays praise music on the wooden piano that moves on wheels across the stage where she sings. Sometimes my father plays guitar with her. I watch people fall down on the ground when the preacher lays his hands on their heads. I remember them laying the spirit-filled people up and down the narrow movie aisles. I watch their bodies twitch and shake like dying carp.

~

"People never fell down," my mother says. But I saw them gathered around the foot of the stage. Passed out on the floor. Was it a special prayer meeting? Were we at some Kenneth Copeland convention? Somewhere else? I don't understand why my memories are so taboo. I thought we shared the same history, but talking with my mother makes me feel like I know nothing about my own experience. Maybe I am not supposed to know. Maybe I am forbidden to eat the fruit from this tree of knowledge. Maybe someone inserted these memories into my brain or deleted some of hers. My mother confessed to me one of the most terrifying moments of her young life: she awoke one night to a grey alien being standing by her bed and she never slept in her basement again.

Maybe my mother is not ready to reconcile these parts of our life. But I cannot remain unconscious simply because my knowing frightens her or anyone else. We may fear to grow, fear to fail, fear to have our perfect pictures of reality fall apart. But the breaking of the bread is what heals us, just as the seed must crack and open to the life within and the old wine skins must be replaced with new ones. It is scary, but that also makes it fun. The soul yearns to adventure, to flow with creation as it weaves the sacred web of life.

~

I remember people speaking in tongues at our church. They raise up their hands and sing in their prayer languages. When they do this, I feel the room grow warm; I hear music circling around my head. One day, it gets so hot I think I might pass out. I open my thirsty mouth and suddenly I begin to speak like everyone else. My heart contains a secret water fountain. An ocean of joy bubbles up within me. I lift up my hands, I throw back my head, and I sing words in a language I don't understand.

I think I finally understand the meaning of life, a mystery I have been trying to unravel in the lonely corners of my bedroom, through the smoke and beer bottles of our tiny apartment, in the furrowed brows of my parents' long faces. I know all there is to know: God is love and I belong to him. (I was told God was a him, so I ran with that for a while). After that, at home I would sneak off to my bedroom and make the room dark like it was at church. I would turn on the vacuum cleaner to cover up my singing to God.

> *O Lord, You have seduced me, and I am seduced.*
> -Jeremiah 20:7a

My best friend, Rachel is more spiritual than I am. When I knock on her door, her mother opens it very slowly and looks at me with half open eyes.

"We are praying right now," she says in a whisper. "Rachel cannot play." The house is completely dark behind her. The black air is thick and heavy. I am always afraid to knock on her door. When Rachel can play we round up the neighborhood kids. We hide behind the shed in her backyard. She leads us all in prayer. We ask Jesus to come into the hearts of our all our friends.

~

I am taken out of public schools soon after I start kindergarten. I think it's because I watched a film about apes changing into people. My mother says my kindergarten teacher was horrible. For some reason I am enrolled in a strict fundamentalist Baptist school where I spend the rest of kindergarten through second grade sitting in a mini cubical so I can't see any of the other children and they can't see me. Recess is granted to those who memorize an entire Psalm—each week.

The name of the private school is *Maranatha!* —a word found in Corinthians, which is neither Greek nor Hebrew, but a transliteration of an Aramaic phrase that means, "our Lord has come" or "our Lord is coming!" or "our Lord, come!" When I grow up I come to love how the various meanings and interpretations give space to a religion that used to fit like a tight itchy hand-me-down dress.

At *Maranatha!* I learn that if a girl wears a skirt above her knee or cuts her hair too short, the principal spanks her with a giant steel paddle. I don't want to get spanked at school. I pull at my skirt and cry in the bathroom. My legs are so long, all of my skirts are just above my knee. I am spanked enough at home. I am two the first time it happens. I am twelve the last. I remember my mother taking my diaper off. I remember the wooden spoons cracking in two. I remember other parents showing off their paddles inscribed with Bible verses. Religion and violence, it seemed, went together. I didn't understand that either. I still struggle with making healthy boundaries—I don't want to use the practice of violence to instill them because I know how much it crushed me. And this felt out of alignment with Jesus' message: love your enemies and pray for those who hurt you.

At school I sing about onward Christian soldiers marching on to God's holy war—which is surely coming soon as tensions rise between the true Republican Christians and the evil Democratic Party, gays, feminists, and environmentalists. I am taught to fear those who are different, those who are dangerous because of the ways they practice love, as if love and violence must go together, as if this masochistic self-hatred is a requirement for salvation. But the people I truly fear are the ones upon whom I must depend.

~

A very short yellow school bus comes to my house on Griffith Air Force Base before the sun's light shines in the early morning darkness. I am one of the youngest passengers and the only one who is dropped off at *Maranatha!* I always sit in the front seat by Kenny, a disabled boy no older than twelve. Kenny has little control over his body, including his saliva. I'm not sure what kind of disability he has, but I sit by him because I don't want him to be alone. Lost in his thoughts, his eyes fill with watery dreams he can only utter in deep moans. He is like me, we are each strange in our own way.

My first crush is on one of the high school boys who sits in the back of the bus. He is the only boy who doesn't tease me. One day I make a bold move that I have been plotting for months. I walk right past Kenny and all the way to the back of the bus and sit down next to my crush. The kids erupt in laughter.

"Why don't you go back and sit with your boyfriend Kenny?"

"Oh, you have a new lover boy?"

I just keep staring up at his gorgeous face. He'll protect me, I think. He shakes a nervous leg up and down. Finally he looks at me.

"What's on your shirt?" he asks.

"Jesus is the Answer," I say.

"Oh, you believe in God?"

"Yes?" I say, not fully understanding the question.

"I don't," he snorts.

"What?!" I think I scream. "How can you not believe in God? God is everywhere! God is in the wind and the trees and all around us!" I hear the laughter again. I keep my eyes on my crush. I put my hand inside of his. I watch the corner of his lips curl into a smile. He shakes his hand free from mine and ignores me the rest of the ride. Stewing in public humiliation I decide here and now that I am going to discover everything that lies beyond the realm of God so that I can find love in this world. This is in kindergarten.

The next time I ride the bus, and every time after that, I sit by Kenny. I yearn for holy things and I think surely this heat is holy, the one that makes my heart throb and long for something beyond myself and simultaneously within. I spend the early morning hours draped over the corner of my bed, face flushed, ears red. I have no words, only deep moans and sighs and watery dreams, like the ones I find in Kenny's eyes.

~

My mother sits very still in our old brown La-Z-Boy rocking chair looking up at the ceiling. She's wearing her bathrobe in the middle of the afternoon. Her skin is covered in Calamine lotion and she gazes at me through swollen eyes.

My father is sitting next to me on the funky 1970s couch which is orange with purple paisleys. He is talking to me, but I don't understand any of the words he is saying. I keep looking at my mother anointed in Calamine lotion, I look out the window behind her, and the warm sunlight, and the open field, and the creek that runs through our backyard, which is apparently filled with poison oak. I see my mother in her big cozy chair, big as a throne, she as an icon, a warning, of how clearly dangerous is the natural world.

My father's face is dark. This is the most serious conversation we have ever had. Ok, it's a one way conversation. He rarely lets me reply. I learn early how to smile and nod and hope this will be over soon. I keep looking to my mother for help, but I can't seem to reach her inside of that pink paste. My father is really smart. He's a scientist. A weatherman. He uses big words I don't understand. I do know that he and my mother are very upset that I watched the movie *Purple Rain* at my friend's birthday party last night. It's like they caught me with all those strange feelings I had when I draped over my bed, when Prince sang, when he took off that lady's shirt and when he kissed her. I get the message: these feelings are bad. Real bad. Shut them down.

~

"Did your parents tell you how babies are born?" My friend Angela was at the party too. She and I push the handle bars of our bikes up the side of her street and take a breather as we recover from the last hill. I watch the wind blow the ribbons on her bike and in her hair.

"No," I reply.

"My parents told me babies come from sex!"

I stop in the street and look up at the bright blue sky and think, "So that's what my father was trying to warn me about!" Angela leaves her mouth hanging open, her eyes fill with wonder. But I remember my parents' rigid faces and I can't make my face look like Angela's. I want to, but I am so afraid that if I do I will end up in big trouble.

~

"Oh my God! David, we hit the dog!" My mother screams. My father is still slowing down when I open my car door and race to the side of the road.

"Jessica, no!" I hear them behind me, but only in a dream-like way. I am drawn to the dog, compelled by its pain. The shoulder of the road slopes down a little hill and into a ditch. I follow the trail of blood until I am face to face with a black lab's angry teeth.

"Oh you poor puppy!" I reach out my hand to the dog. He hoists himself towards me using his two front legs. His back legs are limp and dripping with blood. I sprint towards the car and jump in the back seat. The dog leaps in after me. My brother, sister and I pile on top of each other trying to get out the other door, but we can't get it to open. The dog bites down on my ankle and begins to gnaw. Everything turns slow motion. I can't understand why the dog is attacking me. I love animals so much. They always like me. I just wanted to help. My father grabs a pillow and pushes it on top of the dog wrestling him to the floor from the front seat. My mother runs out of the car, opens our door and the three of us fall into the road.

"I told Tim, they're gonna hit that dog," says Aunt Lisa in her practical matter of fact tone. She grew on a farm and saw animals die and so for her, death was just something normal that happens. For me I couldn't seem to close my heart to the dog's suffering, and it hurt more than I could bear. Uncle Tim walks towards me, his eyebrows lift to the center of his forehead. He speaks calmly, like his father,

"Jess, are you okay?"

We are caravanning to St. James Lutheran Church, to his ordination service tomorrow. Uncle Tim is going to become a Lutheran Pastor just like my grandfather, my great grandfather and my great uncle.

My eyes fall to my bloody socks.

"She should go to the clinic," he says.

"What about the dog?" I cry.

~

My arm is sore from the tetanus shot and it hurts to move it in any direction. My body begins to shake with the chills. I learn that they have to put the dog down to see if he has rabies. I fall asleep sobbing into a pillow because I made a dog die today. If only I would have stayed in the car, they could have fixed his broken legs. I awake to the patterns on the wallpaper dancing around me. I am suddenly freezing, but my skin is hot to touch. I stumble downstairs and wake up my mother who proceeds to shove Tylenol in my mouth every four hours.

She says I'm hallucinating and my temperature is near 104. Meanwhile, my brother Peter is nowhere to be found. His bed is strangely empty.

The next thing I remember, I am standing outside of the house in the cold night. My teeth are chattering as my breath makes clouds in front of my face. I hear the sirens. Everyone is out of the house except for my parents and my brother.

If my father looks like Christopher Reeves as Superman, then my mother would definitely be Maria from *The Sound of Music*. I think they can survive anything, but I begin to worry when the firemen run inside.

~

My grandfather stands on a pulpit so high it hurts my neck to look up at him. His adult words are beyond me. But I see goodness in the twinkling of his eyes and the tender smile he can't keep out of the corners of his mouth. I look down and finger the aqua dots printed on my white satin dress. It's my Easter dress and I wear it proudly for all special occasions.

My parents found my brother Peter up in the attic last night, naked, crying, and sitting on a stack of chairs. My mother said it was like Peter was just waiting to go up in flames. They said it was an electrical fire. If I hadn't kept her awake, if I hadn't killed the dog, she might have missed the popping sounds coming from the ceiling in the bathroom that fell like lit cigars onto the carpet below. The fire chief said twenty minutes more and we would have all been dead.

I watch the men in white robes circle my Uncle Tim. They put their hands on him and push him to kneel. I wonder how he will ever be able to stand up again and carry a weight so heavy.

In the days that follow I hear my mother talk a lot about the spiritual forces of darkness. Her version of the story sounds straight out of a Frank Peretti novel with demons strategizing how to keep Uncle Tim from ordination.

"Satan had planned to ruin Tim's ordination, but thankfully God sent his angels to keep me awake and protect his powerful ministry. Could you imagine the guilt Tim would carry his whole life, knowing that family members died because they came to witness his ordination?"

The dog's sacrifice and my mother's sensitivity may have saved us that night. As my mother comes from a heady family of intellectual Lutherans, these mystical experiences make people feel uncomfortable, and maybe that's why my mother doesn't like to think about those days.

Part I
The tree of Knowledge of Good and Evil

I will take you down
Into the darkness
Of your soul
Into my lair
Where you can see
Nothing
But the images in which you dress me
There, I will take off all of our clothes
So you can face yourself
As you truly are
Naked
And afraid
Of your own shadow

What appears to be a catastrophe, over time, becomes a strong foundation from which to live a good life.

-Dr. Rachael Naomi Remen

Whore

Yellow cornstalks line the horizon ready for harvest. In the northeastern corner of Arkansas just beyond the Ozarks, flowers turn outside my bedroom window. The dandelion weeds, the Queen Anne's lace. In August 1989, around the time of Mary's ascension, I receive a call.

"Jessica! It's for you." My mother hands me the phone, "It's Christian."

"I'll take it in my bedroom."

I run down the hall and lock the door. I have just turned fourteen. I am all arms and legs and the tallest girl in my class. My hair is streaked with blonde and my olive skin glows from summer sun. Looking back at old pictures now I see that I was beautiful. But I can't see that for many years. The development of a self requires healthy mirroring. I hate my geeky self and I am desperately plotting how to become cool and gain friends.

"Hey! What's up?" his voice sounds deep and sexy. He's sixteen or seventeen—I can't remember. He's one of the first guys apart from my family to pay me any attention. He makes me believe I am more than a giant nerd. Now I wonder—was he sent for me? Ordered? Mind-controlled?

"Nothing," I giggle. "Just helping Mom unpack another box—my life is so exciting." I'm the new girl in the small town of Blytheville, Arkansas. With the southern accent it is actually pronounced Blah-ville.

You shall not oppress a resident alien; you know the heart and soul of an alien, for you were aliens in the land of Egypt.

- Exodus 23:9

"Tell me again how a beautiful girl like you just shows up in my world one day?"

My heart pounds. He thinks I'm beautiful? What the heck? No one has ever called me beautiful before. Nerd, prude, dork—that's what people call me—not beautiful.

"You know, when you talk about me, it doesn't really sound like me," I say.

"So tell me all about the real you," I can hear him smiling. I wrap the curly mauve telephone cord around my index finger and wonder. Obviously he has figured out how to be popular. Everyone loves Christian. Even my parents. We were entrusted into his care the first day we showed up at the Youth Center on base. He works there. I guess he's like a Youth Leader or something. He has the keys to a world I want to be inside of. The one thing I want in life is to belong—not on the fringes, not in the shadows, but at the center, near the sun and the bright smiles of my peers. I want to be protected from the people who make fun of me. I want to become a whole new person, one that is likable, even lovable. My fantasy is that Christian will take me under his wings and shelter me from any further assaults, train me in the ways of cool. Me, his little Padawan.

"Okay, Christian, but you have to promise not to tell anyone. I mean it, NO ONE."

"Jessie, I will never tell a soul your secret. What you tell me tonight will be our secret. I promise."

He is so good at making me feel comfortable. How can I resist? "Okay," I swallow down the lump in my throat. My hands begin to sweat. Will he still like me when I tell him who I really am?

Here goes. "Christian, I've never been popular."

"What do you mean?" He chuckles, "You're so beautiful. I can't imagine that."

"I used to wear glasses."

"So?"

"No, these huge blue glasses that covered up half my face. I just got contacts last year."

"You think a pair of glasses could hide those big blue eyes from the world? They're so pretty. I love your eyes."

I can't stop the smile from spreading across my face.

"And I wear generic shoes."

"So?"

"From Payless!"

"So what?! You are probably the hottest girl in the world with your big blue glasses and generic shoes!"

"Shut up!" I laugh. "Everyone used to make fun of me."

Christian is silent. The phone keeps sliding through my hand. I press the number pad closer to my cheek and wait for all of eternity to hear his reply. Finally his voice breaks through the void as if he is commanding an answer from the dead.

"Who made fun of you, Jessie?" The question echoes across a black universe of pain.

"Lots of people…my whole life," I whisper, suddenly finding it difficult to talk.

"Oh, Jessie, how could anyone be mean to you?"

"I dunno," I try to hold back the child-like sobs, but the force is too strong and the dam breaks anyway.

"I've just never figured out why I don't fit in! I think it has something to do with my parents' religion!" Snot falls out of my nose and drips off my chin.

"Jessie, shhhhhh, don't cry. Try to calm down, okay? I don't like hearing you so upset when I can't be there to give you a hug. Is your bedroom door closed?"

"Yes."

"Good. You don't want your parents to hear you."

"I know."

"Jessie, you know I care about you, right?"

Relieved, I croak out, "Yeah…"

I can hardly believe it. Suddenly, my soul swells with hope. It's a new feeling. Maybe everything will finally be all right. I will learn the ways of Christian Roberts. He will take care of me. I breathe deeply, into something I have never known, like I have come home to a place that has never been mine.

"Jessie?"

"Yeah?"

"I can help you. Do you believe me?"

"Yes."

"All we have to do is initiate you," says Christian.

"Initiate? What's that?"

"Jessie, do you know what sex is?"

"Yes," I blush. "It's something married people do."

Christian laughs. "Is that what your parents told you?"

"Yes," I say.

"Well, there's your problem! All the popular people have sex together."

"They do?" I say, truly amazed.

"Yes! Even friends have sex with each other. You don't have to be boyfriend and girlfriend or anything—or even in love to do it."

"Really?"

"Yes! Don't you watch TV or read magazines?"

"Yes, well, kind of…"

"Everyone has sex, Jessie, it's what human beings do."

I think of Madonna steaming up the TV with her hot music videos. I think of all the sexy girls spread out on the covers of magazines with their half open eyes and parted glossy lips. Suddenly the veil is torn in two. *Of course they do*, I think. How could I have not seen it before? This must be the key to life. Sex is how you connect with others, make friends, and become popular—which is the real sin—which is why my parents don't want me to know about it! Oh! I feel so silly. All this time everyone has been sneaking off and having sex together and I've had no idea! How naïve I have been!

"Tomorrow," he says. "We initiate you tomorrow."

I remember that mysterious warmth that grows between my legs and rises into my heart exploding like a million butterflies inside of me. This is what I want. All those butterflies in my chest. Someone to hold me and love me. And maybe this is my part in the crime: I am naïve and curious about sex without knowing how dangerous a woman's curiosity is to the establishment. My mouth turns dry. My body begins to tremble. *You'll finally belong*, I tell myself. *It will be okay*. Something inside of me knows otherwise. It groans and twists my stomach. But I can't reach it. Or maybe I don't want to or I don't know how. Maybe I fear it will want to keep me miserable, like I think my parents do. Or maybe my higher self has agreed to undergo this suffering, like Jesus willingly walks towards the cross.

~

For years I turn to boys and men to save me from myself. This is the awful start to it all. Or maybe it isn't the start. Maybe it begins when I am five, when an experience of divine love enchants me and pulls me into another dimension of reality. Or maybe it goes further back, deep into the annals of history, in the dark corners of the human psyche, to a time long, long, ago when woman was broken and her only means of power came by betraying herself and assenting to the patriarchy.

Religions centered on the worship of a male God create "moods" and "motivations" that keep women in a state of psychological dependence on men and male authority, while at the same time legitimating the political and social authority of fathers and sons in the institutions of society.

-Carol P. Christ

"Are you sure you don't want to come with us?"

My aunt Mary Kay, my mother's youngest sister sits on our couch drinking coffee, her white-blonde hair is wet and smells of fresh flowers. She's just ten years older than me and I think she's cool, but hanging with my family is definitely not.

"I would but I've got plans." I am successful at convincing my family that it's more important for me to stay in town and make friends today.

The doorbell rings around 10 a.m. Christian stands in the doorway. The light behind him makes him glow, like he is Jesus, come here to save me. His broad chest fills out his white t-shirt and his cologne snakes through the air and makes my heart pound. I hope my parents don't sniff out our plan. His rust colored hair feathers back, his skin is fair, his teeth are perfectly straight. He shows them off with an easy smile. A black belt wraps around his waist, holding tight his tapered stonewashed jeans.

"Hi," I say as my heart melts like warm butter.

"Well, hi!" He laughs and makes small talk with my parents. I look past him, afraid I might stare too long. I watch the dandelions sway in the grasses behind him. I pluck one from the ground on the way to his car.

"Have a good time!" My mother and father stand on the threshold of home and world and wave goodbye.

Christian puts his hand on my shoulder and directs me to his old black Mustang. I pretend that I am more woman than child. I smile and throw my head back like the beautiful girls on TV. He turns up the radio and Don Henley sings, "This is the End of the Innocence."

We race down Chickasawba, the old road named after an Indian Chief who is remembered for carrying honey across town to sell it. This road connects Blytheville to Gosnell like a golden thread weaving our mutual pain to our illusionary balm. As the cotton and the soy beans sway, we each look to the horizon and dream of the coming kingdom.

"Dammit!" Christian bangs his hand on the steering wheel.

"What's wrong?" I hide my alarm and try to be nice and sweet. That's what boys like.

"I forgot to tell you, I promised to pick up a few of my friends soon. You won't mind if they come and watch will you?"

"Um…" I didn't know what to say, but I start to have an awful pit in my stomach. I press the yellow flower into my arm so it bleeds on my skin.

"Actually, in any sort of initiation there has to be witnesses," he adds.

"But I thought it was just going to be me and you."

"Jessie, you want to be popular, don't you?"

"Yes, but—"

"So, you won't mind if my friends join us will you?" His tone grows cold and forceful. I know how to fight with my parents. I have no idea how to fight with someone older and cooler than me.

I look at the yellow streaks on my arm and try to ignore my feelings. I am so close to the dream I have always wanted. I know it won't come easy. I know there are sacrifices involved in life. Christianity has taught me that much.

~

According to one account of history, when the drought came, the Native Americans asked De Soto to pray to his God for rain. They admired his shiny armor and his advanced weaponry. They brought two blind men to De Soto and asked him to heal them. De Soto accepted these religious honors and built a fifty foot cross on top of the peoples' holy hill—maybe it was the Chickasawba mound, the one discovered between Gosnell and Blytheville. Maybe the Natives brought the conquistadors atop the hills where they previously slayed the giants. Did the Natives really surrender their power to a stranger they mistook for God? Or did they perhaps pretend as hard as they could while they strategized how to stay alive?

~

"Like who?" I ask finally.

"Like Matt. You've met him before, the skater with the long dark hair."

Yeah, I remember meeting Matt. He did seem pretty cool. And I do have a thing for skaters, especially the ones that have flops—that long hair that covers up one eye—so mysterious. But I just want to be with Christian. I trust him. Maybe initiations aren't for being romantic? Maybe that comes after?

"I guess."

I fall back into the seat and let the familiar haze fill my head. I zone out and follow orders like I'm made to do at home. He turns up the radio, and we listen to "So Alive" by Love and Rockets.

"Look. You can bring a friend too. Do you know someone you'd like to invite?" He sounds nice again. His eyebrows lift.

"Tara." I say. He veers the car around and we return to my street to pick up my neighbor.

I try to act cool and invite her to hang out with some guys and me.

She squeals. She looks in the mirror, fluffs up her brown curly hair and applies some lip gloss.

"This will be a lot more fun that watching soaps with my Mom!"

~

In the distance ahead I see the large barbed-wired fence on the horizon, its metal reflects the last rays of morning sun. Ignited prickly little spears poke into the sky circling the entire base like a crown of thorns. Christian makes the liquid spray all over the windshield. The wipers smear dead bugs all over the glass. We peer at the world through two gray rainbows.

How did I end up here? What am I doing?

I wash the thoughts away.

Christian has impeccable manners.

"Good morning sir," he says to the soldier on duty who guards the base gate. I usually find these guys devilishly handsome. I stare at the gun strapped to his waist while Christian hands him both of our military IDs.

"And one guest," Christian points at Tara, the civilian, in the back seat.

"Off to the Youth Center, Christian?" I am impressed. Who doesn't know Christian? Nobody. This eases my mind. If everyone else trusts him, then I should trust him too.

"You got it, sir." Christian flashes his radiant smile and takes our IDs back into his hand. The soldier salutes us and opens the gate. I listen to the moving metal parts. The high pitched squeaking, the grinding wheels and shaking fences.

Strips of grass with baby trees line the islands between the traffic. Everything is new at Eaker Air Force Base. The buildings, the shrubbery, the concrete, and me. Christian turns left, slows down, and parks his car in the Youth Center lot. The clean brick building still has shiny floors and smells of fresh paint.

"Wait here, okay? Lemme see who's around." He pats the roof of the car like it is supposed to be my head.

"Who's he looking for?" Tara asks.

"The skaters," I say. "Do you like skaters?"

"No," she says. "I like preps."

In a few short minutes Christian returns looking worried.

"What's up?" I say.

"Oh, nothing. I need to go the BX." His hands are shaky and he drops his keys on the ground.

"What for?" I press. The BX is like Target for military folks. It's just down the street.

"Stop asking questions and just go with the plan, okay?"

His snapping comment reminds me of my father. It makes me feel like a little girl. I look back at Tara. Her eyes are wide open and she mouths, "What the hell?" I just roll my eyes back at her like it's no big deal. God, I want him to like me so bad.

He turns the car into the BX parking lot and breathes a sigh of relief when he spots a group of skaters practicing ollies on the curb. I slide down in my seat, wishing it would swallow me whole. Christian rolls down the window.

"Hey you guys!"

He flashes his smile and draws them in like disciples.

"Christian! Hey man, what is up? Who you got in there?" They smack hands and give each other knuckles. Cool dudes acknowledging other cool dudes.

Christian turns to us, "Sit tight, I'll be right back."

He jumps out of the car and slams the door so he can have a private conversation with the skaters. I can only imagine that he is informing them of my desire to be initiated into their club of coolness. I almost throw up all over myself. I told Christian private things I would never tell anyone else. I didn't realize my initiation would involve him divulging my secret insecurities to my peers, in a three-minute conversation in the BX parking lot.

"You okay, Jess?" Tara puts a hand on my shoulder.

"Of course," I lie. She wouldn't understand what I have to do. Her father makes good money. She wears gold necklaces and diamond earrings. She already fits in, more than I ever will.

"Who's the guy with the black flop?"

"That's Matt," I say.

"He's cute," says Tara.

"Yeah." I look out the window and squint. The sun hurts my eyes. I wish we didn't need witnesses. I wish the skaters weren't at the BX. I wish they were nowhere to be found.

Within minutes, the guys pile into the car with us. A strange energy comes with them. They're amped. I don't understand their words. It's filled with a lot of code language and acronyms.

"69, man!"

"No—hand job"

"Hell no. Blow job."

I laugh my fake laugh as best I can and pretend I understand every word they say. One guy reaches out and pinches my nipple.

"Ouch," I say. They laugh. They touch me more. I worry: if I push them away, will they still like me?

"Who's got the condoms?" Christian asks. The guys pull out their wallets and start thumbing through their contents.

"Oh man, I used all mine!"

"Me too," said another.

"The BX sells condoms!"

"Yeah, you go get some," Christian orders.

"Naw, man... you do it. I don't want anyone to see me buying them. My Mom works at the BX."

"I thought you said you always carry condoms?" Christian commands so much power.

"Yeah, but my Dad gives 'em to me, and I'm fresh out. You know, I was hanging with Lana Berry last night!"

"Yeah right!" All the guys laugh and punch him in the arm. I hear she is the prettiest girl at Gosnell High School, and the captain of the cheerleading team.

"Jason, you do it," Christian says to the quiet boy in the back seat.

"I'm only fourteen."

He's my age, I think.

"So! You don't need an ID to buy condoms, dummy!" Christian pulls Jason's hat off of his head and all his blond hair flops in front of his eye. All the guys laugh and wrestle Jason down into the backseat.

"I'll do it," a guy they call Motor says. "I'm 18 and no one will think anything about it."

"Just remember, she's jail bait for you," Christian says. "Sorry, I can't promise you any love today my friend," he teases.

"Do you want the condoms or not?" Motor snaps. He's short, thick and muscular and everyone knows he could mess you up if he wanted to.

"Please?" Christian puts on his irresistible gaze. Motor slams the car door shut.

"Who wants some oral?" Christian turns and winks at me while the guys exchange high fives and whoop and holler. I don't feel the sunshine anymore. I give him a nervous closed-mouthed smile, not knowing what "oral" is. I catch Jason's eyes. He looks just as confused as I feel.

The touching and laughing continues. Tara is stronger than me.

"Get the fuck off me," she says to one guy. "Don't you dare touch me."

Soon Motor is back in the car with the condoms and we drive off.

"Whose parents aren't home right now?" Christian asks.

"I thought you had a plan?" I whisper.

"What honey?" he says. "It sounded like you were talking!" He roars.

"My Mom's off work today," says Matt.

"Yup," said Motor chiming in.

"Well, you know we can't go to my house," says Christian.

I only go to Christian's house once. It's dark and eerie. The windows have thick blankets draping over them, so the light stays out. The house is a dump. Old food is rotting everywhere and his jittery overweight mother gives me the creeps.

Christian has an epiphany, "I know! The high school!"

The car erupts with a round of cheers, like this is the best idea ever. I cannot even begin to understand what he is thinking. We drive off base, turn right at the Sonic and speed down Highway State Road 181 listening to U2 sing, "Desire!"

I sit perfectly still and pretend that I am one of those beautiful models in the magazines with all the guys surrounding her, worshiping her. I don't feel as happy as the models always look. My body is shaking again. *We have to do this.* The thoughts press in on me. *It is the only way. Think how no one has ever wanted to touch you before. They laugh at you. They think you are ugly.*

I have to admit I love this new attention, this ability to attract another human being like a magnet. I both love it and fear it, like a child sitting behind the wheel of a car, wanting to drive so badly without knowing how. The urgency pushes me forward. My secret nerdy identity could be found out at any moment and things could instantly return to the way they were before. I don't want to be an outcast anymore. I have to be initiated so I will belong somewhere, so I will be loved.

~

Dark Sacred Mother, take my hand and the hands of all who dare to descend into the depths of pain, for I know that you behold all of your children with compassion. I know that you have seen all of the suffering that has inflicted humanity for eons. Place the eyes of compassion upon us now that we may look and behold all in deep love as you behold all of your creation. May all who gaze upon these words and hear of this tale and tales such as these find for every wound of their own deep healing. And so it is. Blessed be.

~

A short distance away, on the left side of road stands the brand new high school, large and erect. The landscaping isn't finished yet. Everything is dusty and brown, like a desert. I half expect to see a tumbleweed blow by and Cowboys and Indians to appear. Dirt hangs in the air and scratches my eyes. I taste it on my lips, it sticks to my hair. I let go of my ravished dandelion and it falls to the ground.

Jason, Motor, and the other guys take off on their skateboards in search of curbs and railings to practice tricks. Jason looks back at me. Tara follows him. They both appear concerned. I wave them away. *I'm going to be okay*, I think. *I'm going to be popular.*

"This way!"

Christian runs ahead of me. Matt and I follow him around the side of the building to the back. I'm assuming Matt has been chosen as our star witness. Christian calls me to the rear exit, under the brick awning. We stand on a slab of fresh concrete. I look inside the glass at the waxy clean floors that wait for students to scuff the shine. Matt walks into the field behind us, towards the woods that line the edge of Gosnell school property.

"Hey, check this out!"

Christian points at the peachy condom on his limp penis. I can't help staring at his red pubic hair curling wildly in every direction. I have never seen a man's penis before.

Matt pops his head over the bushes and waves at Christian.

"Yeah, man! Alright!"

"Take off your pants," he orders me. Obediently I unbutton my jeans and pull down the zipper. I try to loosen my legs, but my pants are stuck around my feet. I laugh nervously. I forgot that I have safety pinned the hems tight around my ankles.

"I'm sorry," I whisper. "You know, these dumb pants, they're too short. I have to safety pin them together so they stay tapered under my socks."

Acting like a sex goddess is not so easy after all. Memo to self: *practice getting undressed in the mirror at home—and forget the safety pins next time, you dork!*

Christian presses his plastic penis against my little tummy and starts moving it around. The dry condom pulls at my skin and the smell of it makes my stomach turn. This obviously feels much better to him than it does to me. He doesn't kiss me or hold me. *What is this?*

"How's it going?" Matt yells.

Christian pulls away from me, takes the condom off and throws it to the ground. I don't understand what is happening. I don't know what to do.

"Get some oral!" Matt shouts and they both laugh.

Christian looks at me with two walls in front of his eyes. The concrete sidewalk irritates my sensitive bare feet. My shirt hangs barely below my waist. My underwear and jeans are piled in the corner. He leaves me standing there without saying a word. Maybe I am too ugly to be popular. I gather my underwear and my crumpled pants into my arms and start to get dressed as I blink back the tears of rejection.

And then I feel a hand on my shoulder. Matt pushes his mouth roughly into mine and parts my lips with his forceful tongue. He breathes hot heavy breaths onto my cheeks and holds me tight so I can't run away—not that I would. That would require easy access to my feelings, my confidence, and being wiser and stronger than I am in this moment. I make a quick assessment: the greatest danger is to be forever excluded. So I let him take the lead. This feels almost natural, almost divine, letting the man be in charge, trusting him without question. He pushes me against the brick wall and slides me down to the concrete floor. Pieces of skin rip off my back. I bite my lip and I dream of being elsewhere—in a bed, running through a golden field of grass with the sun on my face and my arms spread wide. He lays his body on top of mine. He's a rail of a guy, with pale skin and black hair, but I am skinnier than he is and I can barely breathe.

He brought Jesus outside and sat on the judge's bench at a place called The Stone Pavement...then he handed him over to them to be crucified.
-John 19:13 & 16

I am watching the backs of my eyelids when I feel him enter me. I don't know what I thought sex would feel like, but I thought it might actually feel good. Instead, it feels like a gun goes off inside of me. One part of me wants to kick and scream and yell, "Stop!" But another, stronger part of me tells me to endure and shut up. That's how we make it through life, right? That seems to be what my mother believes. I remind myself that everything will be okay after it is over.

I am tough like the concrete sanding flesh off my back every time he jams himself inside of me. I am hard like the brick wall my head smashes into as he jerks his body on top of mine. I am so desperate to be accepted that I will endure the pain of this initiation to escape the life I have lived as an outcast. It is almost finished.

I open my eyes and watch his skater hair dance on my face as his body grows sweaty. He doesn't look at me. He keeps his eyes closed. I don't know anything about Matt, the skater. I don't know if this is his first time too. I don't know what Christian told him. Why we need witnesses. Why he is here doing this to me now. I turn my head and watch the trees in the distance, how the wind blows their branches and makes it look like they are sadly waving at me.

I see Christian's red hair above the green bushes, his pale blue eyes flash like glass reflecting sun. I can't behold what's wrong with all of this. I am too caught up in my own self-doubt.

What a lie, I think. *All the magazines. All the movies. All the sexy girls. What a joke!* I want to laugh. I want to cry. I want to scream: this fucking hurts! Except I never say the "F" word. I am a good girl. Or at least I used to be.

Finally, he stops moving. Someone should say something.

"I love you," I fucking whisper it in his ear. I think that's what you're supposed to say after sex. But I know immediately that I am wrong because Matt grabs his clothes and runs away as fast as he can.

You have taken our land and made us outcasts.
                                                    -Sitting Bull

When it is over I try to stand a little taller, but I feel like I might pass out.

Christian walks over to me. The hunger in his eyes has vanished. Now they are like vacant black holes that go all the way back into the darkest darkness of space.

"Don't forget these." He throws my underwear at me and walks away. I don't understand why he didn't initiate me like he promised. Why he sent Matt over instead. Why he is angry at me now.

I see Matt kissing Tara. He puts a hand on her breast. She throws her head back like she's in a movie. I know we're not boyfriend and girlfriend. Still, it bothers me. How I just gave him everything and he still needs something more from another girl? Or maybe this is just how it works when you're trying to be popular? Who knows? I certainly don't. Not in the least.

Dark clouds appear as thunder shakes the earth and lightning flashes in the sky. The heavens open up and it begins to pour. I watch the first drops of rain land on Tara. They make her brown hair wet and curly. She looks more like a woman than I do with her C cup sized breasts. Suddenly I'm filled with a storm of emotions too complex, too raging for me to calm. I am drenched in rage and I suppress it as hard as I can.

All of us pile back into Christian's car. A brand new song blasts on the radio: Tears for Fears sings, "Sowing the Seeds of Love." All soaking wet, we listen in a trance. I try to make the good feelings come—the ones that were supposed to come when it was over. I try not to think about the throbbing pain that didn't stop when Matt did. I try to enjoy the satisfaction of getting exactly what I've wanted for as long as I can remember. *You belong now.* I repeat the mantra over and over in my mind, but it doesn't stop me from falling into a whole new dimension of darkness.

We track mud all over the shiny tile floors of the Youth Center. I escape my "new friends" and hide in the bathroom. I'm still surprised by my reflection in the mirror. *Look at yourself, Jessica. Look how much you've changed in such a short amount of time. The people you left back in Omaha, Nebraska wouldn't even recognize you now. You will never be called a prude again.* I had no idea how truly awful that was going to be.

When we moved here less than a month ago, I vowed to transform myself. No more goodie two-shoes. No more wearing t-shirts that say, I love Jesus. I know that my mother and Jesus are in cahoots, that they love the sweet nerdy girl who will never survive junior high. Today I cut ties. I am a new girl. I am, a woman? There used to be initiation rights for this sort of transition. I think: the nerd is dead and she will never come back!

I close myself in a stall. I just want to sit down. It hurts to stand. It feels like everything inside of me is about to fall onto the ground. How long can I sit here until people start to notice I'm gone?

Someone walks in the bathroom. I listen to the footsteps. The silence.

"You in here, Jess?" Tara says.

"Sort of," I say.

"You okay?"

"Yeah," I lie. "Great."

"Did you do it with Matt?" She squeals. "He is such a good kisser, don't you think?"

"Uh, huh." I hate her.

"Okay, see you soon!"

I hear the click of her compact mirror and the bathroom door opening and closing.

I sigh and drop my head between my knees. And that's when I see it: blood everywhere. This is not period blood. This is something else. My first thought is: *I need to go to the hospital immediately.* The second: *I am dying.* The third is worse: *if I don't die, my parents will kill me.* My hands begin to shake. My heart pounds inside every cell of my body. The air becomes thick and impossible to breathe.

I run out of the bathroom, forgetting all the codes of cool. "Christian! Christian!"

I find him by the concessions stand sitting at a round table with a lot of other guys who are at the Youth Center today. I tug on his white t-shirt that's covered in rain and mud. He pushes my hands off and continues to talk to Matt.

"Christian!" I say even louder. "I need to go to the hospital—something is really wrong—I'm...I'm... bleeding!"

There is just the briefest moment of quiet. I wait for his compassionate eyes to return. Where did they go? He doesn't even look at me.

Finally he faces the boys in the room and yells.

"Oh yeah!" I watch a wide smile grow on his face. "Give me five my man, Matt! You popped her cherry! Way to go!" The big circle of guys crowd together and give Matt celebratory high fives. Jason is not here. I don't know where Tara went either. I stand here alone, stunned, like a deer that just got hit by a car unsure if she's still alive.

"But...but," I can't help pulling at Christian's shirt.

"Jessica." Finally he turns to look at me. "Haven't you ever heard of a hymen?"

"No." I say and I'm sure my face is now as red as my underwear. Christian proceeds to teach me how my body works, in front of an audience of male teenagers that hang on his every word. Apparently my naiveté is hilarious because these guys cannot stop laughing and pointing at me.

I put my head down and try to contain the nuclear meltdown inside my chest. So much for the butterflies. Their delicate wings are on fire. Their weightless bodies instantly turn to ash. I escape to the game room with the ping pong tables. Crying like a baby in front of my peers is not an option. I try to play it cool again. My parents will be here soon and I need to hide everything from them, especially my clothes. I keep looking for Tara. She and I will go to Blytheville schools together so we won't have to see these kids ever again. I just want to get out of here.

"Did you just fuck Matt Black behind the high school?" A pretty girl stands in front of me and I watch her nose wrinkle up. I try to comprehend the hatred in her eyes.

"Yes—but..." she walks away from me before I can explain. I watch her tell her friend. I watch the girls' faces transform. They all stare at me with the same hard look in their eyes. I put my hands over my face. I thought I was the only girl who hadn't had sex. Christian told me everyone did it. Especially all the popular people. What is going on? Madonna's song "Like a Virgin" starts playing on the loud speakers throughout the Youth Center.

"Slut!" The girls in the game room begin to yell at me.

O Lord, You have seduced me, and I am seduced; you have raped me and I am overcome. I am ridiculed all day long; everyone mocks me.
-Jeremiah 20:7

Nowhere in the Bible does it say that Mary Magdalene is a whore. And nowhere in the Bible does it say that Mary the mother of Jesus remains a pure virgin until she ascends into heaven. These are myths that we have projected upon the text—projections that split the images of these women, fragmenting the image of God and ourselves—for thousands of years.

~

I return to where the guys are sitting. I tug on Christian's t-shirt again. He throws my hand off him like I have a contagious disease. I don't care if I'm annoying and uncool anymore. My entire world is falling apart.

"Why are you telling everybody?" I whisper.

"You said you wanted to be popular," he says real loud. Then he smiles at me, that radiant you-can-trust-me-with-your-whole-life-smile, and winks.

"Jessica," He says, "I am making you a legend."

What else can I do? I have already put my life in his hands. I hope against hope and all my reason and all my feelings that somehow he can still save me? It's sort of like trusting that Jesus is the answer to everything. This is called faith.

"Where have you been?" I say when I find Tara at the snack bar.

"Oh," she giggles. "I was talking with Mike outside." Her face is smeared with pink lipstick.

Tara and I make our way out the front door. We sit in silence on the curb watching dirty puddles drown our feet. I wrap Tara's pink hoodie around my waist and I tell my mother that I started my period and it was really heavy this time.

My family of musicians visited Elvis' mansion today. My family usually giggled at me when I sang off key. They paid homage to the King of Rock today while I paid in blood to become like a sinking stone.

"Well, what did you do today?" My father's body is stiff, his skin is pale like it is when his blood sugar is low and he's about to lose it.

"Nothing," I mumble.

My parents look at each other nervously. I think they know something is off. Then Tara buckles over and starts complaining about her stomach. My parents get caught up in taking care of her. I watch the high school move across my window. It's a miracle I am able to hold it together until we get home.

Once we get inside, I run to the bathroom, lock the door and turn on the shower. The sound of the water covers up the moaning noises that escape my mouth as I try to wash my body. I scrub and scrub until my skin is raw. I try to reach the filth all the way down in the depth of my bones.

Victims of sexual assault are:

- *Three times more likely to suffer from depression.*
- *Four times more likely to be suicidal.*
- *Six times more likely to suffer from post-traumatic stress disorder (PTSD).*
- *Twenty-six times more likely to abuse drugs.*

If childhood sexual abuse is not treated, long-term symptoms can go on through adulthood. These may include:

- *PTSD and anxiety.*
- *Depression and thoughts of suicide.*
- *Sexual anxiety and disorders, including having too many or unsafe sexual partners.*
- *Difficulty setting safe limits with others (e.g., saying no to people) and relationship problems.*
- *Poor body image and low self-esteem.*
- *Unhealthy behaviors, such as alcohol, drugs, self-harm, or eating problems. These behaviors are often used to try to hide painful emotions related to the abuse.*

There is a wind that sings songs through trees
moving leaves like tambourines,
a breath that fills the spaces between
the dark knots of branches,
where the air becomes a stage
on which life dances.

Your word descends on concrete
blowing babes from the nest.
The once fluttering heartbeat
drops like a stone in the chest
into a night,
where rocks cry,
and flames speak—fiery things
like alchemy,
transforming leadened flesh
into light,
into wings.

> *I decided that it is better to scream.*
> *Silence is the real crime against humanity.*
>
> -Nadezhda Mandelstam

Daughter

My mother buys a parakeet. I take her out of her cage to play, but her wings have grown and she flies away. I run through the house to see if any ceiling fans are on. That is the rule: I am not supposed to take the bird out unless I turn off all the fans. But I forget. The little bird flies so fast. I cannot catch her. She flies into my parents' bedroom where the ceiling fan is on high.

"No! No!"

I scream as she moves towards the killer blades anyway. I watch as she descends into the whirlwind, as her little body is thrown hard against the wall. Feathers explode and land like snow upon my parents' pillows and blankets. My mother comes to the doorway leaving a piano lesson she was giving to a grade-schooler. She marches in like a soldier, methodically searching for her baby bird. She finds her shaking in a corner and places her in my hands.

"Hold her," she says and then she returns to her piano student. I can't believe she's still alive.

~

I live somewhere floating above myself, above the pain that threatens to annihilate me. I am exiled from my body, from the things that it knows, things that are too shameful to speak. If I try to return, the fiery angel moves his sword. I am not allowed to return to the garden of innocence. Safer to live beyond the skin, I think, somewhere up in the spirit world, in the white clouds, close to the sun where there is no darkness or any kind of sorrow. No one knows what to do with all those emotions. So we don't talk about it. We pretend that they aren't even there. This probably looks like Attention Deficit Disorder. I'm just weird. I always have my head in the clouds. Only, I don't look for Jesus anymore.

The Iroquois tribe lived in New York between Niagara Falls and the Adirondack Mountains. The name Iroquois means rattlesnakes. The Iroquois called themselves Haudenosaunee meaning people of the long house. The tribes were matrilineal; the lineage was traced through the mother line and the men left their families to live with their wives in the long house. The Mohawks were a part of the Iroquois nation and the keepers of the Eastern Door which presently includes the land around the Erie Canal, which was a vital hub for trade even before it bridged the water ways to the west. Ft. Stanwix was erected there in 1758 to protect the "Carrying Place" and its settlers. This fort eventually became the site of Griffiss Air Force Base where my father was stationed when I was five years old.

The Mohawks fought against the colonists with Britain, while other Iroquois tribes fought alongside the colonists. And some tribes vacillated their allegiances depending on the food supply and the present needs of the community.

Others fled their homeland when trouble erupted and followed the Ohio River west. The Umahan, or Omaha, means "upstream people," settled in the Nebraska territory. And the others, the Ugakhpa, or "downstream people" settled in what became known as northern Arkansas. The Natives knew the rivers had power. They were places of prayer, sacred sites especially for the women—who are created of more water essence than men.

It wasn't long before the settlers took away the rivers from the Native Americans.

~

Tribes divide like cliques in junior high school. Who belongs? Who is outcast? Who is strong? Who is weak? Who gets to sit at the popular table? Who eats lunch in the library alone? Who has access to the river of life? Who is cut off and left for dead?

~

The smell of burnt coffee and sweat hangs in the air like the suspended cross in the sanctuary. I am planted in the warm wooded narthex of First Presbyterian Church in Blytheville, Arkansas. My parents think differently about faith now. There's no more speaking in tongues or being slain in the spirit. Now our church is more orderly, more heady, more boring.

It is a sticky afternoon in late summer. Services last exactly an hour or people complain. Perfumed women wearing too much makeup and thick gold chains around their necks chat about the sermon and arrange lunch dates. Wide men in suits loosen up their ties, wipe their foreheads, and make predictions about their favorite football teams. I stand silently on putting green colored carpet, my feet tucked inside a pair of generic black flats. An upperclassman named Heather watches me from a dark corner of the room. She stands there quietly with her laser eyes while I chip the paint off of my fingernails and shift my weight from one foot to the other. The longer she stares, the more polish flies into the air. When she makes her move, her fiery red lips lead the way.

I think I am safe at church where people are supposed to be nice. I wear a black dress with pink and white flowers printed on the cotton fabric. The shoulder pads rise high and poof wide. The pleats at the waistline make the skirt balloon and fall into ripples upon the middle of my calf. My hair is as hard as armor, curled high and sprayed down to perfection. I am the new girl. I am not the prude. But I am beginning to hate the new girl just as much as I hate the old nerd.

Heather's mousy brown hair bobs up and down as she barrels through the crowded room. Her short heavy frame makes my willowy figure wilt.

"Aren't you the girl that fucked Matt Black behind the high school?"

I can't count the number of times people asked me that. In the question, I am the one doing the action. I am the one with the power. I am The Evil Temptress. They see me exploiting my charms and seducing Matt under my magical spell. He is powerless to resist me, cornered, helpless. Do they imagine that I strip him, hold his arms to the earth, that I sit on top of him and ride the waves of ecstasy while he moans, "No! Please! Stop!"? Am I the great Whore of Babylon in the book of Revelation, riding the seven-headed beast around the sky at the end of time, looking for men to devour as I destroy the earth by fire?

I feel awkwardly caught in a myth of epic proportions.

Maybe no one heard her accusation. But I feel everyone watching me in Blytheville, like I am always on stage playing the lead role in a story of which everyone else knows the lines but me. Time starts to move slow. I hold my breath. I imagine heads turning from every direction and freezing their gaze upon my blushing cheeks. I am sure the greeting line behind the pastor pauses, hands are left unshaken, hanging in midair. The minister's clear blue eyes lock on me but I look past him to make sure that my parents are far away. I spot them trapped in the back of the greeting line that cascades down the center aisle of the sanctuary and I sigh with relief.

My father is striking with his jet-black hair, his strong jaw and sharp cheekbones. My mother's white skin sparkles with rainbows in the stained glass light. A crowd of people gather around them. My father is telling his latest repertoire of jokes and everyone is laughing as usual.

I think of the flesh on my back rubbed raw against the concrete, the annoying itchy scab that is still healing. I turn to Heather and all I can think are Jesus' words, "I am who you say I am." I stand there with my mouth hanging open waiting for the sound to come. I look down. Finally my voice betrays me, "Yes."

Heather wrinkles up her nose and says, "Oh my God, you are such a slut!"

What's my line? My heart pounds and pain knifes the back of my throat.

I can't remember what I did next. Did I run outside or into a bathroom? Did I stand there until Heather walked away and listen to the hushed whispers around me? I probably tried to smile and make everyone feel comfortable. Laugh it off like it's just a big joke, like I'm just a big joke. What I do remember is that this was the moment when I realized I was in way over my head and not even God could protect me in his own house. I had walked away from him and he was letting me go.

~

The law mandated profane prostitutes who were not dedicated to the temple of the Goddess in ancient Rome to wear togas like men. They were not permitted to wear fine clothes, royal colors, jewelry or anything that would give them a reputable status. Their hair was normally dyed yellow or red, in Greece sometimes blue. Prostitution outside of the temple was cruel and young girls were often easily identified, abused, and used for sport. Throwaway girls—the ones who must bear the shadows of the community.

~

Traditional developmental narratives describe coming of age as a gradual solidifying and strengthening of the subject—the dawning realization of the self. But the girl chosen as the high school slut experiences coming of age not as the dawning of self-possession and subjectivity but as a darkening loss of self and complete objectification...Her subjectivity is smeared and muddied, crowed out by voices. Any truth of herself that she might try to present to the jury of her peers is canceled out by other testimonies...This is a surreal experience that is difficult to overcome; it's not a a-run-of-the-mill teen trauma that can be easily integrated into a forward moving logic of dawning adulthood... they are in some sense human sacrifices...
  - Emily White, Fast Girls: Teenage Tribes and the Myth of the Slut

My father always drives home slowly after church, like he can keep the future at bay, the dread of Monday, and the hot emotions that trump his meticulous order with inevitable disarray. Whatever peace he feels in church, it seems he wants nothing more than to make it last as long as possible. With his hands on the wheel at ten and two, he can keep us all contained within our perfectly clean car, seemingly in control of everything, down to the syrupy classical music in the cassette player.

We drive a forest green Reliant K-car. I call it the K-Mart car because it has a giant letter K on the glove box and on the rear bumper. The lime green seats are synthetic leather so they burn the flesh of your legs when you sit down on a hot summer day. I hate this car. It announces our poverty to everyone.

My parents are somewhere else, safe inside a heavenly dream where everything makes perfect sense to them. They smile and silently nod their heads in agreement with each other. It's a place I cannot reach—like the shame lodged in between my bones and sinews that won't wash off when I shower. I am relieved that I escaped their inquiries, and at the same time, needy for someone to know exactly what is going on inside of me. My younger brother and sister, Peter and Emily, bob their sleepy heads. They both have light brown hair and my father's hazel eyes, which begin to glaze over and close as Dad's music and tranquil driving lulls us to unconsciousness.

I stare out the window at the houses flowing by. They are strange because most of them have a second smaller house that sits near them like a child who is supposed to be seen and not heard, the old slave houses. Their uninhabited presence is a dark reminder of a not so distant past. I wonder about the stories that unfolded inside their walls, how the frames still hold memories of which no one speaks. Driving down these streets reminds me of the old Roman roads where they hung criminals on crosses to frighten people to submit to the empire.

And God said: Abraham's descendants will be strangers in a land that belongs to others, who will enslave them and abuse them for four hundred years. And I will condemn the nation they serve as slaves.
-Acts 7:6

I don't remember any hills around here, only cotton fields stretching out for miles. There is an ancient hill here though, one shroud in mystery. Large bones belonging to human-like creatures are found inside many of these mounds. Old newspaper clippings report finding skeletons belonging to a race of giants inside these strange hills, especially in North America. But for some reason the once public remains have disappeared from museums. Native legends say these creatures captured their women and children and were cannibals so they fought and defeated them. Some of the giants are said to have bred with humans, maybe these are the Nephilim, the fallen angels. I consider the tall genes on both sides of my family tree and wonder if any of my ancestors were giants.

We drive down Chickasawba Road, splitting the cotton field in two, driving straight into the unknown. This land was once covered in forests, but when the European settlers moved in they cut down most of the trees to farm and sold the wood to make a profit.

The land is naked and vulnerable, like me. I press my hands to the window, longing for cotton like Eve craves forbidden things, like consciousness, and divine wisdom. I have never seen cotton like this before, cotton that is alive and growing. It seems odd to me, that cotton is a living thing, that our clothes have a life before they become shirts and shorts and underwear. I wish I knew how to transform all the wealth around me into something useful because not a stitch of my clothing is name brand. I believe name brands can protect me. I don't know where I got this idea; it seems to be common knowledge that these little logos are powerful symbols that could act like protective shields around us. How could anyone reject me if I looked rich and stylish? I color little blue rectangles on the heels of my generic white sneakers so that from a distance people might actually think they are a pair of Keds. And I desperately want a pair of Guess Jeans with the little triangle on the back pocket, but they are seventy dollars and my mother (who hates material things) says, "No way, no how." Jesus is supposed to be the most important thing in my life. Not fashion. Not friends. No protection for me.

"Get your hands off the windows!" My father yells, "And you get to wash them when we get home too."

~

My sister Emily is in the car with me because she is young and I can still convince her that it is fun to help me do my chores. I spray Windex all over the inside of the car windows and breathe in the fumes like I am smelling sweet perfume.

"Jess—don't do that! You'll die of toxic poisoning!" She's already so much of the caretaking nurse that she will become later in life.

"Oh yeah?" I say. "Then what will happen if I do this?"

I spray Windex all over the crumpled up paper towels and bury my nose in it like an oxygen mask. I take long deep breaths until I dramatically pass out.

"Don't die, Jess! Don't die!"

Emily wails. She tries to perform CPR on me, only she is pushing her hands into my neck while she counts, "One, two, three, four..." She must have seen this on TV, but missed the part where you're supposed to pump the heart not the esophagus.

"Emily! Emily!" I choke out.

She throws the roll of paper towels at me.

"Not funny," she says, but I can't stop laughing.

~

After my father inspects the windows and I watch him rewash them because I did it wrong, I meander into the kitchen to eat. My mother stands over the stove sinking eggs into boiling water.

"Mom, I really need some new clothes," I say. "All my jeans are too short and I don't have any cute tops."

Mom presses her lips together. I push, "I can't make friends with dorky clothes!"

"Jessica—anyone who likes you for what you wear is not your friend."

"But I don't have anything to wear."

"What about that purple top? Or the blue and white striped one?" She takes a knife and starts cutting a loaf of bread.

"They're old." I cross my arms. "And nerdy." I say.

My mother turns to face me.

"Jessica—I was a nerd growing up. My parents hardly had any money. I had to wear hand-me-downs. Plus you don't want to be like all the popular people anyways. They all grow up to be losers."

A lump forms in my throat. She pulls plates from the cupboard.

"But Mom! I'm already a loser!"

"Well, so was I and it didn't kill me," she says. "And what did the pastor talk about today? Jesus didn't have any friends either—not in the end. They all deserted him." She looks through me with her icy blue eyes. "Jessica. You are too materialistic. Those things don't matter. Would Jesus be worried about clothes? How many starving children in Africa are dying right now because they don't have any food? And all you care about is how you look."

"But Mom!" I wipe the tears with the back of my hand.

"Set the table please."

54

I used to like Jesus, but that was back when things were easy, when God, Jesus, and love were the only answers to every question the pastor asked at children's story time. Now I realize that my mother and Jesus want me to suffer, dress dorky, and be made fun of like I was in Nebraska. I used to wear the same outfit every Monday, Wednesday, and Friday and a different one on Tuesday and Thursday. The kids teased me because I had so few clothes—and they were all generic. I can't let that happen here. I like to think I left Jesus on the concrete behind the high school or in the garbage with my pink Pro Wing high top sneakers. Everyone laughed at those stupid shoes. I am doing just fine being an outcast all by myself without carrying the added burden of his gospel too. I drop the plates on the table and enjoy the clanking sounds.

"Careful," my mother warns. But I know that however careful I am, her God can't save me.

~

The sun moves to the west of the sky. I stand in our backyard and look over an acre of land that is temporarily ours. We rent a brown ranch surrounded by country and cotton. Because my father is a commander, we are supposed to live on base, but base housing is full, so we have to live here until a unit opens up. Then we will have to move again. I move all the time.

Life says to me: *Change! Change! Keep changing!* It's exhausting. When I meet someone who's lived in the same place their whole life, I'm like: *wow! What is that like? Tell me more.* I don't know what it's like to live anywhere for more than a few years.

We have never lived on land like this before. My father is so excited about it he and my brother mow an official sized baseball diamond into the grass. Our house is in the Blytheville school district. Already my mother has tried to get us enrolled in the Gosnell district so we won't have to switch schools right after we start, but no luck. After Behind the High School, I'm relieved.

The obsessively straight lawn mower lines on the grass cage our house inside a perfect square. Our backyard stretches out to infinity and cotton. I watch the little puffs of white sway in the breeze and play in the spaces between the heavens and the earth, crossing boundaries and mixing worlds defiantly. I stretch out my hand and touch the cotton with my fingers. It's thick, coarse, and dirty—not soft and gentle like I had imagined it would be. I pick a dandelion, smear the yellow flower on my arm, and remember. I dig a hole. I sprinkle dirt upon the flower until I can't see it anymore. It's like a game of peek-a-boo, a reminder that things lost are still here somewhere, even when they can't be seen. Underneath my feet the ancient people sleep curled up with their bones and belongings, waiting like I do, for redemption.

~

The artifacts found nearby have been dated back to prehistoric times, before the time of Jesus, before the pyramids were built. Archaeologists say the earliest people here developed no written language to tell us anything about them. Their stories are read in the mysterious hills that rise up from the ground like pregnant bellies. They call them The Mound People. Layers upon layers of earth hide their world from us. The Chickasawba Mound was registered in Blytheville in 1978. The locals used to run all over it until just a few years ago. It was looted before archeologists declared it sacred ground when they realized it was once a site once used for burials and worship. Now the land is protected.

Who decides what land is protected and what land is polluted? Which women are sacred, which women are not?

~

The trees are in full bloom above me. I feel the heat return to my legs and run up my thighs where the pain remains. I am not a virgin anymore. With that, there comes a dark sort of wisdom. Not even Jesus had sex—or Mary—so I am taught. I had gone to a place uncharted by the heavenly gods who rule over our family's faith. I was out.

When I had my first period two months ago my mother looked at me with a long vacant expression and silently handed me a box of sanitary napkins, like they were Kleenexes and we were at a funeral. I would have to walk the chthonic terrain of feminine sexuality alone. I place a stick in the grave of the wilting yellow flower.

~

In ancient times a girl's menses was celebrated with flower petals, music, songs and dance out in the caves with women of all ages. Women knew the power of life that flowed through our bodies—men did too—it was held in the highest sacred honor by all. Women are more connected to nature than men; we are not separate from the cycles of creation, we cannot so easily dominate and destroy nature for it also destroys our very essence. Women bleed on average thirteen times a year, just as many times as the full moon appears. The womb is the shape of the universe. Women are more psychic and in tune with the spiritual dimensions when we bleed. We birth not only physical children, we birth new realities. We are the creators of culture, the web, the hub, the center of the sacred cities of light. Much of women's suffering around our menstrual cycles is due to the fact that we have long lost our sacred celebrations of women's mysteries. And that may be by no accident.

~

Inanna, an ancient Sumerian Goddess, possibly a precursor of Sophia, Mary Queen of Heaven, and Persephone, must pass through seven gates before she enters the Underworld. At each gate she removes a piece of her clothing or jewelry so that by the time she stands before her grieving sister Queen Ereshkigal Goddess of the Underworld, she is naked and stripped of all her power. There seven judges condemn her fate. For when Inanna's lover betrayed her, she fell into shadow. In her rage she sent the Bull of Heaven to destroy her betrayer. And the bull died in that fight, the bull who was Ereshkigal's husband. The Goddess' grief is now inconsolable. The judges gaze upon Inanna in all her vulnerability. They look upon her with the eyes of death and then she dies.

This is one of the oldest stories known to humanity: the story of a Goddess who descends into hell and surrenders her life for the sins of patriarchy.

Taking her by the hand he said to her, "Talitha cumi," which means, "Little girl, I say to you, arise."

-Jesus, Mark 5:41

For so many years I have wanted to go back in time and relive the day of Behind the High School differently. I imagine immersing myself in books and writing my first novel by fifteen. Pouring all of my energy into the piano, maybe hitting the big stage at twenty-one. Who then would I have become? Would life allow a naïve girl to roam the flowery fields indefinitely? Or maybe this is the reason the myth of Persephone lives on—to teach us that the earth does crack in two, and dark forces do pull us into the underworld. Maybe these stories are here to wake us up, to help us see the little girls who have been to hell and back are so much more than what has been done to them, so much more than the consequences of rage, so much more than that moment of death when the soul was eclipsed.

~

One problem (among many) with atonement theology is that it can rob people of their personal descents and resurrections. Atonement theology is basically: Jesus died for your sins so you don't have to suffer. Jesus went to hell and beat up the devil so you don't have to go to hell. So many expressions of American Christianity try to keep people in a state of constant happy clappy, up in the clouds, close to heaven, outside of our own bodies. Dogma keeps us cut off from using our sovereignty, our imaginations, and our intuitions to follow the wild soul's creative path. Congregants are often encouraged to cut off their wounded writhing soul in the underworld, to identify with the light. We are taught to stay as far away from the mysterious abyss that is naturally a part of our human condition. But learning to encounter the abyss and relate to our bodies and feelings and the depths of the unknown brings us healing, integration, and wisdom. Some expressions of Christianity can sever the psyche and create a dangerous dualism within ourselves and the world around us. When this happens, other people, other religions or other countries carry our shadow of evil and the only way we can stay out of our own abyss is to enact the drama on the stage of the world, as we attempt to kill off the shameful parts of our fragmented souls in perpetual war with our delicate human nature.

~

When I grow up, when I am a mother, I take a child abuse prevention course. I learn that sexual predators target the most vulnerable children who don't understand sexual boundaries. And children who have been sexually abused often respond with increasing sexually activity. Suddenly I have a name for what happened to me: abuse. The word echoes in my mind. Dots begin to connect: my response was normal. For a moment I can see myself in a different light. Maybe I was a victim of something much bigger than myself. Maybe what happened to me was not entirely my fault.

For a few moments, I taste grace. I try to swallow that truth, to bring it all the way down into my shame-filled flesh because still, at nearly thirty, I feel like I have a magnet that draws others in, that somewhere in my energetic field I am still wearing a sign that says, "abuse me," because I still agree on some level that I am bad and that I deserve it when people treat me poorly, because that had been normal for so long. It isn't until I begin to work with junior high kids—until my niece turns fourteen—that I can finally look back on my young self and begin to see her more clearly, more compassionately. Girls this age are still very much children, just on the cusp of womanhood, about to take a perilous journey through a world that praises their beauty and exploits their vulnerability. I wonder: where are our girl guides? Where are our sacred mothers and sisters who know the way? Where is the circle of women who have made vows not to betray ourselves or one another anymore?

~

After Behind the High School my mind becomes filled with sexual fantasies. I am like a dog licking a wound. I go over and over all the details, consumed by pain, in search of some kind of redemption. Later I learn that people who suffer from Post-Traumatic Stress Disorder relive the painful memories in the days, months, and years after the unbearable incident occurs. It's like the mind replays the trauma, trying to get it right each time. But when the trauma is so severe, the episodic triggers begin to form a cocoon around the victim which attacks any efforts of growth in order to protect the self from any further harm. When this happens, life becomes a fearful colorless existence that whispers, *at least you're safe cut off from all the people who will just hurt you anyways.*

Donald Kalsched, a contemporary Jungian analyst, writes about how the psyche weaves complex fantasies around victims of trauma to protect them from the unbearable. The true self becomes locked away like Rapunzel in a tower, unable to enter the real world, sealed off by a possessive witch who would blind anyone who comes to set the girl free. The trauma inflicted on mothers and daughters goes all the way back to ancient times. Finding healing requires facing the shadow side of our wounded femininity and undoing her dark spells so our lives can have magic again.

I am not sure where my soul had gone to live during those days. I know I was rarely present. I was locked away, buffered in a space where sex, drugs, even religion could protect me from facing the pain.

~

One bright afternoon Brian Anderson walks over to me. I have just applied another coat of baby oil to my skin and reclined on my beach towel. The sun feels good on my body, my hair is wet and my toenails have been freshly painted pink. I am not allowed to wear a bikini. My full swimsuit is supposed to be peach, but it has faded and is now the color of flesh. From a distance I look almost naked, and in the bathroom light I notice that my nipples can be seen through the fabric. I am both embarrassed and excited that I am starting to look like a woman. I long for something out of reach. I constantly wonder why sex didn't feel good. I imagine a future experience, maybe an illusionary world, where sex feels amazing, where it is healing. I want to believe in it, I want to feel my butterflies again.

"Wow, it must take you all day to shave legs that long," I look up at a tall blonde hunk in red swim shorts.

"Actually it takes about two minutes." I put a hand above my eyes to block the sun.

"You wanna go for a ride in my car later?" he shuffles his feet and looks down to the ground.

"Maybe," I look around for a clock, I still have an hour before my parents pick me up. "How about now?"

I grab my things, wrap the towel around my waist and walk out of the pool with Brian. He has his father's car: a small, red, sporty thing. We drive around base for a while listening to the radio with the windows rolled down, playing these unconscious roles filled with power and allure. I assume he is shy because he doesn't say anything. He keeps looking at me and giving me nervous smiles. Brian wears a pair of Ray Ban sunglasses and drives with one hand on the wheel. He meanders around base housing as, "Hanging Tough" blasts through the speakers.

"I love New Kids on the Block!" I say.

"Oh God." He says and changes the channel. "Yes!" He says as he stops on the song "Heaven" by Warrant. He pulls into his driveway and we park.

"I really like you." He puts his hand on my thigh. "But I need to know something. Did you and Matt Black…" He takes a deep breath. "Did you guys do it behind the high school?"

"No," I say. "We didn't," I look straight into his wide eyes. He looks back at me and considers my words, my posture, my face. I am convincing. He leans over and kisses me with his mouth wide open. I open my mouth and he sticks his tongue down my throat. It tastes like lettuce and onions. I assume that he ate a Sonic hamburger right before he went to the pool because the trash is all tangled up with my feet on the floor. He moves his tongue back against my tonsils pulls it in towards my teeth and launches it back to my tonsils again. This weird pattern goes on and on and I have trouble breathing. He leans his face to the side and takes really deep breaths, sucking the air out of my mouth and then breathing it hard onto my cheek. I wonder if this kiss will ever end and if it could possibly get any worse. It can. He puts his hands on the back of my head and pulls me closer. My neck is killing me and his teeth are clanking against mine. I try to repress my gag reflex. I open my eyes and find the clock. My parents will be at the pool in fifteen minutes. My heart starts to pound but I sit there with my mouth open and let Brian do whatever it is he is doing. Finally he sets me free. His eyes are half closed and dreamy looking. I am trying to smile and look pleasant as I wipe off my face.

"Will you go with me?"

"Go where?"

"You know, go steady, be my girlfriend?"

I don't know how to say no. We just kissed. Maybe I am supposed to be his girlfriend now? No one has ever taught me the art of going steady.

"Ok." I say agreeably while I begin to panic. I had no idea how to reconcile my inner world with the outer one. Or that this was the main task of the soul.

I spend the rest of the day wondering how I can break up with Brian Anderson before he tries to kiss me again. When I can't think of anything, I wonder about the space between my deep sensual longings and the awful reality of bad kisses and painful sex. Something is missing. I just know it.

~

I turn to the only person I know who understands stuff like this.

"Lettuce and onions?" Christian says. "That's totally disgusting." Like we were friends. Like the guy who completely humiliated me was my friend.

"What do I do? I cannot ever let him kiss me again!" I press the mauve telephone into my cheek and twirl the spiral chord around my finger.

"Don't worry about a thing," he says. "I've got a plan that will make Brian break up with you before the night is over."

And yes, I really do allow Christian Roberts to devise another scheme to save me. Something, something, Stockholm syndrome. I guess it's a thing.

~

I sit straight up in the movie theater chair, glancing down at my blue and white striped shirt, wondering if it is my bra or my growing breasts that are making my chest look larger and hoping to God it's the latter. Brian's hand is on top of mine and we share a drink with one straw. My hair falls perfectly into place tonight and I spray it down until it is rock hard. It has brightened up so much over the summer; the blonde has turned almost white. I coat my eyes in thick black liner in the movie theater bathroom and add luscious amounts of pink lip-gloss as *Beauty and the Beast* plays on the big screen.

Christian sits on the other side of Brian. I can't believe he brought Matt along too. We just happened to bump into them on the way into the theater. Matt won't look at me. Brian sighs and rolls his eyes when they ask to join us. After we see them, he holds my hand tightly and keeps pulling me into his chest and putting his arm around my shoulder. We sit in the middle of the dark theater, taking up half the row. The base theater is hot and dirty. My shoes stick to the syrupy floor and crunch on popcorn. Little kids are crying. Parents are shushing, grabbing wrists, and running the screaming ones up the aisles. Finally, Christian leans forward and gives me a wink. It's go time.

I stand up and say I'm going to get a refill and I'll be right back. I walk up the dark aisle and head to the concession stand. In a few minutes Christian joins me. We hang out for about ten minutes. Christian gets another straw and sticks it in the cup right next mine which is smothered in my pink lip-gloss. He bites it and curls the end so it's unmistakably used. Then the two of us saunter back into the theater together. I sit down next to Brian and wait until he leans forward to take a sip. Then I pull the crinkled straw out of the cup and throw it onto the floor. He glares at me. I cannot bear to hold his gaze. I toss my hair and pretend to be entranced in Gaston's manly song.

"What the hell is going on?" Brian took the bait.

"Nothing," I say.

"Something is going on."

"I don't want to talk about it now—after the movie."

Christian makes sure to lean forward a lot during the rest of the movie and make eyes at me. Brian refuses to take another sip of the soda or hold my hand.

Outside the theater we stand sweating in the heat of the night.

"What the hell are you doing with that guy?" Brian points to Christian. "Or that one?" He points to Matt. My heart is racing. I'm not good with words, not in public, not put on the spot. I don't know what to say.

"Man, just let her go," Christian says.

"I don't need this shit," Brian says. "Fucking slut." He screeches the tires on his father's car as he speeds out of the parking lot.

"That is one cold bitch," Matt says to his buddies. I smile as if to say: see I'm warm and friendly! I want him to look at me so badly. Does he feel anything for me? How can he not? I long for him in a strange way I can't explain. He throws his board on the sidewalk and skates off into the night.

Christian is warm with me now, "You gotta hand it to me," he says, "I'm pretty amazing. I told you I can fix anything."

I smile and fake laugh. I wish he could fix all the gossip, but I know he wants it to happen. It's all a part of some grand plan that I cannot possibly understand. I must simply trust the guy who's ordering my universe: everything is happening for a reason, even if it has nothing to do with my best interest or the greater good. I seem so wired for this.

~

This is hard for me to remember. To think about how I trusted Christian even after all he had done to me. How he humiliated me and took complete advantage of me. To think I continued to put my life in his hands reveals how little dignity I had, how little respect for myself. Maybe that felt familiar. How lost I was from my own intuition, from people who could see me and value my worth. It explains why for years, I couldn't even think about this time in my life. How I pretended that it never even happened at all.

~

I sit in a gray warehouse somewhere in Blytheville. The orange lamps that hang from the ceiling make everyone look like they took one too many visits to a tanning both. My hands are shaking. I fold the ends of the test booklet and whisper the words as I read.

"Don't worry, honey."

A heavy man sits next to me. He's dressed in overalls, a flannel shirt and he spits chew into a paper cup.

"The last boy who took the driver's test drove straight into that garage door and he still passed."

For some reason I think they allow boys to drive crazy, and not girls. But I drive around the block once and at fourteen I am given my driver's license. To my horror, my father tells me I must learn to drive the K-Mart car, which is a stick. I go at the plastic letter K on the back bumper with a screwdriver, but it won't budge. I drive around town learning to maneuver the car with my father. I stall in all of the busiest intersections. I am convinced: it is my destiny to perpetually humiliate myself in public.

~

"Well, well. Look who's finally showing his face around here," Tara holds the kick ball in one hand and props her other hand on her hip. I watch the cotton stalks bend in the breeze behind her. She stands on the pitcher's mound, her long brown hair blowing in the wind. I am envious of her beauty and strength. We both stare at a cute boy who's sauntering towards us.

"Hi, I'm Buck." *Hi Buck, with sun-kissed skin*, I think. He stretches out a muscular arm and offers me his hand to shake.

"Jessica," I say. "Pleasure to meet you." I look at Tara who looks back at him.

"No, Ma'am, the pleasure is all mine." He kisses the top of my hand. I decide right then and there that I love southern hospitality.

"Where you been all summer?" Tara says.

"Oh, you know, huntin'… fishin'… the usual." His southern accent throws words into corners of English I have never heard.

"And who is this fine young gentleman?" Buck points at my brother who is wearing a baseball cap way too big for his head.

"Oh, that's my brother, Peter." Buck makes his way over to home base and shakes his hand too.

"Cool diamond," he says. "Did you make this?"

"My Dad and I made it together," Peter beams.

"You're one smart kid," Buck says turning Peter's hat around backwards. "Hey, ya'll wanna to see something really cool?"

We follow Buck around to the front yard. Parked in my driveway stands a shiny red bike that looks like a motorcycle.

"It's my new moped," he says. "Do you wanna go for a ride?" He looks at me. I blush and force my smile not to spread it as wide as it wants to go.

"Uh, maybe…"

"Just around the block—no big deal."

"Okay." I look at Peter and Tara.

"Do it!" Tara says clasping her hands together. Peter looks nervous, but he usually looks that way so I go with Tara's advice on this one.

I step on the little black platform and put my hands around Buck's waist. He stands a little taller than me, but I am able to peak over his shoulders as we begin to drive around the neighborhood, which is one street shaped like a U in the middle of a cotton field. This feels so romantic, touching his waist, feeling his muscles. My hair streaks into the air, whipping against the sunset sky. I push my body against Buck's as he kicks his moped into high gear. I think, *so this is what it feels like to be a woman!* We zip around the street one time and I can hear "The Next Time I Fall" by Amy Grant and Peter Cetera playing in the background of my mind. Everything moves in slow motion.

"See? Not so bad, eh?" He brings the bike to a stop in my driveway.

"Wow! You looked amazing," Tara says jumping up and down. My brother tilts his hat down over his eyes and looks away from me.

"Yeah, that was fun!" I twirl a finger around a strand of hair.

"Do you wanna have a try?" He lifts his eyebrows up and offers the handle bars to me.

"What?" I gasp.

"Do-you-want-to-drive-the-scooter?" He emphasizes every word like I am a foreigner, which I am.

"No way," I say. "I'm, umm…I wouldn't know how to…"

"Aw, listen, this is no big deal," he smiles and shows off his cute dimples. "Look, you just take the handle here and twist it. That'll make it go. Just pull on that brake when you wanna stop. Simple as that. I'll ride on back and coach ya all the way through."

"Okay…"

I mount with feigned confidence. He puts his hands around my waist. I want to please him. I turn the handle just the tiniest bit and we begin to move down the straightaway at a snail's pace.

"Come on, give 'er some gas," Buck says.

I twist the handle a little bit more.

"Yeah, all right," he says. So I decide to make the bike go faster and faster, until Buck yells a great, "Ya-hoo!" like some cowboy riding off into the sunset.

I imagine the neighbors all peering from their windows murmuring to themselves, "Who is that? Wow, look at her go!" I race down the straightaway, full of power. I think, *Timber! I'm falling in love!*

But my eyes freeze on the curve ahead and the ditch beyond the road. I see into the future. I see us driving straight into that ditch, unable to make the turn. I continue to fly, dead-locked on that fatal vision. Joy transforms in to terror. Fear consumes me.

"Come on girl, slow it down, turn that wheel," Buck encourages me. My elbows lock. My jaw is set. I freeze. I can't save myself. Impossible.

"Honey, turn that wheel!" Buck says. "Turn goddammit! Turn!" He screams. I scream. We drive off the road at fifteen miles per hour. We catch air at the lip of the ditch and crash into the other side of the bank. Buck and the moped roll over me. Pain knifes my knee, my lip, my cheek, and my elbows. Pieces of Buck's bike fly into the air and land all around us.

In a flash I revert to a much younger version of myself and I begin to cry for Mom and Dad. Peter runs into the house for help. Tara screams like she's more traumatized than I am. Just weeks ago, we were real women. Now here we are, still obviously children. Maybe this is the real reason for our tears: we realize we're not grown up after all. Images warp into spinning colors. The last thing I remember is my father picking me up like he did when I was little, and carrying me off to the ER.

On our way home from the hospital, my father drives our shameful K-Mart car by Buck's house. To my horror, Buck walks out his front door and my father rolls down the window.

I stare at the big band aids that cover my body and sink down into the seat.

"Looks like you wrecked your moped," my father says.

"Yes, sir," says Buck.

"Well that was a pretty stupid thing to do," my father says. "You're lucky I'm not going to press any charges against you."

"Yes, sir."

"Stay away from my daughter from now on, okay?"

"Yes, sir."

I watch Buck turn his back on me. A heaviness fills my chest. I want to bury my face into my hands and sob. But I must be stronger than that. I must carry on. There are other boys out there who can save me. I am determined to find one so I can feel like that powerful woman again. But then I wonder if I could ever hold that energy without driving myself off a cliff.

~

In late August I start school at Blytheville.

Every school day for as long as I can remember begins with morning devotions, which occur at the ungodly hour of 5:30 a.m. The five of us sit in the living room (my brother lies on the floor rolled up in a blanket) and we read the Bible and pray together.

My father leads the sleepy lot. "The Gospel according to Luke," he says enthusiastically. I stare at the digital clock and watch the little blue numbers shake like they're having seizures. Emily snuggles into my mother's lap—a place I don't remember being—my sister's brown pin straight bangs lie crooked across her forehead from her failed attempt at cutting them herself. A pastel colored painting of a dead Native American warrior and his speared horse hangs above my mother's head. His body rests high on a platform suspended by stilts. I can't escape the feeling of death in our living room.

~

Some Native American tribes placed the newly dead high in trees as an offering to the Great Spirit. In the plains however, plentiful forests were more difficult to find so the custom of creating scaffolds became more common here. In some tribes, the warrior's horse is killed and placed beneath the scaffold to accompany his spirit into the afterlife. In others, the wife or other family members are killed to accompany the fallen. I read the Pawnees would tie an unmarried girl they had captured from another tribe upon the scaffold. In the Morning Star ritual the priest would cut her chest to bleed and the men and boys of the village would shoot her body full of arrows. Her blood was thought to bring fertility to the soil. Is this what happens in all cultures who forget the value of the feminine? For wherever patriarchy attempts to rule feminine energy—rather than honor the sacred balance—some little girl will have to pay the price.

~

I hate looking at that dead horse. Why did it have to die? It reminds me of the dead dog we hit. It reminds me of all the pain inside that I am not supposed to talk about.

I try not to look at my father because his short paper thin robe is a million years old—it's blue and brown striped and it falls open revealing lots of graying chest hair. He's more comfortable in his skin than I'll ever be in mine. He holds a cup of black coffee in one hand and sits with his legs crossed. In a booming voice he tries to capture our attention and make the Bible sound much more interesting than it actually is.

"For those who exalt themselves will be humbled, and those who humble themselves will be exalted," he reads.

I can hear Peter snoring from underneath his blanket as I listen to Jesus tell all of his disciples to make friends with the losers in society. I hear, *Thou shalt be a nerd for that is the heavenly will of God my Father.* I'm so not getting into heaven.

After the Gospel is read we recite Psalm 103, which we have memorized because we have been saying it together as a family ever since our daily devotions began. This was also my mother's grandfather's favorite psalm—and maybe this is why we said it. "Bless the Lord O my soul," I say bitterly, "Bless his holy name."

And then we each pray. My father starts and we take turns going oldest to youngest. If he's in a bad mood it will be a very short prayer. If he's in a good mood, it will be very hard to stay awake until it's your turn. My prayer is usually some version of the same one I say every day, "Dear God, thank you for everything. Help me today (and I squirm here knowing that God's will and my will are at odds) to, uh, um, have a good day. Amen." While my brother is mumbling a muffled prayer into his blankets I add in some private pleas about not getting any pimples and for my breast size to increase, for my parents to finally understand how important name brand clothes are, and maybe they could afford to buy me some so I can be protected from public humiliation—even though I know God didn't spare Jesus from that. My thoughts crowd with questions and confusion over why prayer always draws me to a place of anger rather than peace.

After devotions, I take off all my clothes and stare at my naked body in the bathroom mirror going over my many flaws, my boney knees, my tiny breasts, my short hair. I really hope my hormones will kick in soon so I can stop looking like a little girl. Ever since I was five I wanted breasts. I knew they gave women power because of the way my father drools over them on TV.

"Men are visual creatures," my mother defends him. "That's how God made them. You can't blame them for it." I am reminded of what I have been taught: God created woman so man would not be lonely. I get the message: we are here for their entertainment. This dreadful vision of my future does not quite match the dream in my heart. But then again—I don't even have a dream except that I just want to feel safe, be loved, and happy. I just don't know how to get those things in this world without inevitably hurting myself. Maybe because this world doesn't really value those things or women like me, so I have to pretend I am not who I am in order to survive, which doesn't get me any closer to the things I need. Being a teenager is so confusing.

I step in the shower and let the hot water run down my back. I am so tall I have to bend my knees to get my hair wet under the showerhead. I don't even need to wear a bra except to show off the white straps under my T-shirts—proof that I abide by the unspoken junior high dress code.

Today I am copying the makeup of a new model, Cindy Crawford, who is all over the magazines now. I work very carefully using my mother's old Mary Kay mirror that has settings for office, day, and evening. I choose the evening setting because I think I look sexier in the amber light. I apply a base of foundation and powder. Then I choose an eye shadow that matches the deep brown colors above Cindy's eyes. I follow the black eyeliner around her lashes, the rose color on her cheekbones and match the glossy wine tones on her lips. I open the bathroom door and literally run into my mother.

She gasps. "Jessica, you cannot go out of the house like that! Take all that black eyeliner off!" My mother's steely blue eyes cut right through me. They are the same color as mine, blue as the sky with dark navy rims that circle the irises.

"Mom!" I plead.

"You are not allowed to wear your make up like that, now wash it off now! People will think you are a slut." How do I tell her that doesn't matter to me, they already do?

"Smile!" My father sneaks up behind my mother and points a camera at me. Could he be any more insensitive? The flash goes off before I slam the bathroom door in his face and lock it.

"Oh, that's a keeper! I'll save it for your wedding day, so we can show your husband how beautiful you are when you're angry!" He laughs. I hate him. I hate her. And they hate the self I need to make in order to survive in this world. I am so confused. What is the difference between becoming a woman and being a slut?

I wash my face and try not to cry so my skin doesn't look all splotchy for the first day of school. I turn on the radio, *"You've built a love but that love falls apart. Your little piece of heaven turns too dark."* And I begin again.

I never knew what my face looked like underneath my large blue glasses because I am so blind that I can't see anything when I take them off. But I got contacts before we moved and I am beginning to see that I am not so ugly; my cheek bones and jaw are angular like my father's and I have my mother's blonde hair and Nordic genes. I reapply my foundation, adding only mascara and light pink gloss to my lips. I put my black eyeliner, blush, and dark brown eye shadow in my backpack and I decide: I will add the rest when I get to school.

My mother eventually takes me out shopping. I get about four new generic items. I'm devastated we can't afford more. She's angry that I'm so materialistic. She tells me about the hippy days, when they didn't shower all week and she wore the same T-shirt and jeans every day and walked barefoot. She talks about the children in Africa. About Jesus.

I look at the stubble in her armpits and I think, "I can't be like you. I just can't. There's no way I'll survive junior high like that!"

I put on my pleated stoned-washed jeans. I tight-roll the hems and safety pin them in place so they look tapered at the bottom, like the other girl's pants. I know they won't embarrass me today. I put on two pairs of white socks and bunched them perfectly so that they snug up against the roll of my jeans. Ever since tight rolling jeans at the hem became fashionable, I have to wear two to three layers of socks to make up for the extra inches I always have between the end of my jeans and my ankles. I can never find pants long enough. They are all high waters on me. Even though it is hot outside, I wear pants because the kids in Nebraska used to tease me about my boney knees. I never wear shorts, hiding away for years my legs that I later learn—at 40—are actually beautiful. I put on my wanna-be-Keds, my blue and white striped t-shirt, and return to the bathroom to work on my hair.

I have decided that the bigger the bangs the prettier you are. I take a few inches of my hair and roll it into a hot curling iron, apply hairspray, and let it sizzle for a few seconds. I do each section of my bangs until I have a tall sea of waves on the top of my head. I comb it out carefully and spray it all down until it's hard as a rock, strong enough stand up to anything Mother Nature would throw my way: wind, rain, humidity, bring it.

"That's better," my mother scans my face.

Dad offers me his daily forecast, "Watch out for the tsunami rolling in off of Jessica's head today! Entire civilizations may drown in her large tidal waves!" He thinks he's hilarious. I look at my father with all the hatred I can muster.

"Don't. Touch."

~

The fluorescent lights in the bathroom at school make my skin look all purple and blue. I do my best to reapply my makeup without the bronze evening light. The colors still look somewhat like Cindy's. I take a deep breath and walk out of the bathroom with my head lifted high.

"Hey," Tara swings her long curly brown hair through the air and turns to face me.

"Hey!" I yell too loud, unable to control my excitement of seeing a familiar face.

"Don't you look sexy at 8 a.m.! When is your lunch?" She slams her locker and kisses the clasp of her necklace and moves it to the nape of her neck.

I unfold the paper in my hands, "I have second lunch at 11:45."

"Bummer, I have fourth. You should come over to my house after school. I found a box that my brother keeps all his secret stuff in and he's going to be away at football practice until 5:30."

I lift my eyebrows. "What if he finds out we touched his stuff?"

"That's exactly why I want to do it. What's he going to do? Tell Mom that I looked at his porn?"

We both laugh. "True!" I say feeling naughty and intensely curious. "See you later then!"

First period History is awful. The walls are coated in black paint and the hazy light from the rear windows leave the room dark. When the teacher comes in, he doesn't turn on the overheads or if he does, I can't tell. The air conditioning blows down upon us and I shiver through the entire class. I wish I had worn a jacket even though it's already ninety degrees outside. I dig for a pencil in my backpack.

"Hey, you're the new girl ain't you?" A wiry boy with a thick southern drawl taps me on my shoulder.

"I moved here a few months ago," *and don't call me the new girl.*

"You're a damn Yankee!" He slaps his hand on the desk and leaves his mouth gaping open.

"A what?" My heart flutters like a frightened bird.

"You're from the other side of the Mason-Dixon line. I can tell by your accent." He's wearing hunting boots, camouflaged pants, and a black t-shirt with the Confederate flag on it.

I laugh, "Um, I don't have an accent. You do."

"You Northerners. Can't even smell the shit you're stepping in."

"Northerners?" My mouth turns dry.

"Since the war, your kind has been like a disease slowly infesting our land." His eyes close to tiny slits and he throws his torso to the back of his chair and crosses his arms.

"The war?" He can't mean the Civil War; that was so long ago.

"Haven't ya heard of the Civil War, or don't they teach ya'll Yankees nuthin' in school?" His breath smells of chew and there are pieces of black between his teeth.

"For your information, I have learned about the Civil War, and I thought it ended years ago."

He laughs and a few others join in.

Suddenly a pretty blond girl walks through the door with confidence. Her hair is perfectly styled, her shirt flaps open revealing cleavage that can only come from a C cup or larger. All the eyes in the room leave me and turn to her. She rides the waves of all this attention so effortlessly. I'm so jealous. We all follow her walk across the room to the back row where she sits and starts chatting loudly with the girl next to her so that everyone can hear.

"Hi Anne! Did you hear Patricia—the girl with the frizzy dyed hair who is sitting in the front row by Kendra—was fingered by her boyfriend this summer after he was working on his car? Well, she got antifreeze in her hole and she had to spend the whole summer in the hospital where they tried to get it all out, but the doctors say her privates are ruined for life and no one, not even her boyfriend will touch her ever again because they're all afraid to get antifreeze on their wankers and end up with cancer and deformed babies!"

The whole class roars. Patricia hangs her head low. I watch her face flush as she blinks back the tears.

I think, "God I'm so glad I'm not her." But I know exactly how she is feeling. How will we ever survive, I wonder?

~

Hagar is the mother of outcasts. She is the woman who is possibly raped and impregnated by Abraham, the one who endures Sarah's jealous cruelty, she is the one seen as dark and forbidden. She is cut off from the people of God and sent into the desert to die with her child. Did we ever read the story that way? Did anyone ever ask if Hagar if she wanted have Abraham's child? Is this why some Jews, Muslims and Christians fight to this day? Do all rifts in human culture stem from rape?

~

In gym we have to run outside on the track and I am worried that this will be the end of my hair and makeup. The air is so thick with humidity that it's hard to breathe. The cheerleaders are on the football field practicing their builds and throwing the tiniest one into the air. I feel so inferior. I could never be a cheerleader. I am the biggest klutz and my mother says our Norwegian hips aren't made to bend that way. She told me to give up on that idea a long time ago. I internalize: our bodies are different, our bodies are bad. Doesn't the Apostle Paul also say that all flesh is sinful? I believe I am inherently bad. Something in my very nature is rotten to the core. I am sick at the thought of it. Where will I hide it? Already, everyone seems to know.

"Hi!" A girl taller than I am runs towards me. Her long hair is thick and she's starting to bead up with sweat. "I'm Alex," she says breathlessly.

"Hi," I smile. Her eyes are kind. "Alex?"

"Well, Alexandra, but everyone calls me Alex." In the sunlight I can see that she has tried to cover up a few of her pimples. She's human. I like her instantly.

"That's cute. I love it when girls have boy names like Jo or Bobbie. I think it's sexy."

"Really? I've always hated my name." We slow to a trot so we can talk easier.

"No way. It's super cute!" Her eyes brighten and she gives me a little smile.

"Wow! I wish I could do that!" I say as we watch the cheerleaders leap into the air and do the splits touching each of their toes.

"I can't even touch my toes when they're on the ground," Alex rolls her eyes and we both laugh.

"Neither can I!" I say. "It's because they're so far away!"

~

The cafeteria is completely chaotic, people are darting in a million different directions at the same time and everyone is talking so loudly I can hardly hear my own thoughts. Our school is seventy percent black and most of the white kids are wealthy and live in mansions. Many wear gold necklaces and expensive name brand clothes while the majority of the black kids live on the other side of the railroad tracks in run down shacks. The middle class escapes my view and I wonder how I will ever fit in here.

"Over here!"

Alex waves me to her table. I make my way through the crowd. All the black kids are heading the opposite direction from the white kids.

"Why do we sit like this?"

"You're not supposed to talk to them." Alex dips her French fry in ketchup and carefully puts it between her glossy lips.

"Talk to who?"

"The black people," she says.

"Why not?"

"Because."

"Where I come from we talk to everybody."

"I just thought you should know so people don't make fun of you."

"OK," I have suddenly lost my appetite. "Thanks for the heads up."

But I didn't listen to Alex. I did talk to black people which added nicely to my current reigning titles of shame: 1988 Miss Prude, Queen of Nerddom, 1989 Miss School Slut & Nigger Lover.

~

Science class is after lunch and I am having trouble staying awake, except that my teacher is a young woman and she is very beautiful. The classroom is so cold that everyone can see her nipples through her sweater. We are all enchanted by her. I daydream about the day I might look like her. I imagine her exciting single life, her ability to do anything and go anywhere. I imagine her boyfriend taking her home at night. Lifting off her sweater. She teaches us all about the solar system and I travel to heavenly places in my imagination.

~

After school I am exhausted and relieved to have survived my first day. No one asked about Matt Black. Maybe the rumor dried up over the summer like the crinkly corn stalks shriveling back into earth.

"Here it is!" Tara whispers as she pulls out a light blue shoebox from underneath her brother's bed. We open the lid and find tons of magazines, condoms, and a pack of cigarettes. I pull out a magazine with a naked woman on the front cover.

"Oh my gosh! Have you looked at this?" I have never seen a magazine like this before.

"A little," Tara flushes. I flip it open. My ears grow instantly hot. I am staring at a naked woman, she is on her knees and her back is arched so that I can see everything.

"Look at all that hair!"

"It's gross," Tara says.

"Totally," I lie. I wonder if I look anything like this when I bend over. I have never seen a woman from this angle before. I turn the magazine around. I flip through the pages. All the women have large breasts and perfectly peachy skin. I feel ugly compared to these women and still so much like a child.

"Check this out!" Tara opens a condom and unrolls it.

"Iew! Those are so gross!" The smell makes my stomach turn.

"How big was Matt? Did he fit in here?" Tara lifts her eyebrows.

"Oh yeah," I say, even though I never saw it actually.

"Did he look like this?" Tara pulls out another magazine and opens it up to a picture of a naked muscular man whose skin is oiled. He leans on a big rock in the glistening sun.

"Oh my gosh! Not that big!" I say and we giggle.

"What was it like?" Tara tosses her hair to one side. "Was it the best thing ever?"

I don't want to disappoint her. Maybe it was just me. Maybe I am weird.

"I can't wait to do it again."

The next time has got to be better than the first. It just has to be. Somehow. Why else would everyone be obsessed with it?

"He sure was a good kisser," she says with dreamy eyes. And suddenly I am insanely jealous. Matt wanted her. He kissed her. I just laid there for him. Because Christian told him to. So I could be initiated into whoredom. I am repulsive, I think.

"I gotta go," I say. "I'm late for dinner."

~

The following weekend I spend the night at Alex's house. My sudden immersion into Sex Ed is not only intriguing, but also bewildering and horrifying.

Alex lives in a big old Victorian house, where the wood floors creek and the bathrooms are decorated with radiators. Her room is painted yellow and pink and she has big fluffy pillows thrown all over her flowery queen bed. Red leafy branches scratch the window when the wind blows. She flicks a little straw with tiny plastic penis on the end of it.

"They look so disgusting," she says. "Have you ever seen one?"

"Only in a magazine," I lie. "They're so wrinkly and strange."

My cheeks are warm after watching the movie *Dead Ringers* with Alex and her family. My family would never watch movies like this. In the film twin male gynecologists have sex with a lot of their female patients. One of the twins made all these new instruments to operate on women because he began thinking they all had mutilated vaginas.

"Sex looks so fun," Alex says. "I can't wait!"

"I hear it hurts for girls," I say tentatively.

"Really? All the women on TV seem to like it." Alex twists a piece of her hair in her hands and crosses her legs. We have very similar bodies, both thin, long legs, small breasts.

"How far have you gotten with a guy?" I ask.

Alex blushes. "I'm still waiting for my first kiss. What about you?"

"Just kissing," I say. I don't want to tell her about Matt. I want her to like me. "His name was Paul."

I tell her about my first kiss—underneath the chipping paint of our carport where the moving boxes had begun to pile up just before we moved here from Omaha. How he put his two hands on my waist and pulled me close to his body, how I felt millions of butterflies flapping their tiny wings inside my chest. How his lips were as warm as my thighs. About my crazy idea: that if a kiss could feel this good, imagine everything else.

"That sounds so much better than Mr. Sonic breath!" We giggle.

We talk about the different ways of kissing. Mouth closed. Mouth slightly open. French kissing. We practice kissing our hands and the air in front of us.

"My sister just started taking birth control so she won't get pregnant when she gets married," Alex hands the penis straw to me.

"How old do you have to be to get pregnant?" I ask.

"Oh, you can get pregnant as soon as you have your period," she says.

My heart starts racing.

"How do you know when you get pregnant?" I stare at the little hole on the end of the penis straw.

"You stop having your periods," she says.

When was the last time I had my period? I think back. It was before Matt. Before Behind the High School.

"Why doesn't your sister just use condoms?" I ask.

"Well, they're not one hundred percent effective all the time. They can break or have leaks in them, I guess."

I am one hundred percent freaking out. I could be pregnant. At fourteen. My whole life could be over. My parents will definitely kill me. And if they don't, I will want to die. If Christian is so smart about all this stuff, why isn't he worried about me? Do Christian and Matt worry about the consequences of their actions? Do they even care about me? No duh.

I still throb and ache deep inside. I think about those scary operation instruments from the movie and I am convinced that I know what it feels like to have a mutilated vagina.

~

By Monday morning I am exhausted from worry. Before class even begins, things take a turn for the worst.

As I'm digging in my locker before first period I hear the pretty gossipy girl who burned Patricia, "I heard you fucked Matt Black on the concrete behind Gosnell High School."

"What?" My face turns red.

"Everybody in Gosnell is talking about it," her lips curl into a devious smile. "I went to a party this weekend—everybody knows your name, Jessica Zdenek."

"Rumors," I say with a trembling voice.

"Matt said your vagina felt like it was filled with two-by-fours, nails and steel. And Christian Roberts said he witnessed the whole thing."

The lump in my throat becomes a bowling ball. No words are coming out. I turn and walk away from her, my eyes deadlocked on the floor.

"I think it's true," she yells down the hallway. "Slut!" She laughs. Her cackling voice rick shays down the hallway, "That girl is the biggest slut in the history of this town!"

Humiliated again. How in the world do I stop this from happening? I think of Jesus' humiliation and crucifixion. I worry this is God's plan for my life.

Elbows and books are jabbing me from every side. Everyone seems taller than me now. Bodies pressing in on me. I can't breathe. The ceiling starts to spin. I walk until the bell rings and the hallway is empty. I walk to the nurse's office and slide down onto the cold floor. I sit here and wait for some sort of mother to find me, to wrap her arms around me and tell me everything will be alright.

The Vice Principal's office is across the hall. There is a long line of black students standing outside his door. No one says a word. We are all slumped over and looking at the world with half open eyes. We listen to his voice seeping out into the hallway.

"You think you're gonna make something of your life? Didn't your mamma teach you nothin? We're gonna get the Devil out of you girlfriend! Come 'ere!"

We all listen and flinch as her shrilling screams fill the air.

"Yeah, you gonna learn the hard way. And I'm gonna teach you!"

A few minutes later a young black girl runs out of his office, her face wet with tears and snot. A tall black man follows her out standing erect, flattening his gray suit jacket and tie with one hand, in the other hand he grips a large wooden paddle.

"Who's next?" I watch everyone's eyes fall to the ground. I worry we are all doomed to repeat the history of violence done to us.

~

"How was school?"

My mother lights candles and spreads out the tablecloth that reminds me of Joseph's Amazing Technicolor Dream Coat.

"Fine."

The five of us sit silently around our dining room table. I listen to the clanking silverware, the awkward chewing and gulping noises. My father's face looks white with stress. I always know when he is about to explode.

"You left on your curling iron again this morning." He stares at me from the head of the table.

"Sorry." I mumble as I stab my meatloaf with my fork. I hate meatloaf.

"Well, maybe sorry isn't good enough," he says. "Do you know how much it costs to keep a roof over your head? Do you know how much money you just throw away by leaving lights and curling irons on?"

"No." I roll my eyes.

"No, sir!"

"No, sir."

"I think you may just have to go without your curling iron for the week. Maybe then you'll learn to turn it off."

"No, Dad! Please!"

"What, are you too afraid to go out of the house without your silly tsunami?" My brother and sister watch me with wide eyes and open mouths.

My body turns instantly hot. My hands are shaking. I throw my fork across the table.

"I hate you!" I stand up.

My father laughs. "Oh, now you're in big trouble. Not a very smart move. You're not so bright, are you?"

I run down the hallway to my room.

"Where do you think you're going?"

My father chases after me. He catches me in the hallway grabs my arm, picks me up by the elbow and throws me to the floor.

"David, stop it!" My mother runs to his side. I scramble to my feet and crawl into my bedroom as fast as I can.

~

Later that night when it's dark my mother knocks on my door.

"Jessica," she says. "You have to forgive your father."

I don't make eye contact or say a word.

"He needs you to forgive him," she says. "Jesus needs you to forgive him." My father walks into my room and kneels down at the side of my bed. He begins to sob, "I am so sorry, I didn't mean to hurt you."

I rub my arm.

"Please forgive me," he says.

But my heart is hard. *Never*, I think. I will never forgive him. It is the only power I seem to have. *I hate you,* I think. *I hate you for not understanding me and for humiliating me just like the kids at school!*

~

I may not be good at math, but I can add up a few things. If my father gets this mad over a hot curling iron, imagine—just imagine—how upset he would be if he ever found out what I did behind the high school! If I had any doubt before, now I know for sure that I can never tell my parents anything.

~

Today I know my father to be a different man than the one I feared growing up. He had no idea what was going on at school. I know if he did, he would have marched over to Christian Robert's house, just like he marched over to Buck's. I know he would have worked to protect me. He, like so many others, just didn't know what was going on or what to do with my wild emotions. And I had no idea how to tell anyone what was happening. Most children don't.

Father, I wanted you to save me
but you saved your lightning for another rainy day

when I fell away from you
when I lost my point of view

Mother did you even hear me screaming?
Did you stop the spring from blooming?

when I fell away from you
when I lost my point of view

How much farther must I fall?
Must I lose it all?

And who is this that waits for me
in this wound that bleeds
is it just one seed that makes this girl
His queen?

At the core of that father-lover complex is the father-god whom she worships and at the same time hates because on some level, she knows he is luring her away from her own life. Whether she worships him or hates him makes no difference, because in either case she is bound to him with no energy going into finding out who she herself is. So long as she can fantasize her love, she identifies with the positive side of the father-god; once the fantasy is crushed, however, she has no ego to sustain her and she swings to the opposite pole where she experiences annihilation in the arms of the god who has turned against her.

-Marion Woodman

PUELLA AETERNA

Nine weeks into eighth grade, the military tells my father that a housing unit on base has opened up and we are required to move immediately. The base sends muscular guys over to pack up our stuff and load it onto the moving truck. We say goodbye to the cotton field, the baseball diamond, and the cozy ranch house that let us enjoy the illusion of an upper middle class life, even as our K-Mart car told the truth. I promise Tara and Alex I will keep in touch, but we've only just met and once I start my new life, I don't; I have a host of new challenges that require my full attention.

~

Our new house is a small duplex on a tiny square of lawn that takes about twenty minutes to mow. It looks exactly like all the other cookie cutter houses chipped with paint and lined with bubbling linoleum floors. Amenities included driveways covered with open-aired carports and air-conditioning units that perch like fat ugly birds in the living room windowsills.

We are unpacking boxes when the doorbell rings. My mother opens the door. Christian is standing there with a bouquet of flowers. "Welcome to the neighborhood, Mrs. Z," he says with a perfect smile on his face.

"You are the sweetest kid!" My mother presses the flowers up to her nose. "Do you want to come in?"

"Maybe next time," he says waving to me and flashing his straight white teeth. But the next time I see his face it's on my computer screen. He's surrounded by children as a soccer coach. I am thirty-six years old. My hands shake as I dial the number of the local police in his area. My voice cracks as I explain that he abused me when I was a child when he was employed as a Youth Counselor at Eaker Air Force base and my suspicion is that he enjoys having power over vulnerable children. I ask them to please make sure that the kids in his care are safe. I plead with her to just check him out. She assures me, he has no record so there's not much she can do.

~

As soon as I walk onto Gosnell campus I feel electricity run up my legs and straight into my heart. Everyone has been waiting for this moment, waiting to lay their eyes on me, to see me in the flesh.

I am the new girl, again. I should be a pro by now. But I really suck at this.

I walk down the hallway darting my eyes in every direction trying to find my classroom.

"Nice ass," some guy says.

"Yeah, she's got a better ass than tits," another says.

"What tits?" Another guy says, "She's flat as farmland."

"I heard she fucked the whole football team," another says. "And then she blew them." They all laugh.

"I heard she was tight—like slamming your dick between concrete and steel," another says.

"Fuck that," another guy says. "Leave those whores alone or you'll get some nasty disease." He and two other buddies start singing, "Poison," by Bel Biv Devo.

One guy pushes me against the lockers and sticks his face in mine. I can smell the chew on his breath. He wears a royal blue letter jacket with a big yellow G printed on the front. He's a local. He moves his gaze between my right and left eyes, just like my mother does when she's angry with me. He wears cowboy boots with fatigues and a John Deere trucker's hat.

"Cunt," he says.

Brown water from his mouth lands on my face. What do you say in times like these? I don't know. No one has ever spit in my face before. Except maybe my father, when he loses his temper and shoves me up against a wall. Why is this so familiar to me? Maybe it's because I deserve it. Something about me is bad. I just wish I knew what it was so I could fix it. But maybe there's no fixing original sin, especially when you're walking away from Jesus.

My thoughts bring a cold presence into my body: *I am destined to be rejected. Something is really wrong with me. I'm going crazy. Keep smiling*, I tell myself. *Just be nice.*

"Hahaha, that guy is so funny," I say as I wipe my face.

~

First period. I sit at a small sticky desk. My boney knees and long legs jet out from underneath. I stare at a green chalkboard. I feel all eyes on me. My heart pounds like a bird in the paws of a cat. I watch the whirlwind spin around me. I taste the bottomless crescendo.

"What is eight times nine?"

I grasp at numbers that fly away.

"Twenty-seven?" I say.

I hear the familiar laughs. "Girls are so stupid," a boy says.

What if the truth doesn't even matter? What if people are cruel anyway? What if I brought this upon myself and I deserve everything that's coming to me? Blahville-mind. It jumbles my thoughts as I fail to separate logic from the ominous feelings of doom.

The bell rings. The teacher pulls me aside, "I want to have you tested," she says. She sends me to a small mobile home on the perimeter of campus. I scribble answers on paper. *They will know*, I think. *They will run this paper through their computers, analyze all the data and they will come to me and say: I understand completely. I am so very sorry. Here, my child, this is how we can fix everything.* And then someone will give me a big hug.

But I must have answered the questions wrong because all they do is move me down to the lowest level of math one can possibly take in the eighth grade. I don't understand. I even made a few extra mistakes on purpose, just so that they'd really know how much help I need. Apparently math isn't the best language for expressing one's feelings.

~

"Jessica—you were exactly like him as a child!"

My mother and I watch my eight-year-old son zoom around the living room, all arms and legs, a wide smile spreads across his face. He knocks things over all the time, falls down, and doesn't quite know where his body is in space. The doctors at Children's Hospital tell me he has Asperger's—he's on the autistic spectrum, highly functioning though—and that he definitely has ADHD. They tell me it's genetic.

"He's impulsive," Dr. Jeremy says as he spreads his index and thumb fingers across his wiry eyebrows. "We have medication that can help him slow down, help him think before acting, but you'll have to do behavioral therapy to help him learn how to read social situations better."

The medication they want to give him ends up growing breasts in teenage boys. But before I knew that, I listened to my momma bear instincts (having children helped me connect to my deep knowing) and I opted out of medication and I changed his diet instead.

"Yes, Jessica, you were exactly like that."

I think about my inability to fit into some social situations, my physical awkwardness, my sensitivity to fabrics, tags, the way other people's emotions seem to invade my body, and my young precocious mysticism. I watch the way my young son breaks down when he is overwhelmed, the way he self-implodes, the way he punches himself in the head when he gets frustrated, things I used to do too when I was completely overwhelmed. I reflect on how I overwhelmed my parents, who tried to do their best with what they knew to raise me well. How I was often punished for being overwhelmed. How I had yet to develop an awareness of my sensitive gifts and self-compassion practices.

Women with disabilities are raped and abused at twice the rate of the general population.
-U.S. Bureau of Justice Statistics

What many label as a disability in one perspective is actually a superability in another. Perspective is everything. From which angles will we choose to see? ADHD: Attention Directed to Higher Dimensions.

~

The worst time of the day is lunch.

I may have been a nerd back in Nebraska, but at least I had someone to eat with. At least I had other nerd friends. I learn one more thing today: in the hierarchy of cool, everyone is above the slut, even the nerds. I have gone down in status, not up like I had hoped. I am a complete failure.

People are so hungry for me to be the school whore. They think I know everything about sex. But I don't know anything. How come no one teases the guys about their sexuality?

I try to keep my eyes on my food. When I look up, I catch groups of girls staring, whispering, turning their backs on me, laughing. Guys smile wide and lift their eyebrows high and open up their arms to me and then wave me away.

"Just kidding," they laugh.

Still, I try to smile at everyone, like I was taught. "Love your enemies," my mother says. "It's like pouring hot coals on their heads."

As much as I want to bury Christianity, it lives on in me in a twisted way. I can't feel my anger in public. Only at home when my parents provoke me. My father's anger frightens me and I don't want to be like that. I'm afraid of my angry feelings. I'm trying so hard to be cool instead. Trying so hard to earn the love that I can't seem to give myself.

I flop my Styrofoam plate on the end of a vacant lunch table and eat alone. I think about how popular Jesus was with all of his peers, how crowds of people followed him around and hung on his every word. Even if I still wanted to, I could never be like him. The bar is just too high. Jesus was an asexual god and I am the devil's whore. And I'm not even good at whoring. All I know of sex is that it hurts for a very long time.

Everyone thinks I know everything, though. Everyone wants me to know. They need me to know. Why? What is happening to me? The more I try to figure it out, the more my head spins.

Blahville-mind.

"Those girls are so dumb," A pretty blonde girl puts her tray next to mine. "Can I join you?"

"If you don't mind catching my cooties," I say.

"I'm Marissa," she says. "And you're Jessica—the tallest, prettiest, new girl in town." She smiles at me and I laugh.

"Yeah right."

"Wanna see a picture of me and my Dad?" She pulls out a wallet-sized photo from her backpack. She looks about ten sitting on her father's lap. Both of them have long faces and sad puppy dog eyes. I like her instantly.

"Nice to meet you Marissa," I say. She is in three of my classes that afternoon. We sit by each other. We giggle and pass notes. Suddenly I am not all alone in the world anymore.

~

The radio is blasting. Journey is on. Marissa sings along. She sprays her hair and teases out the sides and the top.

"I'm forever yours faithfully," she sings into the hairbrush. I show her the beauty tricks I learned in Seventeen magazine and we both put on deep shades of evening make up.

"What's this?" I ask.

"Sun-In!" she says. "It gives you that yellow summer hair all year long!" She makes a goofy face like she's performing a TV commercial. I laugh.

She never asks me about Matt, even though I know there's no way she's the only one who hasn't heard the rumor. Maybe she knows about the things you just can't talk about. Maybe that's why we like each other instantly.

We're at her Mom's house in Blytheville. It's a tiny old house that smells of cigarettes. Her Mom and her step-Dad, Barney, live here. Marissa's Dad lives in Gosnell. She spends the weekdays with him and the weekends here.

"Blonde girls look sexy in black," Barney says as we present ourselves before heading out for the night. Marissa looks at me and rolls her eyes.

"Barney's creepy," she says when we're alone. We walk from her house into town and decide to go to JC Penny's to look at clothes.

We pretend to have tons of money to spend. We pick out all the latest fashions and try on the fanciest evening dresses. Marissa comes out of her dressing room wearing a red babushka wrapped around her head, a pink and blue polka-dotted moo-moo, and high heel shoes five times the size of her little feet. I fall to the ground laughing. We spend the rest of our time trying to outdo each other in finding the most hideous outfits to wear until we both end up rolling around on the dressing room floors trying not to pee our pants—or someone else's.

After the JC Penny's fashion show we walk through a big field in the middle of town.

"I love coming out here at night and watching the stars," Marissa says. We both look up at the clear night sky.

"There's the Big Dipper," she points.

"Where?" I squint. She connects the dots of light with her fingers, but I can't see them.

"And there's where we come from, the Pleiades!"

A warm feeling comes over me, like I am coming home to a place I've never known.

"What are the Pleiades?" I can't tell which stars she is pointing at.

"They are always sending us love."

When I look into Melissa's eyes I feel I am looking straight into infinity.

Headlights shine in our direction. Marissa runs up to the car and talks with the driver. I hold back. Talking to strangers, running through abandoned fields at night, I'm not used to all this bad girl stuff. My heart thuds in my throat. Suddenly she comes running toward me.

"Time to go!"

We take off running as fast as we can.

"What happened?" I pull strands of hair out of my mouth.

"I just threw an egg on his car!"

"Why?"

"I don't know!" She laughs.

"You just happen to have eggs in your purse?"

"Well, only one. The rest broke!"

She grabs a few things out of her gooey bag and leaves them in the field.

"You're leaving the evidence!"

"I'm invincible!"

The two of us dart across the field, natural runners, alive in our rebellion beneath the stars. We run all the way back to her house and collapse in a heap of laughter on her bed.

"Man, it's hotter than a witch's brew in here!" she takes off her shirt.

"A witch's boob?"

Marissa falls to the ground holding her stomach and wiping tears from her eyes.

"Brew!" she squeaks out. "Brew!"

~

The tree outside of our house turns red. Dark moods begin to sweep over my days like clouds rolling in from nowhere. The littlest things set me off—a look from my mother, the tone of my father's voice. Sometimes nothing at all. Anger rises in my belly. Thoughts spiral out of control. My mother tells me to act nice. Just stuff it. No one asks me what's wrong. I don't know what to do with all this negative energy. I slam doors. I punch walls. I tear up pictures. I yell. I get yelled at. I get grounded for hanging out with Marissa.

Shortly thereafter, my period comes. I breathe out all the air inside of me and hug my legs tight into my chest. "Thank you, thank you, thank you, thank you," I say to my body. My mood lifts a little and the world goes on. But every twenty-eight days or so, the darkness returns and it feels like the world is coming to an end again and again and again. Everyone else may deny the darkness, but my body remembers.

~

I recently learn about something called Premenstrual Dysphoric Disorder, where a woman experiences intense feelings of rage, depression, suicidal ideation, and a myriad of other difficult symptoms in the days prior to her period. One connection that has been made is that this time of the month is an especially vulnerable time for women who have a history of sexual abuse.

Ancient people believed women are closer to the divine realms during menstruation, that a space between worlds opens up and women have the ability to prophesy, especially when we are bleeding. We have lost the mystery of sacred menstruation and the practices of honoring the life that flows through our bodies. Women who live close to one another cycle together with the moon. Imagine women leaving town together to rest and deepen their wisdom while the men took care of all of the civic duties. When the women returned to town, the men appreciated all the work they did, the women shared their wisdom and the whole community was renewed.

The womb sheds skin like the snake. The snake was often associated with the Goddess in antiquity, and also with the Oracle, for it is an animal whose entire belly is connected to the earth. Though many of us were raised to see our periods as dirty, our bodies are actually cleansing themselves at this time. Our blood is filled with natural renewable energy that can be used for healing ourselves and the earth for it contains stem cells. Prior to menstruation, an energy rises within us and urges us to consider the depths of our experiences and to birth new wisdom for our lives and our communities as we consciously shed what no longer serves our highest good. In a culture where we have forgotten how to honor our cycles, the more sensitive women are often medicated or labeled as crazy.

~

On lonely days I make friends with the electric piano in our living room. My mother teaches me piano lessons. She has perfect pitch, a perfect voice, and she knows music theory better than anyone I know. She's been my teacher ever since I was five. But I hate piano lessons. When I sit down to play, I like to let my fingers find the notes all by themselves. I like creating my own music. My heart connects with the sounds that sooth my ineffably dark feelings. Many teachers tried to "break" my ear and teach me how to "think" my way into music rather than "feel" it. But I was a stubborn girl.

"Oh God. Do you have to play that right now?" My father walks in the door, removes his pointy navy blue hat and drops his keys on the counter.

I glare at him. Why are my feelings so offensive? I stand up and walk away, slamming my bedroom door shut. He follows me down the hallway. His shiny black shoes click on the linoleum floor.

He opens my door.

"There will be no slamming doors in this house, understood?"

I just stare at him.

"Do you understand me?" He repeats.

Do you understand ME? I think.

He walks over to me and grabs my chin.

"Do-you-understand-me?" He leans his red face into mine and says every word loud and slow like I'm stupid and deaf.

"Yes," I muscle out of my squished lips.

"Yes, sir," he presses.

"Yes, sir," I mimic.

~

So many of our boys have been raised to shut down their feelings to "be a man." They are taught that a beautiful woman is merely a prize for their hard work. They are taught to distance themselves from anything too sensitive within to avoid the insidiously cruel hazing. We have often revered men for their command and control. We want them to be our heroes and our sure foundations. We don't want to see all that they must hide in order to fulfill our impossible expectations. They have to put their shadows somewhere. Someone has to hold all that has been unintegrated in the masculine psyche and not allowed to shine through the mask. Until there is shadow integration, there will always be a scapegoat; there will always be someone else to hate and to punish for breaking the soul crushing rules of the collective, until there is compassion for what society has asked men to do, until there is healing, until the Divine Feminine returns.

~

"On the spectrum?" I repeat to the doctor at Children's Hospital.

"Everyone presents differently. Your son needs order and predictability or his world falls apart. He's a very bright kid, but he will not thrive in the gray and complex world you and his father live in."

"And this is genetic?"

"Yes. Does he remind you of anyone else in your family?"

I think of my father's perfectly shined shoes, his closet lined with the same light blue shirts and navy blue pants, his intense obsessions with a particular subject for a period of time, how he will read everything on the topic until he becomes the expert, the way he needs to be in control of the conversation, how he melts down at McDonalds because he can't handle all the beeping noises in the restaurant, how my emotionally complex world remains a vast mystery to him.

It was then that I realized that I could no longer run from the rage of my father. Here it was before me in the big blue eyes of my son with white blond hair and a face that looked like mine. And as much as I tried to deny it, it was also in me.

~

"The end is near," the minister says. He pushes his steamy glasses up his nose. "And the people stood by, watching. They scoffed at him. They mocked him. Save yourself, they said, if you can." His white stole swings side to side as he moves his arms with the cadence of his words.

"In him all things in heaven and on earth were created. And we killed him. We killed our savior, Jesus." The pastor looks at me. I quickly look away. "He was with the Father before the world began. He helped the Father bring everything into existence. Together they created the world. And we killed him. But God knew we were going to do this. God knew our hearts were filled with sin. So he sent his son Jesus to be born of a virgin—a pure and blameless woman—"

I squirm in my seat. *I am impure*, I think. *I am not a virgin. I am dirty. I cannot be a Christ bearer. I cannot be holy anymore.* The spirit of my little girl mystic is crushed.

~

I wonder if Mary had any choice in the matter. A cold thought crosses my mind—*did God rape Mary?* Surely she couldn't understand what was being asked of her at that age. Not only to bear a child at fourteen, but to risk becoming a social outcast as well? Mary is shroud in so many mysteries, so many rumors, it's hard to know what really happened. I can relate to that. Maybe Mary was a priestess. Maybe she had more power than we know.

~

"He became human, he entered into our world of sin. And when we killed him, he became the atoning sacrifice for the whole world. We wanted death. But God brought us life instead. God gave his only son that we might have eternal life. Do you want it? The end is coming," he says.

"My rear end," my brother whispers. I snort. My shoulders shake. My mother digs her index finger deep into my shoulder.

"Are you ready for it?" The pastor lets his words hang in the air and steps down from the pulpit.

"...cause it's gonna smell," Peter whispers. I bite my lip and hide my red face in the hymnal.

~

"I am so embarrassed." My mother sits in the passenger seat and rubs the wrinkles out of her forehead.

"I am so ashamed of you, Jessica," my father says.

"But Peter made me laugh!" I protest.

"You need to learn some self-control," my mother says, "and just ignore him."

I shoot daggers at Peter. *Thanks a lot*, I think.

"This is not fair!" I argue.

"Life isn't fair!" My father snaps. "And you have got a real problem respecting authority."

"But, I—"

My father laughs. "What, do you think this is a democracy? This is a one-way conversation, young lady. I talk. You listen. When we get home, I will decide your punishment. Until then, you keep your mouth shut."

He ejects the tape from the player and turns down some unknown country road where we meander through the silence. I hate that he gets to control everything, every turn, how long it takes to get back home. And how I am in control of nothing. I think: *someday you will never control me ever again*. But that day feels a lifetime away. I track my eyes to the edge of the horizon, past the cotton to that one straight line that goes on forever. And that's when it dawns on me: I don't think I can go on.

~

Years ago descendants of the Quapaw, the Kaw, the Choctaw, and the Chickasaw live on this land. Before them, it is probably the Pacaha tribe that greets Hernando De Soto who travels up the Mississippi River as far as Blytheville. De Soto convinces the indigenous people that he is a sun god before he sticks his flag into this ground and spills their blood upon their land. It's not hard. The locals have never seen anyone like him. He revels in power. People who write about him admire his bravery and courage and are disgusted by the earth based "savages" and the "heathens" and the people they call "Indians." Before De Soto dies, one source says that he tells his men to take his body out at night, wrap it up with rocks so that it sinks to the bottom of the Mississippi River, so that he can become immortal. So that the people will continue to fear him. So that even in death he will have power over those he regards as weak.

~

Must we make others fear us in order to have power? Are these the qualities that we revere in our leaders? Is this what we are trying to cultivate in our children? If our children are experiencing problems with bullying, isn't that because our larger culture bullies? We are, after all, the strongest nation on earth, at least that's what we tell ourselves. In order to remain so, there must be weak nations, there must be people to put down in order to remain on top.

~

Why are men perceived as holy even when they become violent, angry, and sexual? I'm thinking of King David who is revered as a great ruler in the Bible. He was a warrior who had a good man killed by ordering him to move to the front lines of battle so he could steal his beautiful wife. He made many mistakes and still he is revered.

But what does it take for a woman to receive our holy projections? Must she remain pure, innocent, docile, silent, and unsexed like the images we've been given of the Virgin Mary? Must she remain controllable and agreeable to men asserting their power over her?

The Goddess was once worshiped in temples, on hills and high places. The oldest cultures of humanity were matriarchal and honored life as expressed in nature and the feminine form. Brothers would raise their sister's children in the house of the mother, that way if the sister's marriage ended, her and her children's stability did not.

King Solomon—the one who wrote the steamy love letters in the Bible and saw Lady Wisdom as God's consort—built one of these high places to honor the Goddess Astarte, the Goddess of fertility and sexual love. But these high places were removed during Josiah's reform.

My family warned me that the Goddesses were the false gods to the one Holy Father God of our Lutheran roots. But something about Jesus' tender message of love and equality, grace and forgiveness makes me suspect that he knew all about the sacred feminine and maybe he was planting her love in the roots of incoming patriarchy. Woman has been demonized ever since Eve bit the apple from the Tree of Knowledge so she could know like God knows. Waking up and becoming conscious, it seems, is the very first sin.

~

"And the categories are: Math, Science, Current Events, Bible, and Music."

My father sits at the head of the table, in control of the conversation, in control of the game. My mother has spread out the Technicolor tablecloth again. A large turkey sits on a white plate and Great Grandma's fine china decorates each place setting. I drool over the sweet potatoes and the stuffing. My hunger is ravenous.

"Peter, my only son, gets to go first."

~

Something was special about my brother. This is the family story. He was sickly as a child and suffered with asthma. A few times he stopped breathing and was rushed to the ER. I witnessed my family protecting and nurturing my brother through many difficult times. Peter's illness allowed us to touch our own fragility in a way that brought sweetness and gentleness into our lives. I would often feel the same tenderness when beholding Jesus' suffering on the cross: it wasn't fair for the innocent to suffer, or for my brother. It turns out that doctors gave my mother some "wonder drug" when she was pregnant with him that caused asthma in children. As he was struggling, my parents got a prophecy or something. They believed that Peter was called to change the world for the glory of God. Sensitive boys could escape the man code of social hazing by becoming spiritual leaders. Here they could hold the tension of opposites for the masses.

My parents weren't really sure what I was meant to be and neither was I. We didn't have the ancient script for a sacred woman's journey, nor permission to use it. We had instead centuries of programmed fears of a powerful woman acting on her own authority outside of the bounds of patriarchy being rebellious and an abomination before God. We had the knee jerk dread flowing from ancient history through our veins warning us what happens to the Jezebels and the Whores of Babylon. We had the silence imposed by doctrinal counsels and the Inquisitions and witch burnings to trigger us even at unconscious levels to stay quiet and leave women's mystical wisdom alone.

Woman was merely man's helpmate, a function which pertains to her alone. She is not the image of God but as far as man is concerned, he is by himself the image of God.

-Saint Augustine

"No fair!" Emily and I complain.
"Math," Peter says smirking.
"Great." I push my body away from the table.
"Name three examples of an integer." I roll my eyes.
"1, 2, 3!" Peter yells.
"Ding! Ding! Ding! You are correct," my father says.
"Music," Peter says.
"Name and sing a line in a song that has a perfect 7th."
"Superman!" I blurt out. "Dund da da da, dund da da da—"
"ERRRR!—only half right—you have to sing on pitch."
"Dund da da da, Dund dad a da." Mom nails it for the win.

"Music for two hundred," she says.

"This is too hard!" Emily whines.

"Okay, who can sing the theme song for the new television show, Saved by the Bell?"

"What show is that?" I look at Peter as he raises his eyebrows.

Emily squeals out the melody in perfect tune.

"Oh my gosh, this game is rigged," I say.

"Final question, winner takes all," my father says. "And the category is Bible."

All of us sit on the edge of our seats. No one dares to take a bite of the mouth-watering food before us.

"Who was the shortest guy in the Bible?"

"Knee-hi-miah!" My brother screams.

"No! Bildad the Shoe-height!" I yell.

"Ding! Ding! Ding! Jessica, you have won an all-expense paid trip to the Bahamas OR you can choose what's behind door number one."

"I'll take door number one, please."

"A new car!"

I run around the table cheering. "Yes! I win! I win!"

~

It's a chilly Saturday night and most of the leaves have fallen from the trees now. I am a few houses away from home, in bed with a complete stranger.

I love the way he looks at me. His eyes are bright like they reflect a light that comes from within me. I didn't know I had any light, but it is there in his eyes that seem to glow in the dark. He doesn't say a word. It's as if we can read each other's minds. He knows exactly what I want and he thinks I know exactly what he wants. He puts his muscular arms around me and pulls me into his warm chest. I love the strength of his body. He smiles at me. He unbuttons his pants and slides them off. He takes my hand to his mouth, then his chest, and then down to touch him.

I retract my hand, smile, and cuddle into his body.

He pulls my chin up and kisses me. He presses his body onto mine.

I relax in his arms, so happy to be held, to snuggle.

He takes my hand again and puts it on top of himself.

I glide my fingers up his back, tickling him, like my mother tickled my back as a child.

He pushes my hand back down and places it firmly on top his erect penis. It's so strange, all these external parts, all this hair. I have no idea what to do next. He pushes me away from him. Throws the sheets to the floor and puts his pants back on.

"What's wrong?" I ask.

"What's wrong with you? You're supposed to know what to do." He walks out of the room, slamming the door behind him. I should have shown him my Queen of Prudes ID.

I walk like I am drunk, but I am not. I've never been drunk. I'm just stunned. Rejected. I thought he liked me. Everyone told me he liked me. I just wanted to cuddle. I lie on a couch and close my eyes. Kids from school pile into the house. Mostly high school kids I don't know. They wear letter jackets and cowboy boots. Hold beers in their hands and talk way too loud.

"There's the little slut," some pretty girl says. People start to look at me. One guy puts his crotch in my face.

"Come on—give me some!" He shakes his hips back and forth.

"Knock it off." A big football player with a kind face comes to my rescue. "Hey—you're friends with Marissa, right? You might want to take her home," he says.

I dash outside. Marissa can barely walk. She's hanging on some guy's arm.

"Get off me!"

I watch Marissa fall to the ground. "Robby," she says. "Robby!" I run to her. "He's so cute," she slurs.

"Come on, Marissa—let's go home." I put her arm around my neck and we trek back to my house. Leaves crunch under our feet, all brown and dried up.

The house is quiet. My brother and sister are sleeping. My parents are gone. At the Officer's Club. Some Christmas Party.

"Why?" Marissa looks at me with her emerald eyes. "Why doesn't he like me?" She sprawls out on the cold linoleum floor.

"I like you Marissa. I like you so much."

I hear keys jingling, the kitchen door opening up, the clicking of high heels getting louder.

Marissa throws up just as my parents appear, and the smell of alcohol fills the air.

"Oh sweetheart!" My mother runs towards her, lifts her head and holds her blonde hair behind her head while she wretches again.

"What's going on here?" My father stands tall like a statue in the corner of the room.

"I think she got into our box of wine. Jessica—go get some paper towels."

My mother touches Marissa so tenderly. I stand there frozen, reaching a hand out, wanting to touch this woman, wanting her to hold me the way she holds Marissa.

"Now!" she says.

~

My father holds a cup of black coffee in one hand, the red Bible in the other.

"You know what time it is, how it is now the moment for you to wake from sleep."

I can hear Peter snoring under his comforter.

"For salvation is nearer to us now than when we became believers; the night is far gone, the day is near. Let us then lay aside the works of darkness and put on the armor of light; let us live honorably as in the day, not in reveling and drunkenness," my father pauses and looks up at me, "...not in debauchery and licentiousness, not in quarreling and jealousy. Instead, put on the Lord Jesus Christ, and make no provision for the flesh, to gratify its desires. The word of the Lord."

He shuts the book with one hand in dramatic fashion.

I look up at the picture of the dead Native American warrior and his speared horse. *Do not gratify the desires of the flesh*, I think. *If I want to be holy, I must kill those instincts.*

My mother's eyes are puffy behind her thick glasses. I can't tell if she's been crying or if it's just her allergies. I know what they want from me, but I can't give it to them. I don't know how to lock down my inner world and perform like a good solider. I don't understand my role. Where are my guides through this initiation of puberty? I look out the window and watch the wind move the empty branches on the trees.

"Jessica," my father finally says. "You are not allowed to hang out with Marissa for a month—understood?"

"Yes, sir," I say, pushing my voice through the familiar lump. I retreat into my room and turn up the radio while I get ready for school. Aerosmith's new song plays, "Janie's Got A Gun."

~

My mother buys a miniature poodle. Tupa means 'little bit' in Norwegian. My great-great grandparents set sail to America from Norway in 1869. In the 1862 Homestead Act, our government gave Native American land away, like they had always owned it, like it was theirs to give. My ancestors leave in May and arrive in Quebec in early July. Legend has them leaving and arriving on both countries' Independence dates. My great grandpa Hjalmar is born on September 25, 1881, six days after the death of President James Garfield, who was shot earlier in the summer. Hjalmar's parents build their homestead in Astoria, South Dakota. According to my grandmother, Ole Rolvaag interviewed Hjalmar's older brother Sven about his father to create the character Per Hansa in his novel, *Giants in the Earth*. My great grandfather lives to one hundred and three. I remember visiting him in the "old folks' home." He calls me Julie, my mother's name. His ring and pinky fingers curl up and dig into my back when he gives me a hug—a Viking gene apparently. My mother's ancestors are musicians, teachers, and Lutheran clergy. Hjalmar is a minister like his father. He knows many languages. He pastored two churches where my grandmother grew up, just thirty minutes from where I live now.

~

I wonder how we as ministers, shamans, and holy ones reconcile the history and sorrowful spirits that cry out for redemption from the earth below? How do we transform the violence of our collective past? How do we stop repeating history as it reaches into our present lives aching and begging to be healed? Do we just ignore it? Really?

This is what I have been taught—don't talk about it. But the silence seems to only make the unconscious grow more wild for voice. How do we release the trauma from the fields we live in? Fields that push us to shut down the light of our soul, social pressures that ask us to stop feeling, stay busy, don't ask why, just obey. For what end? And for who? And who benefits? Certainly not all beings. Certainly not. Who is really in charge here? And why do we continue to let them be?

~

The dog poops all over my room. It's obvious even to her where all the shit belongs: put it on me, the bad girl. My mother is so sweet to the dog, like it is a child, her little baby. When did I stop being her little baby? When did I become a place for her to put her fears? We come home one day and discover that the parakeet's cage has been left open and Tupa ate the bird.

"It's instinct," my mother shrugs. "You can't be mad at a dog for that." I receive more insidious messages: *instincts are destructive and deadly. They will kill our pets and our soul. Shut them down.*

~

I have the piano when my father is at work and I have my guinea pig, Cupcake. She squeaks when I walk in the room. She nuzzles her nose into my armpit and snuggles with me when I am sad, which is often now.

I also have my brother. I teach Peter how to fix his hair. We listen to New Kids on the Block. My brother can really sing. We practice the latest dances. We learn all the lyrics to Ice, Ice, Baby. If I can't be cool, maybe he can. I vow to help him navigate this cruel world. I try to train him, like my mother is training Tupa.

~

I sit on the bleachers in the gym, self-conscious under the fluorescent lights. I pull out my compact mirror and apply another coat of powder. Marissa's not in school today and I am lost without her.

I watch the circles of girls gathering around each other. I compare myself to each one of them. My whole life I have been doing this, trying to solve the mystery of what is wrong with me. This is what I have learned so far: my hair is too short, my teeth are too crooked, my legs are too long, my feet are too big, my knees are too bony, my hips are too skinny, my breasts are too small and my clothes are too generic. And this is the worst part: I have no feasible plan for fixing any of this.

Girls slit their eyes and stare at me. *Why do they hate me? They've never even talked to me.* This phenomenon begins in Arkansas, but strangely, it continues throughout my life. I begin to develop a fear of women, especially groups of women who gossip. I fear they have all the power to shape who I am with their stories; that my real self will never be able to escape the webs they spin.

"Hey," a tall skinny boy walks up to me. "You OK?"

"Sure," I say studying his face. "You, uh, look familiar."

"Yeah." He pushes his glasses up his nose. His blonde hair is long on one side and shaved on the other.

"You were there that day," I say. "Jason?"

"Yes, that's me. I was there," he repeats. He looks at me like he can really see me. His gaze is unflinchingly kind.

"Hey, I don't know what happened. But if you ever want to talk about it, I'm here."

"OK," I say. "Thanks."

~

I'm falling behind in the lowest level of math. I sit down at the dining room table with my sheet of homework. It's dark outside. My father sits beside me, his lips push together tightly, his eyebrows in a furrow.

"OK," he says. "All you need to know in math is how to add, subtract, multiply and divide. Simple as that."

"Not so simple," I say.

"Sure it is. First copy the equation here." He points to the clean sheet of paper. I write the numbers.

"Wait. Wait. Wait. Is this the only pencil you've got?" He inspects the end. "It's not even sharpened," he frowns. He gets up and returns with a perfectly sharpened pencil.

"Now. Write here." He points at the paper.

I copy the numbers. I flip them around.

"Wow. That's not even the right equation," my father grabs the pencil out of my hands, turns it upside down and gives it back to me.

"Erase that."

I try to rub the numbers away, but the eraser catches on the paper and wrinkles it up. Just like my future son, I struggle with fine motor skills.

"Really, Jessica? This is ridiculous. Didn't you ever learn how to use an eraser?" He flattens out the paper, rubs the eraser perfectly until all the lead is gone and blows the debris into the air.

I begin again. The lead snaps.

"God," he says, "you're pushing too hard!"

I crumple up my homework and throw it across the room.

"I hate math and I hate you!" I run into my bedroom. He storms after me. I lock the door. He pounds on it.

"Jessica Jean, you will open this door right now."

"Leave her alone," I hear my mother say. "Let her cool off."

~

I'm falling.

A shiny blade sits on the edge of the bathtub. I've never seen a blade like this. I pick it up and turn it. The light shines off the metal and into my eyes. I don't have to live like this, I think. I could just stop it all right now. All the pain would just go away. I could just cut the Blah-ville out of me.

I take the blade and push it into my wrist. It's dull. There is rust on the end. I push harder. I move it back and forth. I watch the beads of red appear. I am not sure how this is supposed to work. I rub the blade up and down.

~

In some Native American burial rites, the women gathered around the corpse cutting their bodies and pouring their blood over the dead to mourn on behalf of the entire community.

~

I am afraid of death. I am afraid of pain. And I am afraid of God. I remember the story of the talents: Judgment day. I hear a booming voice in my mind.

"What have you done with the gifts I have given you?"

I reply, "I have no gifts. I'm just a stupid girl!"

Will God have mercy on a stupid girl? I sit and think about it. *No. There's no way God would do that.* All I see is fire and brimstone, hell and horns and little red devils. I stop. *Is there a place in this world for a stupid girl? No.* I return to moving the blade back and forth. Hopeful. Afraid. Torn between life and death. *Maybe if I could find someone to love me, maybe then I would be okay.* I stop. I rinse the blade out in the sink and return it to the side of the bathtub and try to clean up my arm. But what I wish I thought was: *maybe I need to learn how to love myself.* Sometimes children need it modeled to them first. I forgive myself for not knowing any better.

~

I sit at the piano. My fingers find the keys that make the sounds to match the feelings inside. I can tell it irritates my mother. She disappears in the kitchen. I play louder. I press my hands into the bass clef. Suddenly she appears beside me. She grabs my wrist and turns it over.

"What is this?" Her eyes are like daggers. I can't find an ounce of compassion in them.

I don't say a word. The music should have said it all.

"Jessica Jean, you tell me what this is!"

"It's nothing!" I yank my arm out of her hand. Of course it's nothing. The dark feelings no one wants to deal with, the ones that are not allowed to incarnate our words, how can they even be real if they are never spoken?

What I don't understand is that her anger masks her fear. And she has no idea what to do. And neither do I.

~

The pastor is right, the end is near. Beginnings and endings are always close together. I pick up the telephone to call Marissa, but my mother is already on the line. I put my hand over the receiver and press the phone into my ear.

"We want to send her away," my mother says. "To boarding school. To a school for troubled girls."

I take a deep breath. *Why don't they ever ask me what's wrong? They don't care*, I think. But now I wonder if they were afraid of my feelings because they didn't know how to navigate their own. Did they have anyone to model that for them?

"Can you make any recommendations?"

"Hold on." It's my uncle Dan. I hold my breath.

After a few minutes he comes back. His voice is strong and clear.

"She can come and live with us."

Someone will save me after all.

~

It happens so fast. Within a week I am all packed and ready to go. I kiss Cupcake goodbye.

"I'll be back, I promise," I say through the lump in my throat. I pull my suitcase to the driveway and survey the gray world. A little light lines the horizon as the sun begins to rise.

"Time to go," my father says. His shoulders slump. I wonder if he is more disappointed in me or in himself. My father believes there are clear obvious answers to be found in life. Right now there are none. I am broken and no one can fix me.

I assume my father favors my siblings because they are better at math and science and I have too many feelings. When I grow up, he tells me how proud he is of me. I remember it came with a caveat.

"I was worried because you were such a strange little girl," he said.

And I remember feeling his fear when he looked upon me. I remember holding it, incarnating it, because it had no other place to go.

He puts a new mixed tape into the cassette player. My father doesn't know how to talk about feelings, neither does my mother. That's what music is for. It sings out into the darkness and calms the anxious waters. I listen to the contours of his heart, the delicate piano playing, the harrowing melodies, the uplifting power chords. I know he's trying to reach me. To tell me he cares. But I can't bear it. He plays all my favorite songs. The old ones from my childhood. Amy Grant. Harry Nilsson. The Beatles. I bury my head in a pillow, like a small boat hiding among the rocks. All the way to Littleton, Colorado, I wade the waters of a mercurial sea, fearing the lighthouse and each passing storm.

Part II
The Tree Cut Down

Light a lamp for me
here in the dark
I can't see the moon,
or my mother.
Even the evergreen branches scratch my skin,
the dirt and needles stick to my feet.
Am I leaving
or returning
or turning round again?
A candle in the night,
one light to lead me home.
All I need,
is a thought,
a word,
a seed,
some new beginning.
Enough to save the world.

Leaving behind nights of terror and fear
I rise
Into a daybreak that's wondrously clear
I rise.

-Maya Angelou

NEW GIRL

I move west looking for gold like the old panhandlers who came before me. I don't need to be rich. I need to know something of value. I need to know that I have worth.

Four candles are lit on the advent wreath that sits on the long dining room table in the Franklin's home. I can taste the evergreen in the air. The biggest Christmas tree I have ever seen stands in front of the bay windows; little fairies seem to dance around the tree among the soft white lights. The angel on top nearly touches the cathedral ceiling. My siblings and I soon realize the necessity of such a large tree: our cousins get a million presents.

We finish opening ours long before they do and we watch with growing jealousy as they unwrap each additional one. Peter begins a tally. Emily falls asleep on my mother's lap. I stare at my little stack of gifts. They symbolize the lack of love I feel. My parents rarely buy me anything I want. We get practical things like socks and reams of paper to load up our school binders. And underwear. I mostly dread my father's underwear gift to my mother. It's usually some piece of lingerie and Dad often crosses the line by oversharing something about their sex life. My mother is sure to remind me of the children all over the world who don't have enough food to eat this night and how I should be more grateful and less selfish. My cousin Erika is Peter's age and her sister, Kirstin is Emily's age. I am the firstborn grandchild on my mother's side of the family, which means I set the example for the next generation. I do so by rolling my eyes often.

When all the wrapping paper is on the floor and the advent candles are blown out, I retreat upstairs to my new room. Kirstin moves out of her room for me and into a bunk bed with her sister Erika. I put my hands against the large window above the bed. Even in the dark I can see the snowflakes falling outside. They're huge, like the ones we used to cut out in school and hang from the ceiling. They cover the foothills in the distance, and the mountains beyond.

My family leaves a few days later. We give awkward goodbyes. Their eyes are hard, impenetrable. Everyone seems stuck in so much shame.

"You be good," my father says to me.

His shoulders hunch over again. I'm not sure if my mother even hugs me. I hold on extra tight to my brother. He knows something is wrong. My sister knows too, but in ways she cannot express. For now and for many years, she will hate me for what I have done to our family, how I am ripping it apart in my rebellion. It is only in the eyes of my brother that I feel truly seen. His forehead wrinkles with worry.

"I'll be okay," I say. "You will be okay too," I add. But I have this awful feeling that I am abandoning him. "Keep up your dancing," I say, "See you in May." I watch the backs of their wrinkly shirts walk away from me and I know that I am officially in exile.

~

Why exactly are the Israelites in exile? The writers of the Hebrew Bible grapple with this question in depth. Some conclude that the Israelites have committed a grave sin for which they are being punished. Several writers in the Old Testament point towards the sin of idolatry, of mixing with other cultures and Goddesses, of veering away from their own purity. At the same time, one of the most sacred practices highlighted throughout the Bible is that of welcoming strangers and outcasts. There is a religious tension between purity and welcome. What the descendants of the Abrahamic faiths often forget is that the practices of purity are actually rooted in the ancient Goddess cults which revere cycles and connection to nature and the honoring of balance rather than domination. Aphrodite, the Goddess of Love was known as a Goddess of renewal, as were many of the Goddesses associated with the celebration of Spring's return. These rituals were later Christianized and celebrated with Jesus' death and resurrection. Aphrodite's temple was torn down and replaced with

The Church of the Holy Sepulcher in the early 300s which still stands today in the old city of Jerusalem.

~

"We need to lay some ground rules for your time here," Uncle Dan says. He sits at the head of the table and punctuates the air with his fork. I stare at my plate of bacon, eggs, and toast. I don't know why, but suddenly I miss my family. The unfamiliar makes my stomach churn. I may prefer the hell that I know. I wonder how far away my parents have driven. If there's any chance they could still come back and get me. But I know that the angel with the fiery sword stands between us now. I know I cannot ever return to the way things used to be.

"First of all," Uncle Dan takes a moment to swallow his eggs. His sandy brown hair matches the color of his mustache exactly. I wonder how his skin stays so tan—even in the middle of winter—as if light shines from within him.

"The most important thing is that we respect one another and that we learn how to be a family together while you're here."

I sip my orange juice. "Uh huh," I say.

"Secondly," his eyes are wide with life, "we have arranged for you to see a counselor every week."

"Do my parents know about this?" I fiddle with the coaster beneath my cup.

"They have agreed to this too." I sigh and wonder how in the world my father agreed to let me do something he thinks is completely bogus. He must be feeling pretty desperate.

"Okay," I say. "Anything else?"

"Yes," he talks slowly and calmly. "We would like for you to join the confirmation class at our church. We have talked with our pastor and she has agreed to confirm you in May with the other kids if you join the program now." He looks hopefully at Auntie Jo.

"I think you'll really like our pastor." Auntie Jo talks in a quiet voice. I can't read her very well.

"It's a woman?" I never had a woman pastor. Growing up, I heard a lot about the sin of a woman being put in a position over a man. This sounds rowdy. Rebellious.

My aunt and uncle wait for my reply.

"Okay," I say as I take a bite of my food.

~

My body is adjusting to this new environment. The arid climate makes my lips crack when I smile. The skin on my back and fingers break when I bend. It's a thirsty land, like me, a desert aching for living water.

~

In the 1860s Richard S. Little moves to Littleton, Colorado from Wisconsin to irrigate the land. Just a year earlier the Pikes Peak gold rush begins. When they find gold, they break the treaties they made with the Natives, demonstrating that the powerful don't have to follow their own laws. Mr. Little's men begin digging ditches to move the water from the Platte River to Denver and the surrounding areas. The open wounds of the earth now carry water to wherever the conquering people decide. I wonder if anyone ever thinks to ask Mother Earth permission before doing whatever they want to her body.

~

"So, tell me about Arkansas," the short female counselor says.

"It's weird," I say. "Like, they still believe in slavery and stuff."

"Really? How do you know this?" she asks.

"They called me a nigger lover because I talked to black people."

"Oh my gosh." I think I shouldn't have used the "N" word when she lifts her eyebrows. The little woman looks burdened with all the suffering of life already.

"Jessica," she says, "Tell me why you think you are here."

I look out her window at the view of downtown Denver. I see a few skyscrapers, but no mountains because we face east.

"Um... because my parents couldn't handle me?" I put a strand of hair behind my ear.

"And why do you think your parents couldn't handle you?" She leans closer.

"Um... because we always fight?" My fingernails look awful! Did I remember to pack any nail polish?

"And why do you always fight?"

"Um… because they don't understand me?" I wonder if Auntie Jo has any nail polish I can borrow. I don't think she paints her nails though—much less hot pink or fire engine red.

"You know you can tell me anything," she says. "Jessica," she leans forward. "Why did you cut your wrist?" Icy fingers dig into my lungs. I turn over my arm and look at the red scar. My head hurts. Why did I NOT cut my wrist would be so much easier to answer.

"Um… because everybody hated me in Arkansas?" I look out the window again. I can't even be sure of my feelings or my interpretations of reality. I see a homeless person pushing a shopping cart on the sidewalk below. I think: my problems are so insignificant.

"I'm sure everyone did not hate you—but you felt like a lot of people did, didn't you?"

My chair grows incredibly stiff. I try moving around. I just can't get comfortable. "Um… I have no idea."

"Do you think it was because you're so pretty?"

I laugh. "I'm not pretty!"

"Of course you are, Jessica. You're so tall and thin and you have gorgeous big blue eyes…"

My hands are shaking. My heart is pounding. I look around her cozy little office like I'm looking for some cue cards. I stare at the small red elephants standing on the coffee table and the colorful tapestries hanging on the wall. Nothing comes to me. Only the wordless growing cold.

"Do you want a Coke?"

"Yeah, that would be awesome," I sigh. She leads me down the hall to the snack room. I stand head and shoulders above her. She puts two quarters in the machine and hands me the can that rolls out.

"Thanks."

I realize this is going to be a lot harder that I thought.

~

"Your mother told me that you're not allowed to wear black eyeliner," my Auntie Jo says in a quiet voice. Her face looks similar to my mother's. They have the same color eyes, but Jo's are veiled in more pensive shelters of bone. Her dark brown hair frames her face so simply, like it takes her no effort at all to be beautiful. I imagine her teenage life in the 60s filled with so much more freedom than mine.

"What?" I throw my arms down into the sides of my body. "She lets me wear it!" I protest, "Just not so dark." But Jo doesn't even blink. She just keeps looking at me with her thoughtful eyes. I go back to the bathroom and turn the radio up loud. Duran Duran sings, "I Don't Want Your Love." I hate my mother. All the way across the country she is still able to ruin my life.

I make my hair extra big instead. I curl my bangs as high as the mountains around me. I use half a can of hairspray so nothing will make them fall down. When I come out of the bathroom my aunt and uncle look at me for one very long second. Their lips part. But I know instantly that they are nothing like my parents because they don't utter a single word. Years later I learn Auntie Jo used to rat her hair and wear white lipstick and black hoodies. I wonder if she thinks of those days as she looks at me now. They give me a safe space to create a self—without black eyeliner.

~

Uncle Dan and I walk out the front door to the driveway. They own a big brown house on the corner of the street. Across the street there's a playground, wide-open land, and endless prairie. In the distance little rooftops decorate the bottom of the foothills and surround us like a mother's arms.

"Have fun, Jessie!" Erika waves to me and smiles. Her bright blonde hair hangs straight down to her shoulders. She has her father's hazel eyes and tan skin. Her optimistic happiness annoys me because it's something I don't feel I have access to. I force a smile and wave.

We climb into the Franklin's blue Taurus sedan and drive down West Quarto Avenue to West Columbine Drive and all the way to Deer Creek Middle School.

"I'd like to introduce you to my brilliant niece, Jessica!" Uncle Dan quickly has the office staff laughing and smiling. He's like my father in this way, a bridge, a community builder.

He seems to know almost everyone in the school district on a first name basis. He's lived in the area since his kids were little. Uncle Dan works as a guidance counselor at Englewood High School and Auntie

Jo is a highly sought after elementary teacher in the Cherry Creek school district.

I cast a furtive look his way. *Brilliant?* I mean, I appreciate him trying to cover for me, but I know it will just be a matter of time before I disappoint everyone. We walk the halls together. Shake hands and smile at teachers. The school is open and spacious. Natural light flows in through skylights and large windows. It's so different from the musty enclosed rooms of Gosnell Junior High. I actually feel smarter here. I actually start to hope again.

My class schedule is Earth Science, Typing, Art, Lunch, Language Arts, American History, and Math. As I peek in the classrooms my heart begins to race. All the other kids are probably twice as smart as me. I wonder if I'll make decent grades or any friends at all.

The last room we visit is outside in a trailer, my Earth Science classroom. We walk up fresh wooden steps. Windows open to the world on both sides. I can see the mountains. "He's supposed to be one of the best teachers here," Dan smiles at me.

"Yeah, but I hate science and I'm not very good at it either."

"That may be so, but I believe in you Jessica, and I think you'll be great at it if you put some effort into it."

~

The Franklins immediately go to work on building up my self-esteem.

"Now, where did you get this idea that you're a ditzy blonde?" Jo says. Erika makes me stand in front of the mirror and tell myself that I love math and I'm good at it. Jo buys me a journal and encourages me to write. But I can't shake it. My smile fades and my heart is like a black hole. My fingers tremble. I'm just lying to myself. No matter what I think or say, I can't escape it. I can't escape the way I feel in a crowd. The way I close down. The way the fear grows around me because I know how quickly people can turn on me, how easily they can humiliate me. How simple it is to measure me up, strip me down and be reduced to nothing in everyone else's eyes. How I have no skills to protect myself from that happening over and over again. I wonder if this is a past life thing. Was I burned at the stake? Or is it just the dread I trigger in everyone as I feel their separation from love as much as I feel my own?

"This isn't working," I tell Erika. "I've always been stupid." My eyes well up with tears. I can't explain it to them. They'll never understand. I made one big mistake and a million others leading up to it. How am I supposed to be smart all of a sudden? I'm afraid. Afraid that I'll do more stupid things. Afraid that I can't prevent it because I'm so naïve, so needy for love, so needy for touch. I can't stop dreaming of guys, of imagining the perfect one protecting me in this unpredictably dangerous world.

~

"You alone are the most high, Jesus Christ, with the Holy Spirit, in the glory of God the Father, Amen."

The congregation sings. Dark wood and brick decorate the small sanctuary of Epiphany Lutheran Church. It seats a little over fifty people on any given Sunday. We sit in uncomfortable creaky pews. The ascending ceilings touch at a narrow point above us. Beams and banners hang in the air. Small stain glass windows let in a little light. Green cloths cover the liturgical furniture. A woman stands in the pulpit, dressed in a white robe, adorned with a green stole that matches the altar cloths. She has long wavy hair and wears big nerdy glasses like I did back in Omaha. She looks nervous. I wonder if she worries about men doubting her ability to be a pastor, like the men would at the churches I grew up in.

"Out of darkness we are called, into light, into the richness of God's Kingdom," she says and smiles.

She talks about the three kings. She asks us what gifts we bring to Jesus. What gifts we can share with the world. I hate thinking about these questions. I always draw a blank when adults ask me what I want to be when I grow up. I just want to love and be loved, that's all I want.

In the greeting line I shake her hand. She reminds me of myself, and parts of me I fear.

"It's so nice to have you with us," Pastor Virginia says.

"Thanks," I say, suddenly aware of how incredibly uncomfortable I am in my own skin.

Confirmation turns out to be a class of four of us. We don't make much eye contact with each other. All forced to be here, ashamed and embarrassed by this certifiably uncool situation. We sit around long tables that extend down a room way too large for our group. It's cold and I tuck my hands inside the arms of my fuzzy pink sweater and stare at the Lutheran Book of Worship.

"Let's read this together," Pastor Virginia says. My eyes glaze over as I recite the Nicene Creed printed on the delicately thin page.

"I believe in one God, the Father Almighty, maker of heaven and earth, of all that is, seen and unseen."

I recite the creeds. I memorize their words. They don't reach my soul or my wounded mystic. I learn to cope with the numb feelings in my body, this desert within. I learn to see this as the normal condition of the spiritual life. Like a small coin, the Kingdom of Heaven is easily lost.

~

I wake up at 5:30 in the morning, but not for family devotions now. I make a sanctuary of my room. I light the soft lamp and tune into the radio station that plays the latest music. Martika sings, "Toy Soldiers." I lay the sacred objects on my desk like an altar: foundation, powder, blush, eye shadow, mascara, lipstick, blow dryer, curling iron, hairspray. My arsenal of protection. I must make an invincible mask.

~

How harsh is the public eye that one must build a false self in order to survive? It's as if the Inquisition lives on today in junior highs across the country, in our workplaces, in the court houses, our collective PTSD that continues to seed trauma into our future as it attempts to reconcile the wounds of the past. The still undiscovered soul is waiting to bloom in the mud. Millions of little baby Christs we so easily nail to the tree. "I only want to grow up!" the soul says, and for thousands of years she has been told: *No—it's not safe!* For there have been few divine mothers to be found, few dark shells to protect you while tender and young, few compassionate arms to hold you when hurt. Praise and rewards are given to the ones who feel the least.

Nature which would heal us has been polluted. We have willingly destroyed that which we need to grow into our dignified forms in our misguided quests to sever ourselves from our annoying, weepy little souls.

~

A picture of my family sits on my desk. It was taken on a weekend, right after school started, on a warm sunny day when the leaves turned vibrant. We drove around exploring the Ozarks in the northwestern corner of Arkansas. My father had several different sites picked out for our annual Christmas photo shoot. Of course it had to be perfect and better than last year's. He brought all his gadgets: the tripod, the extra batteries, the cables. He set the timer and counted aloud for us so we all knew when to smile. He must have taken over a hundred pictures. We smiled until our faces hurt, until we couldn't stand up anymore, until we were rolling around in the grass and throwing leaves at one another.

We listened to Supertramp on the drive home as the sun began to set behind the cliffs. We all sang along to the music. My father turned up the volume. My mother added harmonies and tapped her bare feet on the dash as she sang, "Goodbye stranger." I leaned my head against the window and felt the warmth on my face. I even smiled, truly smiled. Not the kind of forced smile that social situations demand, where you think it in your head and send the signal to your mouth, but the kind that begins radiating in your belly and lights little sparks that fire up inside your chest warming your entire body until the corners of your lips spread wide to your ears. But, that was before Behind the High School. Before everything fell apart.

I turn the picture down. I can't afford to feel my feelings. *It's not safe!* I pick up a can of hairspray and make my hair as hard as the rocks in my stomach.

~

The air is cool and crisp like fall, even though it's January. I watch my breath make clouds around my face as I walk to school. The sky is clear and crystal blue. White snow decorates the mountaintops on the horizon. I walk listening to the sound of my knock-off Eastlands scuffing the concrete. I like the quiet. The closer I get to Deer Creek

Middle School, the faster my heart begins to pound. At the sight of the crowd gathering, icy fingers dig into the back of my throat and scratch their way down my esophagus. I think: *Don't feel and don't say anything stupid.*

I squeeze my way through the crowd, avoiding eye contact with everyone. I hold my head high, pretending I need nothing and no one. I find my locker in the commons area. Gray carpet covers the floor. Natural light pours in through the large windows. Kids are grouping off in various cliques. I note the turf of the preps, jocks, druggies and nerds. One wild boy bounces from clique to clique. Waves of laughter erupt in every group he greets. From the sidelines I scan the room, wondering where I might fit in. I can't quite tell the difference between the rest of the cliques. Everyone looks well-dressed and upper-middle class. Who would have guessed this school had the highest suicide rate in the region? A few years earlier a kid walked in here and shot two of his classmates. Years in the future, another terrible shooting happens about a mile away, at Columbine High school, where many of these kids will go after I leave.

I hang my coat in my locker, slam the door and exit the east side of the building to the Earth Science trailer. The atmosphere is light and warm here. My heart slows. The teacher makes a special point to shake my hand and welcome me. His smile is easy. Brown shaggy hair falls around his face and his beard is grown out. He is dressed like he's ready to go hiking after class. After the general introduction, he tells us to talk in small groups and get to know the people at our table.

"Well, I'm Mel," the girl with long auburn hair says. Her brown eyes flash with sass. "I had an amazing Christmas break with my family in Vale. I like to snowboard in the winter and ride horses in the summer." She turns to the girl next to me, "What did you do over break, Brandi?"

Brandi is a thin girl with stringy blonde hair that hangs at her shoulders. She hunches over and wears more eye makeup than I'm allowed, but probably the same amount of hairspray.

"Nothing," she mumbles.

"Ooookay then," says Mel. "Mitch?"

I fiddle with my pen, twirling it around, biting it on the tip. My chest is about to explode. *Be cool*, I tell myself. *Please, dear God, just let me be cool.*

"And finally, the new girl. Where are you from?"

"I'm not from anywhere," I say. "I'm a military brat."

The three of them just stare at me.

"A what?" says Mel.

"My father is in the Air Force—we move every three years," I say.

"Ooooh, so your family just moved here?"

"Not really," I back peddle. "I'm living with my aunt and uncle right now. We, uh, well, my parents and I, uh, we don't really get along."

"Ah ha! So you're a BAD girl!" Mel says with a devilish grin.

"No—I…"

"They sent you away!"

"Not really, see…"

"Okay everyone! Open up your text books to page five. Let's see how the Industrial Revolution has changed our modern world and explore the current threats our civilization faces as our natural resources begin to run out."

~

Typing class is boring. The teacher commands us to type one or two letters over and over and over until we can do it with our eyes closed. We type on a beast of a word processor. Listening to the rhythmic clicks of everyone pressing the keys at the same time is enough to drive me mad. I beg the clock to release me, but time only slows down in this room.

My favorite class turns out to be Art. The teacher keeps the fluorescent lights off so that we use only natural light as we work with our materials. The only windows are small and in the back of the class, so the room is filled with comforting shadows. I don't worry about whether my make-up is blended in or if others can see the new pimple that popped up on my chin. We begin the course with pottery. My hands get lost in the wet clay. I make bowls, cups, ashtrays, plates. I create objects for holding substance. Sometimes when they're fired in the kiln, they don't come out all beautiful. Sometimes they crack and fall into a million pieces. You just never know which ones are going to make it through the fire.

After lunch I struggle to stay awake through language arts until we get to the section on Anne Frank. I am amazed how a young girl's writing can inspire the world. I see pieces of myself in her curiosity and I feel the dread of her inevitable doom. Reading her words kindles a fire within me. I want to write, not only for me, but for her, for all girls whose lives have ever been threatened in this mad world.

I begin to journal. I start to write poetry. I find another place for the feelings I fear.

~

After school I retreat in the cool basement of the Franklin home, down where it's dark and quiet. I like the feeling of being in a cave, of being sheltered and protected. The cat, Glenna, hangs out with me. Sometimes Kirstin joins me and we dress up in costumes and act out funny scenes together. Other times I lose myself in the TV images, recognizing pieces of myself in the stories.

I become obsessed with this movie, Dream a Little Dream, and the young actors Corey Haim and Corey Feldman as they wonder: is it better to live in a fantasy world instead of this complicated life? People affected by trauma must ask themselves the same question. Will we let trauma seal us off in a private enchanted inner world or will we work to connect our inner world with this one? Will we incarnate our soul and let our light shine on the earth plane?

~

Corey Haim committed suicide in 2010. Corey Feldman has since spoken out about the rampant childhood sexual abuse that happens to many young actors in Hollywood, how they both experienced abuse. How Corey Haim was passed around and abused more than most. How they both could not speak about any of it. How to this day he can't even name the man that continues to abuse children. I am drawn to these teenage boys because at a deep level, I sense they know what I know.

~

In my bedroom hangs a poster of the New Kids on the Block. They smile at me like they know me, like they understand my deepest feelings. The Franklins are nice, but how does my messy pain fit into their perfect life? I hope there are people out there who can understand the dark sides of me.

I walk to the playground across the street. The afternoon is warm for January, maybe fifty degrees. The sun shines bright as it begins to set behind the mountains. I sit on the swing and drag my feet in the rocks. I like looking at small things. The way the blades of grass bend in the same direction. The way the dirt clings to my shoes. I breathe in the crisp air. I feel it fill my lungs. There is so much potential here, and at the same time, so much holding me back.

"Hey—you new around here?"

I literally fall out of my swing and land at the feet of an adorable boy with dark curly hair who is looking at me with his sparkling green eyes.

"Heh, heh," I stand up and brush off my pants. "Uh, yeah, I'm new..." *Perpetually*, I think.

"You're the one asleep in typing class?"

"Oh no, I just close my eyes when I'm bored."

"I'm Derrick. Derrick Connor."

I smile and look down, "I'm Jessica," I whisper.

"You know you shouldn't close your eyes in class," he says.

"Why not?"

"Because you have the most beautiful eyes I've ever seen."

Suddenly I am hungry with thoughts of Derrick, as if he's balm for a wound he can't possibly heal. He writes me notes. He meets me at the park. We cuddle in his bed and kiss. It is a beautiful kiss, innocent, tender and wonderful. I feel the butterflies and I know there is hope. His affection helps me feel more confident.

~

My Grandpa Erling comes to visit. After dinner we go for quiet walks together. He fills the spaces with deep breaths and little phrases like, "Yep...So..."

We watch the sky darken, the stars light up the night. He seems happy just to be with me. We don't have to say anything. I don't have to pretend. I can just be me and not worry about being in trouble for it.

Grandpa drives me to counseling. My favorite song comes on the radio. Jo makes me listen to classical music when she takes me, but Grandpa turns my favorite song up louder.

"This is a wonderful," he says. He beams at me and I'm suddenly proud of my good musical taste. We soar peacefully down the highway listening to Phil Collins sing, "Another Day in Paradise."

~

"It's an easy blue," Erika says.

I look back at the green hill and wonder if I should believe her. I only learned to ski a few months ago.

"It really is," says Kirstin. "Even I can do it!"

I look at them in their cute matching ski outfits holding their poles and gear in just the right way. They have been skiing since they were three. They are adorable, all smiles, dimples in their cheeks. I am incredibly insecure and maybe just a little jealous. I am going to prove that I am good enough to hang with them.

"Okay," I say, "but if I die, it's all your fault."

The girls laugh and disappear on the small winding trail in the woods. I follow them. It's fun at first. The trail has all these little bumps. The bumps get bigger and instead of skiing over them, I begin catching a little air on the tops of them. I slow down. I imagine falling and cracking my head against one of the trees and I catch myself thinking negatively as my counselor has been teaching me. I practice the positive self-talk I have been working on instead.

You can do this, I say. *Just focus. Just breathe.*

I hold my poles tight to my body. I bend my knees and lean into the jumps. There is a rhythm to it. Bump. Bump. Bump. Bump. I feel the ground connect with my skis, I glide and lift and land again. Okay, this is not so bad. I grow more confident. The bumps grow bigger.

I can do this.

Bump. Bump. Bump. Bump. I start to love the feeling of my feet connecting with the earth, the way the energy shoots up my legs and sends joy into my heart. This is scary, but it is also fun. Joy and fear are closely related, I think. One gives way to the other. Bump. Bump. Bump. Bump. I choose joy. I choose joy.

    I can't see Kirstin or Erika anymore. I don't understand how they made it out of here so fast. Oh well, I am skiing a blue! Just wait until I tell my friends at school. Before I came to Colorado I didn't know how to ski at all. I feel proud of myself. I think: *I can learn new things!* My chest expands with hope. Bump. Bump. Bump. Bump. I am almost out of the woods. I can see the clearing ahead. One last bump: this one is the biggest of all. I am a little scared, but if Kirstin and Erika did it, then I can do it too. I pick up speed. I bend my knees deep. I put my poles nice and straight behind me. I listen to my skies glide over the snow. I smile and glide up the hill. When I reach the top, the sight in front of me transforms all of my joy into sheer terror: this is not a bump. This is a certifiably huge Olympic-sized ski jump.

    I remember when my brother and I used to play this skiing video game on our Atari. We'd hold the little stick shift and push the big red button. We'd make our skier do amazing tricks, leg kicks, spins, and flips. Most of the time the skier completely wiped out and we were disqualified. But it was so funny watching him wipe out. We'd do it over and over again just to see how badly we could make him crash. Who knew one day I would be that guy! I really don't want to be that guy. Too bad Peter isn't here to watch. This is going to be a good one. The mountain goes straight down. My skis lift off the peak and I fly into the air. I'm at least ten feet above the ground, maybe more.

    "Ahhhhhhh!" I scream.

    It's all slow motion now. I do some spread eagle move. I point my poles high into the sky, I stretch my legs out wide. Maybe a miracle will happen. Maybe I will actually land this jump. People who are skiing down the mountain actually stop and turn to watch me.

    "Ahhhhhhh!"

    I want to fast forward to the part where I'm drinking hot chocolate in the lodge. But my mind goes backwards instead. I am on the moped again, headed straight for the ditch. Why do accidents keep happening to me?

    My right ski hits the snow first. Then my rear end. The ski snaps off of my boot and lodges itself into the snow as I go rolling down the mountain with the one ski on. I roll into a snowball. I lose both my poles, my gloves and my hat, my sunglasses and my dignity. I roll all the way down to the bottom of the hill. I roll into a small crowd that has gathered to watch, and wouldn't you know it, I land at the feet of a really cute guy.

"Are you okay?"

"Yeah, I'm totally fine," I lie.

We both turn and look back up the hill at all my things scattered across the mountain.

"Oh God. Did that just happen?" I ask. I look up and see Erika and Kirstin standing on the side of the jump waving. I glare at them.

"Come on, let's go get your stuff," he says.

I walk up the mountain with the one ski on and I decide this is the hardest work out of my entire life. The cute guy helps me gather my things. We trek all the way back to the stupid jump, to Erika and Kirstin. I'm so beat by the time I get there that I'm too tired to dish out any crap.

"Jessie, you were supposed to ski around it," Erika tries really hard not to giggle. Kirstin has already buried her red face in her gloves.

I say, "Wow, that WAS an easy blue!"

We fall into the snow clutching our stomachs. I'm wiping tears from my eyes. The cute guy decides to ski with me and vows to protect me from any other hidden ski jumps. The rest of the day, in the lodge, on the slope, on the ski lift, people say to me, "Hey, you were the girl that took the jump!"

Hell yeah, that was me.

~

I get a D in math my first quarter. Uncle Dan gets me a tutor who sits with me calmly and helps me figure it out. I bring it up to a C by the time I finish the second quarter. I learn how to type. I experience that feeling of working hard at something and mastering it. I end up getting an A in my Earth Science class. I remember when I brought home my final report card. Uncle Dan was so proud of me. His eyes grew wide and he smiled and gave me the biggest hug. It wasn't a perfect report card. Two of my other grades had slipped. But he looked for the positive and he noted that my efforts had made a difference. These were all brand new feelings for me. A sense of accomplishment. A sense of pride. I started to feel more optimistic about my future. I started to let myself believe that I could make something out of my life.

~

May comes quickly and before I know it my confirmation day arrives. I stand in the bathroom in my brand new dress. Fuchsia flowers and green leaves hanging on me like I am the blooming spring herself.

My parents return to Colorado to celebrate this day and bring me back home. After a few awkward weeks, I make friends in Colorado. Without all the rumors and shame floating around, it's much easier than I feared. I go to sleepovers and toilet paper neighborhoods with twenty other girls. We go shopping, see movies, swap clothes, all the normal things girls do at this age. My friends even kidnap me on my birthday, and take me out for breakfast and then to school in my PJ's. I felt I belonged and it was wonderful.

The Franklins model a peaceful home to me. They treat me with dignity and respect and most importantly: they listen to my feelings. For a time, I know what it is like to be my best self—they see her and hold up a reflection of me that I can live with and be proud of.

It isn't all perfect. Sometimes I fought with Kirstin. I was jealous of Erika and some days I shut her out. I cuss once at Uncle Dan. But their response to me is gracious. They love me anyway. They forgive me. And I learn that love can survive the thorns.

I continued to meet weekly with my counselor, but I never told her about Behind the High School. I work so hard at convincing her nothing happened, that I begin to believe it too. The thought of my parent's reaction still terrifies me. I'm afraid to even think about the summer of 1989. I have a new story now and I am sticking to it: deny everything.

~

Pastor Virginia puts her hands on my poofy hair, and I'm surprised that I really don't care if she messes it up a little.

"Stir up in Jessica the gift of your Holy Spirit: the spirit of wisdom and understanding, the spirit of counsel and might, the spirit of knowledge and the fear of the Lord, the spirit of joy in your presence, both now and forever."

And then, everyone says, "Amen."

I turn to face my family. My grandparents are here too. All of them look at me with smiles on their faces and tears in their eyes. I see that they love me. I don't understand all the words at my confirmation, I don't even know if I believe them. But this I know: something in me has changed. In this moment I am happy—truly happy.

If my body is church
Then my arms are doors
Swung wide
And waiting to pull you close to my heart

Come sit here and wait
For the music to start
For the quiet to come
So you can hear what I have to say to you

Watch the cynical parade
Recess from the sanctuary
And hold tight to my promise of bliss
Until the veil is torn in two
And my taste is upon your tongue

For once the water drops into the wine
There is no separating you
From God

Sexuality and spirituality are pairs of opposites that need each other. Sexuality is of the greatest importance as the expression of the chthonic spirit. That spirit is the 'other face of God,' the dark side of the God image.

-Carl Jung

CHEERLEADER

The summer I return from Colorado, my family moves again.

I am informed that the first base housing unit assigned to us is not the appropriate housing for the rank of Commanders. Now we live in a larger newly remodeled home, with new carpeting in the bedrooms, central air, and a storage unit in our carport. And I have my own room.

I spend every weekday morning that summer at the pool doing laps with the swim team. I swim my heart out. It feels so good to be in my body and to put all of my emotions into the exercise. If I am having a bad day, I can cry in the water without anyone noticing. All of our eyes are red anyways from the chlorine.

I can swim. I place in meets in the backstroke and the breaststroke. I discover new aspects of myself. I grow in confidence. I learn more how to navigate the raging sea inside of me. My body is becoming less awkward and I am looking less like a child and more like a woman.

~

My parents and I continue to fight. Times like these I really miss Jo and Dan. They knew how to navigate these emotions better. They could guide me in a way that kept my best self intact. My parents and I spiral out of control together. My resentment for them grows alongside of a hatred I have for myself and we drift around a black hole of emotions not knowing how to pull ourselves out.

~

My father holds his coffee without taking a single sip as we watch the morning news together. Iraq has just invaded the little country of

Kuwait. I watch as the tanks drive across the land, the long cannon leading the way. I don't understand the global significance or the burden that sinks into my father. I don't understand how he must soon decide which personnel to deploy from his unit. How his choices could turn wives into widows and leave children without fathers.

I understand invasion though. I understand the dreadful weakness of being conquered, the feeling of someone more powerful than you driving a flag into the ground of your being and declaring it as their own. I know the desperate tears that cry out for someone in the world to help, like Persephone cries for her father Zeus when she is raped in the underworld. And I know what it feels like when Zeus looks away, when he decides he is unwilling to rescue his daughter from Hades who has claimed her as his own.

~

I am terrified of starting my freshman year of school. I have to return to Gosnell Junior High. I am worried that all the ground I've recovered will be taken from me.

But it doesn't happen. Marissa and I pick up right where we left off. We become the best of friends. Both she and Jason share history class with me. The first time Jason sees me, his eyes grow wide.

"Jess!" he says. "So good to see you!"

He runs towards me. I almost hug him. He seems to want to hug me too. But he keeps an awkward distance. Still, he's friendly, smiling at me in the hallways, saying hi. Sometimes he writes me silly notes in class that make me laugh.

~

Marissa makes me go out for track with her. Running helps channel my emotions too. Coach Stanley takes a special interest in me. He tells me I have talent. Marissa and I warm up together doing laps, catching up on the latest gossip. Marissa is a distance runner, slow and steady, but with my long legs, Coach assigns me to run all the sprints. At first I'm disappointed because I can't run as much with Marissa. But then I start to love the high I get from all the adrenaline. My favorite is the 4 x 100 relay. Coach puts me on the last leg and I get to cross the finish line. I run as fast as I can. It focuses me. I run until I can't think about anything else and everything goes quiet and all I hear is the wind in my ears and my breath leaving and entering my body. We place. We win medals. I throw up on the other side of the finish line.

"Good job, Jessica," Coach says. "I am so proud of you!"

I love hearing him say that to me. I love pleasing men and getting their approval. Like I'm still trying to earn my father's affections, still waiting to be rescued from my dark underworld.

~

Marissa and I share lunch together. Now I am better at blocking out the others who still look at me strangely and wonder about the girl who blew the whole football team. Every now and then someone asks me, "Hey, didn't you fuck Matt Black behind the high school?" I used to crumble when confronted. Now I look at them like they are the biggest idiots in the whole world and say, "No. How can you even believe that?" The force of the rumor has broken. I have a feeling that my classmates know something about why I had to leave.

I see Matt Black sometimes when I go to the High School for Spanish class. But Christian Roberts is gone. I haven't seen him since I returned. There is only one rumor that circulates about why he left: he molested a young girl and was brought back to another state to face charges. Good, I think. They got him. I imagine him rotting in jail for the rest of his life.

~

When I am in my late twenties, I take a course on sexual abuse prevention training and I learn about all the characteristics of a child predator: they are often well liked by a community, they are charming, they work hard in secret grooming children and paying them compliments, winning their trust by getting them to reject their parents' values and do things that would be too shameful to ever speak of. The more I learn, the more the memories of Christian return to haunt me.

~

I never have a real conversation with Matt Black. Jason tells me Matt felt manipulated by Christian and forced to act in ways that he didn't want. The two of them skate together sometimes. Jason tells me Matt didn't know it was my first time. He didn't understand why Christian was telling him to do this stuff and he was afraid of the consequences if he didn't do what Christian told him. The few times I see Matt, he tries to smile at me, but he's very shy and looks away. There seems to be shared feelings between us: shame and regret.

~

In early fall my mother makes a hair appointment for me with a new stylist in town. She's excited because he is really edgy and hip and she's been letting him cut her hair any way he wants. She wears it short now, with it sticking up in all different directions.

Before I go in for my appointment a concerned lady at church pulls me aside.

"Just be sure you keep your mouth shut when he's washing your hair. You don't want to get any of his saliva in your mouth—you never know—he's gay—he might have AIDS."

"What's wrong with being gay?" I ask my mother on the way to the salon.

"It's a sin," she says. She stares straight through me. I remember Pat Robertson saying that AIDS was God's judgment on gay people, that they deserved what they were getting. But that didn't feel right to me. That didn't match the gentle love I felt from God as a child. My mother tells me that AIDS is a moral sin.

"You only get it by doing bad things, so don't do bad things and you won't have to worry about it." I think that doesn't discount rape—but women are blamed for that all the time.

"People can have sex with anything, Jessica—even trees," she says. "God didn't create us to do that. Do you understand?"

But I don't understand what trees have to do with sex and AIDS. And I hate her judgmental gaze and her inability to have a conversation with me. It's always a lecture with my parents: they are right and I'm an idiot.

When I grow up, I think maybe she wasn't really talking to me all those years. Maybe she couldn't really see me. Maybe I reminded her of something she feared. Something in her past. Something in herself.

Billy the hairstylist is a handsome guy who wears ripped blue jeans. He looks like George Michael with his hair greased back wearing a little earring and a gold necklace. He squeals when I walk through the door.

"You're gorgeous! Oh! I cannot wait to style your hair!"

He inspects my split ends, compares the varying lengths, touches my chin and cheek bones and puts his finger to his lips and thinks for a few seconds.

Finally he says, "I want to make you look like Madonna."

He pulls out US magazine from June and shows me the cover. Madonna's hair is platinum blonde, soft curls frame her face and stop just short of her chin.

"OK," I say feeling super insecure.

I have been trying to grow out my hair for years. I don't really want it cut short, but maybe he knows better than me. I'm just so good at giving up what I want. I hardly have an "I" to advocate for.

My hair is already really blonde. He gives me a perm. The chemicals burn my scalp and when he unwinds the rollers, some of my hair falls out.

"You're a sensitive one, aren't you?" he says.

The perm took really well. Spiral ringlets curl tight and fall about two inches from my chin. Billy blow dries my hair and takes a razor to clean up the back of my neck. He spins me around to face the mirror.

"Darling, you are going to make the boys fall to their knees at the Homecoming dance!"

I smile, unsure what to think about my new hair. I want to feel what he feels about it. I want to feel gorgeous like he sees me. But all I feel is nervous.

At home I lock myself in the bathroom to critically inspect my new hair in private. I decide that I absolutely hate it. And while I'm at it, I also hate my knees, my flat chest, my stupid clothes and my family. I spend the next week crying about it all, thinking my life is completely over and the world is really coming to an end this time.

My parents and I fight wickedly. Everyone lashes out. I feel knocked down and depleted. And then a few days later I have my period and the universe realigns again. I begin to worry that my parents are starting to think I'm crazy. I hear people at church complain about rabid feminists. Christian radio and talk shows, and my family's dinner conversations start to worry me. I am anxious that my emotional needs will never be understood or met. I get the message over and over: *shut down your feelings, ignore your instincts, get with the program.* I know there are many things that my parents just cannot help me with. I worry that if I am honest about my feelings, they will send me away again. I worry if I open up, I will pull everyone into these yawning jaws of death that open inside of me. But the more I try to deny my feelings, the crazier I feel. As much as I want to forget the darkness, my body knows. Once a month, I am reminded. I am asked to return and care for the girl who is wounded. But I am terrified of her. I don't know how she and her big feelings will ever make it in this world.

~

My mother is sewing me a blue gown for homecoming. It's strapless; the front is shaped like a heart over my breasts, sewn extra tight so it doesn't accidentally fall down. A guy named Chris asks me to go with him. He thinks I'm beautiful. I hear new rumors now: do you model? Some guys still try to put me down, but others seem suddenly entranced, like they worship the ground on which I walk. It's strange, how difficult it is to be seen for who you really are, to just be a girl and simply be human.

Marissa has her hair cut exactly like mine. Our hair is now the talk of the school. Everyone tells us that we look like the Madonna twins. People don't know what to do with us. They mostly leave us alone in our mysterious allure.

~

The leaves turn again. I always feel like something exciting is about to happen when fall is in the air, even though the colors only signify that death is on its way. It's strange how I am drawn to the darkness, to danger.

My homecoming date arrives at my house for pictures. He's really too nice for me. He's sweet, but nothing about him stirs my butterflies. He wouldn't understand me, I think. He's all sunshine and I'm all storm clouds.

I work on my hair for an hour and it turns out beautifully. The tight spiral curls have relaxed a little and now they fall softly to my chin. I have given up on the tsunami and have let my bangs grow out to frame my face. The royal blue dress that my mother made matches the color of my eyes. Tonight, for the first time in my life, I feel like a princess.

The dark comes early now and the sky is already black when my father drops us off at the school gym. Chris takes my hand and helps me out of the car. The place is packed. Everyone is buzzing with excitement. What a night this will be!

We go straight to the long line for pictures before our hair gets tussled and our clothes wrinkle.

"Jessica!" A few girls scream and run up to me. One says, "You look so pretty!"

I smile, "So are you! Oh my gosh! What a great dress!"

I keep looking for Marissa, but I can't seem to find her anywhere. She is supposed to be here already.

After pictures, Chris puts his hands around my waist and leads me into the glowing gymnasium. There's orange Christmas lights hanging everywhere, pumpkins, big leaves taped to the walls and barrels of hay laying all over the floor. We dance every slow song together. Chris is a quiet prince charming. He can't stop smiling all night long. The school photographer comes over and snaps our picture. I don't know how it happens but my smiling face ends up on a full page of the yearbook. My peers have decided that I am not the lowest common denominator anymore. Now I try to distance myself from anyone at the bottom of the totem pole and I hate how I turn betray myself and others in order to survive in the world like we do.

We exit the floor for most of the fast songs. I don't really know how to dance. I join in for the Kid N Play, the Vanilla Ice, and the Humpty Dance, but the Lady Pirates Pom team takes over the dance floor. They do all their routines to the songs they have choreographed. I watch them move and feel inferior. They seem so comfortable in their own skin. I am jealous of the way they shake their hips and effortlessly smile. I start wondering again why everyone thought I was the whore. I don't move like that. I don't even know how.

Another slow song comes on. Chris lays his head on my shoulder while we dance to Whitney Houston singing, "Where Do Broken Hearts Go." I look across the room and I see Jason here with his date, Allie. I watch the way he looks at her. How his hands rest on the small of her back. Her long curly brown hair hangs just over his hands. Her dress is short, revealing her long skinny legs. My heart stops at the sight of them together. I don't understand why, but I don't like seeing him with her.

"Let's get a drink," I say as I pull Chris off the dance floor. I find Marissa standing by the snack table. She's gorgeous in a short sparkly gray dress. Her eye shadow is dark and her hair is teased out to perfection. But her body is stiff and her face is long like it was in the picture she first showed me when we met.

"What's wrong, Marissa?" I put my arm on her shoulder. I can see she's has been crying.

"Nothing," she says.

"Where's your date?"

"He left." Her eyes are vacant as they trail across the room.

"Let's go home," I say. "Do you want to spend the night?"

She sniffles and looks at my with her puppy dog eyes. "Can you spend the night at my house?"

We call our parents and finalize the details. Chris seems to understand and the dance is beginning to break up anyway. He gives me a kiss on the cheek to say goodnight. My mother picks up Marissa and I. We swing by my house so I can change and grab my things and she drives us to Marissa's home in Blytheville.

The house is quiet when we arrive.

"Is anyone here?" I say.

"Just Barry," she says. She peeks into his room. "Stupid doof," she says. "Listen to him snore!"

We raid the kitchen for snacks and change into our pajamas. Marissa doesn't tell me what happened. She usually keeps her boy situations to herself. She's more subdued tonight than normal. We talk about what everyone wore. Finally Marissa says, "Do you want to see something crazy?"

"What is it?" I say intrigued.

144

"Be very quiet," Marissa puts her index finger over her lips and tiptoes into her parent's bedroom. She opens the top drawer of their dresser. Both of us keep an eye on Barry to see if he stirs. He is snoring with his mouth open. Marissa pulls out a VHS tape and tip toes her way out of there.

"I cannot believe you just did that!" I whisper. She puts the tape in. We curl up with blankets and pillows on the living room floor.

It's a silly movie. Two pretty girls are sitting in their parent's kitchen. No one is home but them. They keep talking about how bored they are. One girl asks the other if she would like to have some real fun. They both seem really dumb.

"What is this, Marissa?" I laugh.

"Just watch," she says.

"I love bananas," one girl says. I watch her peel it open and lick the banana rather than eat it. I don't get it.

She rubs the banana down her neck and says, "Gosh, it's sooo hot in here!" Then she lifts off her shirt. At first I am shocked. I pull the blankets up over my eyes. But then I am drawn to her. She is so beautiful. Her body is the most perfect body I have ever seen. I cannot take my eyes off of her. I watch the girls make out. They are both moaning and moving and kissing and something weird starts happening inside my body as I watch. I'm trembling all over. My skin turns incredibly hot. I don't understand what is going on. I try to relax. I take deep breaths and then all of a sudden an incredible wave of sensation washes over me.

"I have to go to the bathroom," I tell Marissa and I run out of the room.

I lock the door and sit on the toilet to catch my breath and think. I check—no I didn't pee my pants. It's something else. I am afraid, but excited, even elated. What just happened? I explore myself with my fingers. I find this place that is different from the others within the flowery folds of my skin. "Oh!" I think, "This is where the butterflies come from!"

~

The next night I lay in my bed at home with the door locked. I allow my fingers to find the magical place again. I feel my skin turn warm, my legs relax. I explore and move until I it happens all over again. I have discovered the best kept secret of all time! Tone Loc, Samantha Fox, Madonna: I get it! I dance alone in my room with the radio blasting. I practice moving my hips while I sing into my hairbrush. I buy Cosmo magazines and I am initiated into many mysteries.

~

How many children are initiated into the mysteries of sex by stumbling upon porn where they witness acting, objectification, and a superficial sexuality? What would a sacred initiation to sex look like? If we reach back into our collective consciousness, would we remember?

~

The days become long and I am easily distracted at school. My thoughts slip into erotic daydreams.

"Jessica!" My math teacher shouts. "Aren't you going to answer the question?"

"Uh…what was the question?" The whole room erupts in laughter.

"What is the common denominator of these fractions?"

"Uh…I don't know," I say. I'm so funny. Har. Har. Har. I roll my eyes and glare at everyone.

The teacher returns to his lecture. A skinny greasy guy with long hair sits in front of me. He turns around and just looks at me through his half open hazy blue eyes. I think he's on drugs. He wears a black heavy metal shirt and ripped black jeans.

"What?" I mouth as I wrinkle up my forehead.

Finally he licks his lips and blows me a kiss.

"You're so fucking hot," he whispers.

"Mike!" The teacher slams a book down on his desk. "Get to work."

~

A folded note is passed down the row to me in History class. I carefully open it under my desk. It reads:

Jess,

> *You look really pretty today. Did you have a good time at Homecoming? You looked so beautiful that night. Too bad we couldn't have danced together. I would have liked that. Sorry I haven't talked to you as much lately. Allie didn't like me talking to you. But we just broke up. I'm so glad it's over. Hey, let's hang out sometime after school.*
> *Your friend always,*
> *Jason*

I fold the note back up and slip it into my pocket and think, "Yes. Let's hang out."

In Science class I write him back:

> *Dear Jason,*
> *Thanks for your note. Sorry to hear that you and Allie broke up. That must have been tough. Can you hang out tonight? Want to meet me at the park between our houses at 7:30?*

Jason sends me one more note:
> *See you then, Blue Eyes!*

~

My parents have Bible study every Wednesday night. I take a shower right after they leave. I shave my legs. Rub baby oil all over my body and sneak a few squirts of my mother's nice perfume. I throw a bandana over my hair so I won't have to worry about fixing it.

"Peter, I'll be back before Mom and Dad get home, okay? Can you cover for me with Emily if she's suspicious?"

"Don't get caught," he says.

"You're the best."

I tussle his hair and skip all the way to the park. Only the street lamps illuminate the sky. I sit near the top of the slide and wait. What if he doesn't come? I begin to pace around the platform. I bite my nails. And then I hear his skateboard rolling down the street. I can hardly contain my excitement. I jump off the playground equipment and try to walk calmly towards him like a sexy super model.

I trip over a pothole and go down.

Jason buckles over in laughter.

"Oh my God, are you okay?"

He's trying to show concern but he cannot stop laughing.

"Shut up!" I say, but I'm laughing too.

He reaches his hand out to me.

"Come here," he pulls me up towards him. I fall into his chest and he puts his arms around my waist.

"You are very tall," I say. "I'm not used to looking up at too many people."

"I am," he smiles. We stare at each other for a few long seconds. Then he leans in and kisses me on the lips. It's a sweet kiss. Just long enough to be romantic and not too long for me to worry about his tongue sneaking down my throat.

He sighs. "I've wanted to do that for a very long time."

"Oh, really…" I smile. "Then how come you didn't?"

"Jess…we have so much to talk about," he says.

"But," he pauses.

"What?"

"It's f-f-fucking cold out here! Come on, let's go back to my house."

I'm a little unsure. I look back down my street.

He kicks up his skateboard and tucks it under one arm.

"Race ya!" He looks at me with wide eyes and takes off running.

"Oh no you don't!" I nearly beat him, but his legs are really long.

"Ha!" He reaches his own driveway a few seconds before me.

"Come here again," he says and I run into his arms where we kiss one more time.

He looks at me and smiles. His green eyes are warm and thoughtful. He rubs the back of my head.

"Oh Jess," he says.

"What?"

"I'll tell you later. Come on, let's get some hot chocolate!"

I meet his mother and father. They are both very nice. His father seems to like me more than his mother though. I can tell she's not sure about me. I'm not really sure about me either. Later Jason tells me that all the officer's wives have heard the rumors about me too. We hold on to our warm mugs and eventually retreat into his bedroom and to listen to music.

"Have you heard of Morrissey?" he asks.

"Nu, uh."

"What?! Oh my God, you have to hear this."

He turns on the music and hands me the lyrics to, "Everyday is like Sunday." I listen to the melancholic voice sing.

"Happy music," I tease. "I like it."

"Jess," he says leaning forward. "I've wanted to talk with you for such a long time. I can't imagine what you went through last year. I was really worried about you. I thought about you all the time. I wondered how you were. What you were doing. I didn't know if I would ever see you again."

"You're so sweet," I say, not sure where he is going with all of this.

"You can tell me anything you want, if you need to talk. I don't really understand what happened that summer day, but I have a feeling it was really bad."

"Oh, Jason," I sigh. "It was awful." I tell him everything. How Christian tricked me into thinking it was an initiation, how pathetically naïve I was, the turn of events with Matt, the fall out…well, he knew the rest of the story.

"Come here," he says. And he just holds me. "I am so sorry that happened to you. I wish I was older and smarter that day. I wish I could have stopped it. I didn't know what was going on. I'm so sorry I wasn't able to help you when you needed it most."

No words pass between us for a while. I am able to let it all out with him. I sob and smear snot all over his hoodie.

"Gross," he laughs. I laugh.

"You know me and Allie…" he starts.

"Ugh. Do we have to talk about you two?" I sniff. He hands me a Kleenex.

"Jess, I want you to know that I have cared about you for a long time. I didn't know you'd be coming back. I should have waited for you. When I saw you at Homecoming with some other guy, I could hardly stand it. I want you to be my girl, Blue Eyes. I've wanted that for a very long time."

I leave him hanging for as long as I can.

"Well, then you'll have to get used to me putting snot on your sweatshirts."

He leans in and kisses me on my forehead, my two cheeks, my chin and my nose.

"I am never washing this sweatshirt again," he says.

"Ha! You'd better frame it. Crap! What time is it?"

"Almost 9…are you okay?"

"Jason, my parents are going to be home soon—I have to run!"

He laughs, "You mean you were sneaking out?"

I look at him deviously, "Of course."

He walks me to the front door and I say goodbye to his parents.

"Next Wednesday," I say. "Same time. Same place."

"Good thing you can run fast," he says. "Now go, go, go!"

I kick it into high gear.

"And watch out for the potholes!"

~

Enki, a watery Sumerian god, is known for bringing new life into dry places, like a river in the desert. His renewing energy helps bring Innana's rotting corpse back from the underworld and into the land of the living.

~

For many years of my life, Jason is the only person who knows what happened. When he listens to me that day—and doesn't judge me or reject me—vital pieces of me come back to life.

~

When I study psychology later I learn that patients with PTSD experience triggers that send them straight back to the source of pain. Often it is not one event that breaks people apart, but the constant re-experiencing of memories and patterns of behavior that bubble up in nightmares and relationships. These triggers have the power to unravel our protective false selves, to pull us down into the dark rabbit hole again and deal with truth that we once found unbearable. Triggers ask us to face again that dreadful moment when the soul was eclipsed, when we experienced the divine connection sever and we knew all too well our mortality. When we behold the fragmentation, the polarization of what once danced as one, we can begin to reconnect the dots. Even the earth we have chosen to hold our garbage remembers: she was once a sacred garden.

~

I wake up screaming at night, unable to remember my nightmares. My jaw is tight from grinding my teeth. My days are filled with sexual fantasies that serve to shield me from the unbearable pain. I want to experience the joy of life. I want to feel redemption.

~

One reason Jesus is so feared by the religious authorities is because he breaks all the rules. He touches the unclean with his bare hands. Jesus hangs with the outcasts, the nerds, and the whores. He believes in their potential. He sees the divine ones hiding behind the masks of unbelief. He brings God all the way down into the messiness of life.

~

Jason and I take things slow. I spend a lot of time in his arms, snuggling and feeling safe next to his body.

"How far did you and Allie go?" I ask.

He trails his green eyes around my face, brushing my hair back and sighs.

"It doesn't matter, Jess."

"Come on, Jason, I don't care, I just want to know how far you've been with a girl—you know how far I've been…well, everyone does."

I look down at my pink fuzzy sweater and pull at my sleeves. He puts his hands over mine and brings them up to his lips and kisses them. We sit in silence.

"You really wanna know, huh?"

"Yes!"

"Okay, Jess. Third base."

"Really? What was it like?"

"I don't know. I didn't really know what I was doing. It was weird, I guess."

"I wonder if things would be weird with us?" I lean into Jason's chest.

"I don't want to hurt you, Jess."

"I don't think it's supposed to hurt. Maybe if we went real slow?"

"You really want to try?" He looks at me curiously.

"I don't want to be afraid anymore."

"Come here, Blue Eyes." We lay on my bed together and he hugs me tight.

"I love you, Jess, you know that, right?"

I smile up at him, "I hope you will show me."

~

It is a Wednesday night in winter when we plan to try. I can hardly think straight all day in school.

"Where did you go, silly girl?" Marissa says.

"What?" I dip my french fry in a glob of ketchup.

"You're so dreamy today," she says.

"I'm in love!"

The two of us giggle and she tells me all about her latest crush. She describes the details of Shane's muscular arms and his tender kisses. She always dates older guys who are in high school. There's a neediness to her relationships with men. She clings to them so tightly and they all push her away. It scares me to witness this. Probably because I can't bear to face it in myself.

~

After my parents leave, I soak in the bath. I add scented salts and oils to the water. I am preparing to emerge as a new woman.

I light candles around my room and dim the lights. Turn the radio on. Lock my door. Jason knocks on my window and sneaks into my bedroom. He slips his feet out of his shoes like he is standing on sacred ground. He's nervous like I am, but when we kiss and look into each other's eyes we relax and smile. Not many words are spoken this night. We are both very shy to be naked, so we stand very close and close our eyes. Tom Petty sings, "Free Fallin'."

I pull him down to the floor. He lays his warm body on mine.

"Are you sure?" he keeps whispering.

"Yes," I say. "Yes."

We giggle and fumble with the condom.

"You tell me to stop if it hurts, okay?"

"It's not going to hurt," I say.

"I love you Jess, no matter what," he says. He kisses my cheeks, and puts the side of his face against mine. I soak in his heat. Feel his breath on my skin. He moves slowly. My body stiffens at first.

"Is this okay?" he says.

I take a deep breath and try to relax.

"Yes, I'm okay."

I hug him tight and watch the beads of sweat form on his back.

"He loves me," is all I can think. "He loves me." I can't remember ever feeling so much love.

The whole room grows warm. I hear music circling around me. I open my thirsty mouth. My heart contains a secret water fountain. An ocean of joy bubbles up within me. I lift up my hands. I throw back my head. What is this ecstasy? I remember it from a long time ago.

~

We're both giggling and putting our clothes back on. I feel renewed. I can't stop smiling.

"Let me walk you home," I say, not wanting him to ever leave my side again. We climb out my window into the cool dark night. We walk holding hands, bumping into each other, exchanging dreamy looks and laughing about the most random things. He kisses me goodbye at the playground. And that's when I see the headlights beaming in my direction.

It's the K-Mart car.

My parents drive up beside me. I watch in horror as the window rolls down.

"Jessica Jean, what in the world are you doing out here at night?" My mother's cold eyes instantly drop the temperature to a shivering degree.

"Get in here," she says.

"No, Mom, I can walk."

I take off running ahead of them. All I can think about is those burning candles, my dim room and the condom wrapper lying on my bedroom floor! My father speeds up so we arrive at the house at the same time. I sprint up to the front door but my mother grabs my arm.

"What's going on?" She demands an answer.

"Nothing!" I insist.

"Then why are you out here?"

"I just wanted to go for a walk."

"At night. In the dark." There is no way she's buying this.

I watch my father open the front door. I have to get in there before he does.

"Oh Mom, I have to pee real bad!"

I loosen her grip and force my way into the house and down the hallway. I grab the doorknob. *My door is locked!* Peter is in his room. He takes one look at me and knows in a flash that I am in desperate need of help.

"Can you unlock my bedroom?" I whisper. He jumps out of his chair.

"Jessica! Come here!" my father commands.

Peter runs into the bathroom and starts shuffling around the drawers for a bobby pin.

I walk slowly down the hallway to the kitchen. My parents set their Bibles down on the counter and remove their coats.

"What is wrong with you? It's after curfew!" My father says, "Do you want me to get written up? Have me get in trouble by my commanding officers because I can't control my own daughter? What the hell is going on?"

Peter is now at my door jiggling the handle. I stand in the kitchen doorway to block him from my parent's view.

"Dad, I'm sorry," I say.

"We saw him," my mother says. "We saw you with Jason at the park."

"We were just talking," I say.

I hear the click as Peter unlocks my door. My father hears it too.

"Why is your bedroom door locked Jessica Jean?"

My heart is pounding so fast I can hardly breathe.

He walks towards me.

"Excuse me," he says, but I don't let him pass me. I run down the hallway as fast as I can. I open my bedroom door and grab the condom wrapper lying on the floor and shove it into my pocket. My parents are standing in my doorway just one second later.

"Why are all these candles lit?" My mother's voice is shrill.

"I thought it would be relaxing?"

"And why is your window open?" My father's face is red.

"Because I was hot?"

He walks over to the window and sticks his head out. I kick my underwear under my bed.

"Peter!" My mother puts a hand on her hip. "Was Jason in this house tonight?" He comes over and looks them in the eyes.

"No," he says.

"Listen young lady," my father says, "you are walking on very thin ice, do you understand me? I do not trust you one bit. You had better watch out." He points his finger an inch from my nose.

"Yes, sir," I say.

"And no more candles." My mother blows them out and picks them all up. "And you're grounded for the rest of the week for sneaking around past curfew."

I close my door and slide all the way down to the ground clutching my knees into my chest and sighing deeply.

~

Jesus says, "Let the one who has committed no sin, be the first to cast a stone." The angry crowd slowly steps away. One by one they set down their heavy rocks and let the adulterous woman live.

Many young people engage in sexually risky behaviors that can result in unintended health outcomes. For example, among U.S. high school students surveyed in 2011:

- *47.4% had ever had sexual intercourse*
- *33.7% had had sexual intercourse during the previous 3 months, and, of these*
    - *39.8% did not use a condom the last time they had sex*

- - 76.7% did not use birth control pills or Depo-Provera to prevent pregnancy the last time they had sex
- 15.3% had had sex with four or more people during their life

Sexual risk behaviors place adolescents at risk for HIV infection, other sexually transmitted diseases (STDs), and unintended pregnancy:

- *An estimated 8,300 young people aged 13–24 years in the 40 states reporting to CDC had HIV infection in 2009*
- *Nearly half of the 19 million new STDs each year are among young people aged 15–24 years*
- *More than 400,000 teen girls aged 15–19 years gave birth in 2009*

To reduce sexual risk behaviors and related health problems among youth, schools and other youth-serving organizations can help young people adopt lifelong attitudes and behaviors that support their health and well-being—including behaviors that reduce their risk for HIV, other STDs, and unintended pregnancy.

-Center for Disease Control and Prevention

With Jason and Marissa I feel I can be more of the real me—or at least a me that I like. Still, I don't know how to be me in the rest of the world.

One day a girl that I do not know walks up to me and yells in my face, "Bitch!"

I turn to look at her. Suddenly a crowd gathers around us. Someone yells, "Chick fight!" and more gather around.

My heart is pounding, my veins turn to ice. I stand there frozen, defenseless. She glares at me with hard brown eyes and leans in towards me like she might throw a punch. Her frizzy hair is exploding everywhere. I've never even talked to her before.

Someone elbows me, "Come on—tell her off," they say.

"Oh yeah," I squeak. "You…uh….you wanna make something of it?" I croak. The crowd cracks up and disperses. Some pat me on the head as they leave. The girl smiles at me smugly and walks away. Why do random people hate me? And why can't I defend myself?

Similar problems happen in class—even when I'm paying attention. I'm so guarded. There are times I know the answer, but I just don't know how to put it into words. My voice sounds so funny, like it doesn't belong to me. I can't translate who I am on the inside to fit an expression that works on the outside. I become a very quiet person. I immerse myself in the piano at home. I keep to myself, only talking to Jason and Marissa. I am afraid to branch out and make new friends. I am afraid of being publicly humiliated. A voice within says, *Never again!*

~

"Come on, J!" Marissa begs. "Please try out with me!"
"But Marissa, I'm not good at that stuff! I've never been!"
"You haven't even tried," she presses.
"But my Mom says my body can't do that kind of stuff."
"Who cares what your Mom says. You don't!" She smiles.
"True."
"Just try it. Try it for me, please?" I can't resist her puppy dog eyes.
"Okay, Marissa—I will try for you. This doesn't mean I'm actually going to try out." Marissa squeals and jumps up and down.

After school she comes over to my house and we stretch in my backyard. "See? I can't even touch my toes," I say.
"You will, you just have to stretch every day."
"Marissa! I have NEVER in my whole life been able to touch my toes! They're just too far away!"
"Bend your knees silly dilly. Stop complaining."
"Try this one," she says. "Defense, defense, push 'em back, push 'em back, defense, defense, go!"
I study her feet and arm movements.
"That's a lot to do at the same time! Should I chew gum too?"
"Come on, let's try it together." I follow her feet, my hands? Forget about it. I think I got the chant though.

"Okay, that wasn't the worst thing ever. How about a leg kick? Watch." She launches her leg up to her head, practically doing the splits.

"You are incredible, Marissa, but I could never do that."

"Just kick your leg as high as you can, J."

I launch my leg up and knee myself in the face.

Marissa falls to the ground laughing. I buckle over and cup my nose.

"Man that hurts," I say.

"I knew you could do it," she squeaks.

~

Marissa and I practice every day. I learn all the chants and my leg kick is much improved. She is planning on trying out next month, I'm not. But everything changes when Marissa walks into school one day with the saddest face I have ever seen.

"What happened?" I ask her.

"Nothing," she says.

"Come on, tell me."

"I'll tell you at lunch, okay?"

The day drags on. I have an awful feeling in the pit of my stomach. I want to know what happened, but I am also very afraid to know. I meet her out by the concession stand at 11:30.

"We're moving," she says like it's no big deal.

"What? When? Where?"

"This weekend," she says. "To South Carolina. I don't know. Barry got a job or something and we all have to go."

"Wait. How can that just happen? How can you just say that? You can't go Marissa! You can't! You're my best friend and I can't live without you!"

"Oh, J," she wraps her arms around me. "You'll be okay. You're so pretty and funny."

Tears are streaming down my face. I don't even care about my makeup anymore. "No. No, I'm not." I say. "And I'm only funny by accident!"

Marissa wipes the tears off my face and kisses my cheeks. "I'll write you and call you," she says.

"God, Marissa. I cannot imagine my life without you. You're the only girl who understands me."

"You'll make new friends," she says. "I just know it."

I stare at the gray sky and the jagged clouds that move across it. A little sun begins to shine through and lights up the air.

"You have do one thing for me," she says.

"Anything."

"You have to promise me that you will try out for the cheerleading team."

"What? Oh God. Marissa. Why?"

"Because, I think you can make it. I hear that they are getting rid of the dance squad at the high school and they're going to blend it with the new cheer squad and it's going to be bigger and they'll dance and cheer!"

Just looking at the joy in her face makes me excited, even though I could care less about all that.

"Okay, Marissa. I'll do it for you."

Now the sun is shining bright. We are starting to sweat in our jackets.

"It's hotter out here than a witch's boob!" Marissa says and I laugh and sob and make a big snotty mess.

~

Tryouts come way too fast. I am still in shock that Marissa is gone. I show up at the gym with my hair pulled back in a ponytail, in shorts that make me feel nauseous because they reveal way too much of my legs. The girls look at me with hard glaring eyes. Some of them pretend I don't exist. I'm used to that now. Many of the girls have been cheerleaders for years. Others are dancers or gymnasts. Few of them are happy that the school is combining the two groups. Girls from the high school cheerleading squad come over to teach us the moves for the tryouts.

"You will be judged on how quickly you can learn the moves and how well you perform under pressure," says Mrs. Perlis, a short woman who is almost as wide as she is tall. Back in her glory days, she was the cheer captain.

I do not belong here, I think. I tell myself to breathe. I remind myself that I'm doing this for Marissa and no one else.

"Good luck," says Heather with the fiery red lips. She tosses her brown frizzy hair over her shoulder and flashes me a devilish smile. No one wants to stand by me. Screw them. I'm not here for them. I'm going to do my best and pay close attention.

Lana Berry, the legend, the most beautiful popular girl in the entire school teaches us our first chant.

"You have to have control of your body," she says. "Hold your arms straight and still. Don't let them fly around. Stop them here," she demonstrates. I like the way she teaches. It's direct. I discover that I like learning how to put my body into a form. I've always been such a klutz.

I pick it up the first chant right away. "Be aggressive! B-E aggressive! Be aggressive! B-E aggressive!"

Yes. I think I will, I decide.

"Now for the jumps," Lana says. My heart drops into my shoes. These are hard.

"Before we even try some of them, I want to practice the set up. Start with your hands in a V above your head. Now come onto your tip toes. Next you circle down with your arms and cross them in front of your body. As you do this, squat down. When your arms fly back up again, you use this energy to jump. Let's try that and just see how high you can go jumping straight into the air. Keep it simple."

I'm able to practice that. I see how her approach helps gain momentum and each jump I am able to lift a little higher off the ground.

"Now, let's try the herkie," she says. I watch her carefully. How she sets up her approach. This time when she jumps, one leg goes straight and the other turns down and bends at the knee.

"We all have a better leg, so just choose a side that works best for you." At first I can't remember which leg to straighten and which leg to bend. Several of the girls catch sight of me jumping with both knees bent and snicker. After some practice, I can get my legs doing two different things. But I'm sure I look like a big dork. My legs are so long that I can barely lift them.

The hardest part for me is learning the dance. Lauren was the head of the dance squad in junior high and Mrs. Perlis asks her to create a dance for try outs. Everyone loves Lauren's dances. She uses rap music and copies Janet Jackson's moves. Lauren's not the typical pom pom girl. She's a little heavier, she has a long face, and a large nose. But she carries herself with such unique confidence and grace, it's hard to keep your eyes off of her or to even think about disrespecting her. In fact, we all want to be like her. She turns on her boom box. MC Hammer's song, "U Can't Touch This" blasts out of the speakers. All the girls squeal. We watch Lauren do all these funky moves. Everyone is so pumped to learn. I follow along, but I don't feel the rhythm exactly right. I'm a little behind the beat as I struggle to remember the next moves. She shortens the dance for our tryouts tonight and the girls break off in to various groups to practice.

I find a corner all by myself. I just need to think it through first. The girls laugh at me for being alone. I don't care. I imagine Marissa here with me. I imagine the things that she would say to encourage me. I'm pretty close to getting it. The hardest part will be trying to perform it under pressure, the place I usually crumble.

Mrs. Perlis blows her whistle.

"Ok, girls this is how it's going to work," she says. "First, you will all perform the dance together. We want to see what you look like in a team setting. Then we will call you each by name and ask you to perform two cheers, and a few jumps, okay?"

The buzzing of the gym lights fills the nervous silence.

"Ladies," she says. "If you want to be cheerleaders, then you'd better learn how to cheer!"

All of us scream and pump our fists into the air. All this excitement feels so forced and unnatural to me.

"Now get out there and show me you can dance!"

We run to the center of the gym floor and line up just like Lauren showed us. We stand frozen with our arms to our side, our legs wide and heads down. I count the beat, I wait for MC Hammer to start singing, and I count *five, six, seven, eight* and I'm in on time! I squat and move my hips, I jump and turn and do the running man. In the middle I get lost, but I catch up by looking at Lauren.

"Break it down!"

We all dance and shake on our tiptoes. I have no idea what I look like, but I keep doing it. I forget how the buildup goes near the very end, I miss a few steps, but then I nail the last few beats and I hold the last pose strong. It could have been so much worse.

"Okay, girls," Mrs. Perlis says. "Not bad, not bad at all."

"Taylor Green! You're up first."

I sit in the corner and watch Taylor try out. She's already a co-captain with Lana, but everyone tries out, probably to show the rest of us the standard. She performs perfectly, nails the chants, the jumps.

At the very end of her try out Mrs. Perlis says, "And a cartwheel please."

A cartwheel? I think I'm going to throw up all over the gym floor. I cannot do a cartwheel to save my life. The tryouts move faster and faster as each girl is called up. Watching them all nail their cartwheels is making my head spin. How did I miss the time in my childhood when I was supposed to learn this? I want to walk out of the gym right now. I'm not going to make it anyway. I take a deep breath. *I will do this for Marissa*, I remind myself. *And then, I will leave.* She's getting close to the end of the alphabet. *Oh God. Help me not to pass out.*

Before me, Allie Walker tries out. My stomach twists in knots as I watch her smile and perform all the moves with ease. I imagine Jason kissing her. Going to third base with her. She's so bubbly and happy, I can't compete.

"Okay, last one. Jessica Zuhh….how do you say your last name, honey?"

"Zuh-den-ick," I say it real slow, like I have a thousand times. "Or you can just call me Jessica Z."

"Okay Jessica Z, show me an offensive chant."

"Be aggressive! Be, be aggressive! Be aggressive! Be, be aggressive!" I nail it.

"And show me a defensive chant please."

"Defense! Defense! Push em back, way back! Defense! Defense! Push em back, Woo!"

Not too bad either.

"Okay, let's see your herkie."

I concentrate on prepping perfectly, but I end up jumping straight up into the air and land back on my two feet.

"Oh I forgot to move my legs," I laugh nervously.

The girls on the sidelines giggle. I try it again. This time, I do my best. Still, not a great jump, but it was a jump that I couldn't do this morning.

"And your cartwheel," Mrs. Perlis pushes up her glasses and glances at her watch.

I take a deep breath. I try to do what the other girls did. I run a bit, plant my hands on the ground and then I roll into a summersault and crash into a few of the girls on the sidelines.

"Oh God," a few them say as they push me away.

"She'll never get in," I hear one girl whisper.

At least it's over, I think. That's all I came here for. I start packing up my things and head for the door.

"Aren't you going to wait to see if you made it?" Lauren asks.

"Trust me, I'm not going to make it, I say."

"Girls. Sit down please." Mrs. Perlis says. "I know that this is the hardest moment for you all. I know that some of you have put a lot of time and energy into your practice. I also know some of you are coming here with very heavy hearts because we are combining the dance and cheer squad. I want to thank you all for your bravery and for your courage to come here today to work hard and to do your best. After some difficult deliberation we have made our final decisions."

She pauses for a few very long seconds and then she shouts, "You all are going to be the next Lady Pirate Cheerleaders, class of 1990-1991!"

Half of the girls run to the center of the gym screaming and jumping up and down. The other half walk away and mope on the bleachers. I sit down on the floor where I am, completely in shock. I cannot believe this just happened. I am going to be a cheerleader.

"Thank you, Marissa," I whisper. I fold my hands together and press them to my forehead.

~

I saunter over to Jason's house. I know he's waiting to see me, probably looking outside of his window watching for me. I try to sway my hips like the supermodels do. I toss my hair over my shoulder and pretend that I am looking at something really interesting across the street. I imagine him drooling over me. Excited by the way I move.

By the time I see the orange flag, it's too late. My arms and legs get all tangled up in the little pink bicycle in front of me. The bike and I fall in one awkward mess in the middle of the sidewalk.

I look around. I don't think anyone saw me. But then I hear loud laughter coming from inside Jason's bedroom. Damn. He was watching after all.

He runs out the front door—his face is all red—he is still unable to talk as helps me up.

"Oh God, Jess," he finally squeaks out, "that was the funniest thing I've ever seen in my entire life!"

After surviving my disastrous cartwheel, I can definitely survive this.

~

Jason's mother helps bandage my cuts and scrapes and serves us milk and cookies. I tell Jason all about the tryouts.

"What? I didn't even know you were trying out. Why did you do that?"

"I didn't think I was going to make it, Jason. Marissa taught me all this stuff. You should have seen my cartwheel!"

"Jess," he says, "you're not a cheerleader."

"What? What do you mean by that?"

"They're all jocks and preps. You and me, we're different from them."

"But I don't want to be different, Jason. I want to fit in. It's what I've always wanted."

"You DO fit it. You fit in with me. Those people are mean, Jess. I'm worried about you."

"Oh, Jason, I'll be fine." I kiss him on the cheek. But already I can feel him pulling away.

~

"Way to go, Jess!"

My father picks me up off the floor and swings me around. I look into his eyes and see something new. I see pride. I smile back at him. Something escapes my heart. I think it's love.

"Thanks Dad."

"When's your first game?"

"Not till next fall."

"I can't wait!"

My mother watches from the distance. She bites her lip and looks away. I wonder if she feels bad for telling me I could never do this. Or if she thinks that I still can't. Or if she is upset that she never did. I think: I'm going to show her that I really can do this.

~

It's tricky, stepping into a stereotypical role, filled with a lot of expectations about what it means to be a woman. Are we merely ornaments for men? Competing for their attention? Wearing little skirts to make the games more interesting? I am not aware of all these tensions at the time. For now, all I know is that I belong somewhere at school. I have a place. I have a uniform. I have power. I am not on the fringes any more. I am at the center. And I am making my father proud.

~

To truly belong is to be at home in the body and in a community that recognizes your divine place in the order of life. And yet—the risk of being vulnerable in a community not yet awake is often too high. How easy it is for some of us to change our hair, our clothes, our walk, our language, to gain the acceptance of the still unconscious crowd. But there are some people who can never change the signs that mark them as different—although some have tried to transform the color of their skin, to disguise their ethnic origin, the way they move, or the joy they carry in their heart—no matter how hard they try, some cannot so easily escape the fears projected upon them—fears of the other, fears of the unknown.

~

This summer I am the busiest I have ever been. I spend the mornings doing laps with the swim team and afternoons at cheer practice. After swim lessons I have a secret ritual. I walk over to Jason's house and knock on his bedroom window.

"Hey Blue Eyes," he says as he puts his glasses on. "How are you today?"

"Okay…"

He lifts my chin.

"What's wrong, Jess?"

"It's nothing," I say.

"It's not nothing," he looks at me with his green eyes framed by thick black eyelashes. I put my finger on his cheek and catch a stray.

"Make a wish," I say and I blow it away.

"Come here," he says. He leans out his window and kisses me. I was so cold a moment ago, standing here with my wet hair and swimsuit, my damp towel hanging around my waste. His body is warm. His lips are full. He is so gentle and tender. Time stands still. The butterflies take flight. This. This is all I want: to be with him forever.

"Come in today," he says.

"No way! We'll get caught!"

"No we won't. My parents are gone."

He pulls my arms and helps me scale the wall. I'm halfway through the window when I fall in, knocking him over and his stack of CDs too.

"Oh, Jess," he laughs. "Come here," he pulls me under the covers with him. I lay my head on his chest and snuggle up to his warm body.

"Why do you have all these posters up?"

All these beautiful mostly naked women look at me with half open eyes, and perfectly proportioned bodies.

"Cuz they're hot!"

I look at their full sized breasts, their long flowing hair, their perfectly clear skin. I pull the covers up higher.

"What," he says. "You're just as beautiful."

"No I'm not," I say.

"Shhhh." He says and kisses me.

He helps me out of my swimsuit. We're old pros at this now. We move slowly, kissing, letting our hands explore each other's body. I am so needy for his love. I can't handle the insecurities that arise within me when I think about him looking at another woman the way he looks at me. I can't imagine being with anyone else. I want to marry Jason and spend the rest of my life with him.

"Oh shit!" Jason pulls the window shades down. "Your mother is walking across my front lawn!"

We lay there like dead fish with our mouths hanging open.

"What can she do?" I whisper. "No one is here to let her in."

We hear her knock on the front door. She knocks again louder.

"Get in the closet."

Jason shoves my clothes into my hands and we dive into the darkness together and shut the door.

"Oh, God," Jason says. "I think I left the door unlocked." We wait in silence for an eternity.

"Shit. She's looking inside my bedroom now."

I couldn't move if I wanted to. My heart feels like it's going to explode.

"Okay, she's gone."

"I almost died," I say as my wobbly body spills out of his closet and onto his bedroom floor.

~

A fifteen year old girl's parents hold her down and pour acid over her face and body after they suspect her of having illicit relations with a young boy. The girl is left to suffer overnight and dies the next morning at the hospital. The parents defend their actions as preserving her honor.

~

Jason begins golfing a lot in the summer and it's harder for our schedules to match up. I pester him with my anxiety.

"Why do you have to play golf all the time anyways?"

"Is it more fun than me?"

"I don't get it."

"What's the point of it?"

"You just don't want to be with me."

"I must be boring."

"Maybe I'm getting on your nerves."

"Are you mad at me?"

"Why don't you talk to me as much anymore?"

"When can we hang out again?"

"Can you call me tonight?"

"Can you write me a note today?"

I'm desperately trying to get closer to him. But the more desperate I am, the more he pulls away.

~

I'm breaking the ice with the cheer squad, but I don't have any close friends yet. I spend the late afternoons playing the piano. I have several melodies that I'm working on and one song under my belt. I bring my finished melody to my new piano teacher. My mother gave up teaching me because we fought too much. My new music teacher is so proud of me.

She says, "Jessica, you have a real talent for this! Maybe this is your calling in life."

The little butterflies inside me flap their wings with joy. I can't help thinking about what she said—maybe this *IS* my calling in life. I put even more time into practicing. I hum tunes throughout the day. I try to find the melodies to my favorite songs on the keyboard. It's so amazing when someone believes in you. They help you believe in yourself.

~

When I'm really lonely I spend time in my room snuggling up with my guinea pig, Cupcake. I feed her lettuce and scratch her head while she nuzzles her nose into my armpit.

"You have a way with animals," my mother says as she walks past my room and catches a glimpse of me. She comes in and sits by me on the bed.

"She's so cute, your little Cupcake," she says. "She loves you best."

"I love her so much," I say. "I can't believe we have had her since I was ten! She's been with me through so much."

"Did I tell you? Tupa is pregnant!"

"What? What does this mean?"

"It means in November we are going to have a bunch of little puppies around here!"

"I hope they like me better than she does," I say.

Mom laughs.

"Jess—they will love you."

~

Jason and I are standing outside of my house on a late summer night.

"Things are going to be different for us this year," Jason says.

"How so?"

"Well, you're a cheerleader now."

"So?"

"And I'm a skater."

"So?"

"Jess, it means we hang out in different crowds now. My friends hate all those people. And all those people hate my friends."

"No they don't."

"Yes, Jess, yes they do."

Jason puts his hand on the rim of his Michigan State baseball cap and flips it around.

"God, you're adorable." I say. "Don't you want to see me walking around school in a short skirt?"

"Well, of course I do. But I don't want anyone else looking."

"Oh, do I detect a hint of jealousy?"

"I'm not jealous, Jess. I just don't want people treating you bad."

"They won't, Jason. Not anymore."

"How do you know?"

"Because," I say, "I think the girls will have my back."

"How do you know?"

"I don't. Oh Jason, let's not worry about this. Hey! Okay, let me show you what I can do!"

"What," he looks bored.

"I can do a real good leg kick now!"

"Really…"

"Yes! Watch!" I want to make him smile, so I launch my leg up as high as I can. The only problem is I kick it so hard that my other leg follows the first and I land flat on my butt.

Jason falls to the ground laughing. He can't even talk to me he's laughing so hard.

"Come here you goon," I say as I crawl over to him and steal his hat.

~

My mother starts ordering clothes from a Victoria's Secret catalogue that my father signed up for so he could look at all the beautiful models. She lets me order some clothes too. And she buys me a pair of Guess jeans! Though I'm really into leggings now with big shirts hanging over them. My perm never really goes away. My hair is now wavy, longer and natural looking. This summer I got to buy a new bra size! I'm so excited to be filling out a B cup. Finally. By the time school starts, I feel like a whole new me.

~

Every school day I arrive an hour early. The cheerleaders practice in the gym before first period. We are all careful to do our best, work hard, and not sweat too much either. I've been stretching every day for almost four months, and now I can touch my toes! I'm determined to do the splits by the end of the year so I can show my mother and prove her wrong about what my body can do.

On Fridays we wear our cheerleading uniforms to school. Some of the girls complain that my skirt is too short.

"The real problem is that my legs are just too long," I say.

Still the whispering continues. I am stretching with Taylor and Lana when Heather joins us.

"Tell us about Matt Black behind the high school," Heather says with a devious smile.

"Shut up," Taylor says to her.

"How could you ever believe such an awful rumor," Lana takes my hand.

Heather nervously walks away.

"We got your back," Taylor smiles at me.

"For sure," Lana says.

I am in awe of their protection. I will continue to lie to keep it.

~

Tenth grade is in the new building. I have to look at the concrete slab where I lost my virginity almost every day. Sometimes I stare a little too long.

"What are you looking at?" Taylor closes our shared locker.

"Oh nothing." I say, shooing the memory of that pitiful girl away. In order to survive, I must keep up the lies. I hate myself for it. And I hate the girl who still writhes inside me.

~

I'm excited to walk around the school in my cheerleading uniform. *This must be why my father loves wearing his military uniform*, I think; you know who you are in one. You know what you're supposed to do. All the hazy confusion and work that goes into making a self is covered up. Here is a self, as simple and as bright as day, with all the shadows hidden away.

I imagine Jason seeing me for the first time in my uniform. I fix my hair extra cute, pull it back and tie matching ribbons in my ponytail. I want to wow him. After all, I am his girlfriend. Why shouldn't he adore me?

I bump into him at his locker.

"Hey you gorgeous hunk," I say.

He turns around and says, "Hey," with half open eyes. He doesn't even look at my uniform. And then he walks away.

"Jason!" I call after him.

"I'm late for class!" He shouts back. I blink back the tears.

Our first big pep rally is this afternoon and I'm so nervous. I had hoped he would help me feel more confident. Instead, he crushes me.

"What's wrong Jess," Lana walks up to me.

"Nothing. I'll be fine." I smile.

"Boys are nothing but trouble," she says knowingly. "You'll be great today. You've improved so much! I'm so proud of you!"

I dab my eyes. "Thanks, Lana." She gives me a smile and a wink.

"See you soon, sweetie!"

~

The energy in the gym is frightening. The boys are obnoxiously loud, throwing paper balls across the bleachers. The girls look bored out of their minds.

Someone yells, "Lady Pirates suck!" and everyone laughs.

We stand frozen in position ready to do our first dance. Lana is front and center. She turns to us and whispers, "Let's show them they're wrong."

She turns back around and we press our knowing smiles into our cheeks. We have been practicing all summer and we are ready for this. Mrs. Perlis hits play and the overhead speakers start blasting the music.

"Can't Touch This," MC Hammer sings.

Rows of us turn together at every other line. We are perfectly in sync. The audience is silent. One row starts dancing then they freeze, then the next, then the next. At the chorus we all bust out the Hammer Dance. The stadium goes wild. I catch Jason's eye. He's hunched over resting his chin on his hands. He looks mildly interested. We dance our hearts out. All of us are smiling and giving it our all. At the very end, we launch Lana into the air. The stadium is on its feet, cheering and screaming.

~

That night at the football game my parents come to watch.

"You are really good!" My father's eyes are glowing. "Most cheerleaders can't tell when to do the right cheers, but you watch the game and you initiate all the right chants. Tell me, how'd you learn how to kick your leg so high?" He beams at me.

"I love you, Dad," I say.

"I'm so proud of you, Jess."

~

"How come you never come to the football games, Jason?"

"I told you," he said. "Our crowds don't mix."

"You're my crowd, Jason. We mix and I miss you." He's silent and so disinterested in me lately. I wait for him to look at me again.

"I think we need a little time off," he says. I notice his eyes have changed. They aren't sparkling and they look distant.

"Jason—what can you possibly mean by that? No. No. I don't want any time off. I love you!"

"It's just that you're so busy with cheerleading. And..."

"And what?"

"You're so different at school now."

"What do you mean? I feel great. I feel so confident. I don't feel so lost anymore."

"You've changed," he says. "When you're with me, you're the real Jess. When you're at school—you're someone I don't know."

"Jason—you're breaking my heart. Please don't say that. Is there someone else?"

"Well—no, not really."

"Not really?"

"Well... it's just...we're fifteen, Jess. I'm not ready to be tied down for the rest of my life yet."

"Tied down? I thought what we had was special."

"Jess—it is—it was... but, maybe we could just have a little break and see how things go? Okay?"

"Okay—if that's what you want..."

"It is, Jess."

The walls of my heart cave in and my chin starts to quiver.

"I have to go," I whisper.

I run out of his house and all the way home. I run as fast as I can. When I get home I fall into the grass and pound my fists into the earth.

"Why!" I yell. "Why! Oh God, what do I do? Please tell me what to do!"

My mother opens the front door.

"Oh Jessica!" Mom runs over to me. "Jessica, Jessica," she puts her arms around me. "David!"

"He broke up with me. Jason broke up with me," I wail.

My father comes running out the door.

"Help me carry her inside."

They pick me up and bring me into my room.

My mother tucks me into bed and brings me a cup of warm milk and honey. She pushes my hair away from my face.

"You'll have other boyfriends," she says.

"Mom." I roll my eyes. "I don't want any other boyfriends. I just want him!" I start sobbing all over again.

"Shhhhh." She says. Maybe, he's just having a bad day. Or maybe he's insecure because you're doing so well in school. Maybe he'll change his mind."

"Maybe." I hope.

Dad says, "Do you want me to kick his ass?"

"Yes," I say and smile. I'm not use to having my parents on my side like this. They help balance the blow.

~

In most of my relationships with men, I feel most loved and cherished when I am weak, in need of sheltering, and protection. But when I heal and grow stronger in their caring embrace, they tend pull away. I want both: I want to be strong and sheltered and loved passionately. Is that possible? My mother often warned me not to scare men away. But I don't want to hide in my relationships, I hunger for true intimacy. Still, who can meet me in my fire?

~

Things change at school when people realize Jason and I are not together anymore. Suddenly I am surrounded by scary boys again. They whistle, make catcalls. It reminds me of last year. I am nervous. I don't know how to handle all of it. I smile and giggle and try to pretend that everything is fine, still unsure how to be strong without raging like my father and totally losing it in public. My mother reminds me that our stoic Norwegian ancestors taught us to be nice because the harmony of the community depended upon us.

"Hey, gorgeous." A hunk of a guy leans his head on my locker. He doesn't look like he's in high school. His face is covered in stubble, his cheekbones are hard and his arms are muscular.

"Johnny Diamond," he says and smiles.

"Hi," I look at him quizzically.

"Look darlin' I want to take you out on the town for a night to remember. Please say you'll go on a date with me this Friday."

"A date?" I look down at the books in my arms. I guess I can date now, I think. Maybe this is just what the doctor ordered. Maybe if

Jason hears I'm going out with other guys, he'll get jealous and want me back.

"How about Saturday at 7—I have a game on Friday." I scribble my address on a piece of paper.

~

In the old French fairy tale of Bluebeard, the wealthy aristocrat seems to have everything going for him; even his strangely blue beard doesn't keep the ladies away. He offers his bride respite in his mansion and gives her the keys to every room but the cellar in the basement. The curios maiden cannot resist and when her husband goes away on a trip, she finally pries open the forbidden door. There she discovers every wife who came before her, chopped up into pieces, their blood pooling all over the floor.

One interpretation of the story is that Bluebeard represents an aggressive force within the psyche that attempts to dismember and kill the naïve feminine. Maybe this serves to initiate us into our full potential. Maybe it's just the sort of dismembering that patriarchy has done to women throughout the ages. In our waking up, we face how we have compromised our own souls and the essence of our very being in order to survive an age where sacred feminine wisdom was repressed, chopped, and locked up in the basement of our culture. The Bluebeard lives in all of us. Any time we cringe at our own natural wild selves. Any time we want to destroy parts of creation to have our own way instead. Any time we'd rather stay asleep in the dream of our lives and forget about what's really going on below. When we remain unconscious of this inner destructive figure, we tend to unconsciously attract relationships that are dangerous to ourselves and our potential—and we are initiated into a great awakening.

~

On Friday we're all in our uniforms again. I walk to my locker and see Allie standing there with blue and gold ribbons flowing in her long spiraling hair. Jason walks right past me, puts his hands on her hips and slides them all the way down to her feet and whistles.

"Jason!" She giggles.

"Damn," he says and walks away.

I'll show him, I think. I make sure to tell all my friends that I have a date this weekend so it will get back to him and he'll know.

"Jessica—not Johnny Diamond," Lana says.

"Why not?" I say.

"He's trouble—big, big, trouble."

Good, I think. Cause I'm ready to make some.

~

"A movie?" my father says. "Tell him to come inside."

Johnny walks up to the front door. His leather jacket reeks of cigarettes. My mother's eyes nearly fall out of her head.

"Listen, Johnny," my father talks in his commander voice, "I want her back by 10:00 p.m. Not one second later. You go straight to the movie, you come straight home. Do you understand?"

"Yes sir," Johnny laughs. "No worries, Sir. Not one second later," he says. The southern charm is a little too enchanting for us all.

I fold myself into his little sports car. The seats are all torn up and the engine is loud. He puts his hand on my thigh.

"Hey," I say.

"Hey yourself," he says leaving his hand there and squeezing me. He turns the music up loud. Slayer's "Seasons in the Abyss" assaults my senses. We drive with the windows down out the base gate, down Chickasawba road towards the movie theater in Blytheville. Johnny turns right into a forest preserve area.

"Hey—where are you going?"

"I'm going here, bitch," he says and laughs.

"Take me home," I say.

"Girl, if you wanna go home, then you best get out of this car and walk home."

I look at the dark trees around me. I don't even know where I am.

"Yeah, that's what I thought," he says. He opens a bottle of beer and starts chugging. When it's empty he throws it in the back seat, which is filled with lots of other empty beer bottles. I have never been this scared in my life—I wonder if he is he going to kill me.

Johnny chugs three more beers and I watch his personality transform.

"Get in the back," he says.

"No," I say.

"Look girl—you are gettin' in the back one way or another. Either you go there, or I'm gonna take you there and it ain't gonna feel nice if I have to do it."

I look out the window again. Maybe I should just run. What if he chases me? Where will I go? There's not a soul around here for miles. He's got the car. He promised my father we'd be home at 10:00. I crawl in the back seat.

"That's a good girl," he says. "Now take off your pants."

"I don't really want to," I draw my legs up into my tummy. He jumps in the back seat, unfolds me and lies on top of me. He holds my legs down with his knees. He unbuttons my pants and starts sliding them off of me.

"You ain't escaping," he laughs.

I just want it to be over. If I stop fighting it will be over faster. And then I can go home. I lay still.

"Good," he says. At least he has the decency to put a condom on. I turn my head to the side so I can't smell the beer or cigarettes on his breath. I stare at the ripped open seat, the frayed black synthetic leather and the exposed dirty yellow foam.

"Oh yeah, girl," he says as he moves. "Don't tell me you don't love this. Come on, tell me you love it," he says.

"I love it," I say like a robot.

"You can do better," he says as he holds my arms down.

"I love it," tears are rolling down my cheeks.

"That's a good girl," he says. An eternity passes. When he's done he hops out of the car and chugs another beer and smokes a cigarette. I pull up my underwear and button my jeans and curl into a little ball. I still want to run into the woods. I want to die. But I'm so good at over-riding my true feelings as not to upset anyone or make a scene. He probably has no idea.

"Get back in the front seat," he starts chucking all the empty beer bottles into the woods. He drives so fast down Chickasawba. He has got to be drunk, I think. The crisp wind blows my hair in every direction. I cling to the door and the dashboard. He turns the music up louder as we race down the dark highway.

"Broken glass reflections show your flesh eaten away, beyond the gates I'll take you, where the blood forever rains…"

At least he's taking me home, I think. At least he didn't kill me. My body is still stiff with fear as he pulls into my driveway.

"Just in time," he smiles. I open the car door to bolt.

"Hey, hey, not so fast," he says. He grabs my arm and squeezes it hard.

"You tell anyone—and you will regret it," he says. I pull my arm out of his grasp, run into my house and lock the door.

~

Bluebeard chops up another bride and locks up her bloody body in the red room with all the others that have come before her. He's so charming, just like Christian Roberts. No one knows who he really is, many don't want to know, because more than truth they prefer charm. Only the sensitive woman knows, the one who is awake to her instincts. She is the animating spirit who is able to rescue her dismembered sisters and put their bodies back together. She is the one who knows the way to escape the powers of evil and destroy the red room forever. Someday I will be that woman. But today, I am cut into a million little pieces and locked away, waiting for a stronger version of myself to come to my rescue.

~

On Monday morning I wake up and find my father sitting on the couch with tears running down his face. My mother runs up to me.

"Oh, honey—" Her eyes fill with tears. "Cupcake died last night. Your father just buried her in the back yard."

I walk right past them and pour myself a bowl of cereal. I sit in silence and stare at the back of the Corn Flakes box.

"I'm so sorry, Jessica," my mother says. I hear my father sniffling. "She was the best guinea pig in the whole world."

"I don't want to talk about it!" I yell. I slam my spoon down on the table and run into the bathroom to get ready for school. I push all thoughts of Cupcake away. I don't cry for her until I'm in my twenties when she appears to me in a dream. I decided a long time ago that this kind of pain is off limits. I toss her memories in the trashcan of denial with Johnny Diamond, Christian Roberts, Matt

Black and Behind the High School, my dorky self who loved Jesus, and those stupid generic pink high top sneakers.

~

After a game one Friday night, the cheerleaders take off with the football players in sports cars and pickup trucks. We go to the woods and make a big fire. I take my first sip of alcohol. I get drunk. Heather hands me a cigarette. I smoke it. I cough. I am in the front seat of a truck with a boy I cannot remember. He kisses me. I lean forward and puke all over his floor bed.

"Sorry," I slur.

He's too drunk to care. "Damn, that's ok."

We pile into Heather's red convertible and all the cheerleaders head to Lauren's house for a sleepover. They turn up the radio real loud.

Garth Brooks sings, "Friends in Low Places." Everyone sings along. I lay sprawled out in the backseat with my hands over my ears.

"Don't puke!" the girls giggle.

"Oh my God, she is so drunk!"

~

Tupa has her puppies right before Thanksgiving. She has four of them. Emily, Peter, and I play with them on the lawn. We watch them chase leaves and let them lick our faces. We are devastated when we realize my mother plans to sell them all.

"We can't have five dogs!"

"Why not?" We beg. "Because!" She laughs.

One by one, the puppies disappear. Every time one gets sold, our whole family sits in the living room and cries together. We are down to one puppy now. He's been around the longest so my mother finally names him Thor.

He is the biggest puppy of the litter, so it's fitting, even though he's a miniature toy poodle. He's all black with a little white scruff around his chin. He likes me best. He sleeps at the foot of my bed at night and cuddles up with me in the morning. After Thanksgiving he still hasn't been sold.

"You can keep him, Jessica," my mother says. "He's yours."

~

Two fire trucks and several cop cars light up my street and draw the neighborhood to gather on my front lawn.

My new best friend, Jenny Lee grabs the cute fireman's arm and pulls him into my kitchen where I stand frozen, watching the black smoke fill our base housing unit.

"It's there!" She yells and points at the stove.

"I can see that," he laughs and sprays the fire extinguisher inside my oven. The other men come running in the house behind him. They all look at my oven and at us and start cracking up.

"What are you two trying to bake?"

"Cookies!"

Jenny Lee presents the tray of crispy chocolate oatmeal blobs to the officers.

"Normally I would, but..."

"You two are quite the Holly Homemakers!"

Another pipes in, "You'll make some man real proud!"

"What's all this white stuff on your counters?"

"It's baking powder," I say. "I heard that puts out grease fires!"

The fireman buckles over again. "It's baking SODA!"

"Next time, try to put the soda ON the actual fire! You dumped it down the vent!"

"Well, that's where the smoke was!"

They are dying.

"These are actually not bad," says Jenny Lee crunching on a cookie.

The officers say goodnight and advise us to take another home economics class. One snags a cookie and agrees with Jenny Lee.

"Not too bad!"

We can hear him crunching the cookie all the way out the door.

Jenny Lee and I try to clean up the kitchen before my parents come home from their Bible Study.

"They are going to kill me!" But when they walk in the door and hear Jenny Lee's animated version of the story they are in stiches. Humor covers a multitude of sins.

"It's my fault!" My mother says, "I left the meat we had for dinner in the broiler!"

Normally they would have a big fight right now. But Jenny Lee says, "So, that's what gives these cookies a bacon flavor!" And we're laughing too much to get angry.

~

I'm sitting in the front seat of Kyle Fletcher's blue sports car watching the sun set.

"It's beautiful," I say. He leans over and kisses me. Kyle is a football player and an upperclassman. He's super cute, but he never talks. He sticks his tongue inside my mouth. I have learned to do this a little better. It feels not terrible. He puts a hand on my breast. I pull away. I don't want to just make out. I want to talk and have a relationship with someone. I'm learning how some people think some girls are for relationships and others are just for sex. Once the making out starts, I begin to panic. I don't want to have a repeat of Johnny Diamond. For the first time in many, many years I start to pray: *Dear God, please get me out of this. Please help me. I don't want to have sex with Kyle. Please help!*

Kyle lifts my shirt off. He leans my chair back and crawls on top of me. He takes his pants off. He moves himself against me for a while. I can't feel anything. I glance down and see that he is completely limp. He zips up his pants and jumps out of the car. He starts punching and kicking the bumper and shouting.

"Fuck! Fuck! Fuck! Fuck!"

I put my shirt back on and giggle. *Thank you, God, I think. Thank you, thank you, thank you.* I cannot wipe the smile off my face as he drives me all the way back home.

~

The year flies by. It's warming up outside and everyone is excited for Prom. The elections are today and we have to vote on court and all the other categories in our yearbook. Earlier in the week they handed out the first ballot where everyone got to write in names. Today we choose between the top picks.

In math class we vote. I have an A in math now. My teacher is a woman and she explains everything in a way I understand. I open up the ballot and nearly fall out of my chair. I can't believe it. There is my name next to Lana Berry in the category of *Most Beautiful*. I remember when I first moved here and I just wanted to be normal. I felt so ugly and awkward. Now here I am, a cheerleader who is nominated in the yearbook. I did transform, just like I dreamed a long time ago.

As an underclassman I get into Prom with my date Jose, a sweet shy kid who I see as my ticket in the door. I ditch him half way through the night and he watches me from the lonely bleachers as I dance with the cheerleaders and hog the floor with them. We do all of our routines to the songs we've danced to this year and I enjoy the feeling of belonging—even at the expense of the outcast. *Better someone else than me*, I think. I still have a lot to learn about how to have compassion on myself. The root of all evil is not money; it's self-hate.

~

Everyone at school is buzzing about the big news.

"Can you believe the base is closing?"

People are darting from locker to locker, making sure that everyone has heard. Desert Storm is over. The Cold War has come to an end and the government is closing Eaker Air Force Base.

Jason walks up to me, "Jess—did you hear? We are all being relocated this summer!"

The thought of a town like Gosnell existing without any military kids is inconceivable. We make up about half the population of the school. The news overwhelms me. I have worked so hard to become someone here. And now I'm about to lose everything. I cannot make any words come out of my mouth. I just stare at him with wide watery eyes.

"Come here, Jess," he says and he pulls me close. I had forgotten how he smelled. How my head felt against his chest.

"We only have a few more weeks together," he says. "Let's make them the best they can be."

He writes me notes every day, several times a day. He writes out all of the lyrics from Timmy T's song, "…one more try, I didn't know how much I loved you, one more try let me put my arms around you.."

~

"Nebraska?"

I fall on the floor and hug my legs. "Why are they sending us back there?" I pound my fists into the carpet.

My father looks at me tenderly.

"I know moving is hard," he says.

I run into my bedroom and slam the door. I scream into my pillow. I have to go back. I have to go back to my Queendom of Nerddom.

Wherever you go—there you are.
               -Confucius

"Did your Dad get orders yet?" I ask Jason. I'm so afraid to voice the question.

"Not yet," he says. We lay in my bed together listening to Phil Collins sing, "A Groovy Kind of Love."

My one hope is that Jason gets stationed at Offutt Air Force Base too. Then everything will be all right. He brushes my hair back and looks me over with his green eyes.

"You're so beautiful, Jess." I smile. Tears run down my face.

"What happened to us?" I say. "I have missed you so much."

"I've missed you too, Jess." He says. "You know, I never stopped loving you—"

"No," I laugh. "I didn't know that." I start to bawl.

"I'm so sorry," he says. "This year was hard for me. It was hard for me to watch you change so much."

"Just tell me how you want me to be, Jason. I will be anyone for you," I say.

"Just be Jess," he says. "Be my Jess." He moves on top of me and kisses me softly. It all feels so natural. My body aches for him. It's been so long since he's touched me. Our hands walk down the old trails of our bodies and find the familiar places.

"I love you Blue Eyes," he whispers into my ear. "I will always love you," he says.

~

On Friday we perform our last pep rally. We toss Lana higher than she's ever been. I show off all my perfected jumps. I'm practically doing the splits in the air like I can do on the ground now. My mother can hardly believe it. We close with our final dance to Janet Jackson's Rhythm Nation. All the lights go off. The music is pumped through the speakers. Some of the girls have tears running down their cheeks already. None of us can ignore it: this is the last dance for the 1990-91 Lady Pirates.

Lauren works with us to get the moves just right. We study Janet's videos and learn to move like her. The crowd goes wild. We nail it.

After the dance the cheerleaders gather in a big circle. Mrs. Perlis congratulates us on a year well done. There's not a dry eye in the room. Everyone hugs.

"Good job, Jessica," Heather says to me.

I think back to the time when I was so afraid of her. Now here I stand, so tall and strong next to her. I see the respect in her eyes as she looks up at me.

"Thanks, Heather."

"Jessica, come here please," Mrs. Perlis says. I run over to her. "I just wanted to tell you that if I had an award for most improved, you would get it. I am amazed at all your hard work this year. I know that you have to leave us, I also wanted you to know, that if you had stayed, I would have made you co-captain next year."

"Thank you Mrs. Perlis!" I say and I give her a big hug.

"Best of luck to you kid," she says.

In the locker room, I carefully fold up my uniforms, unsure of who I will be without them.

"I will miss you so much!" Taylor runs over to me and hugs me.

"Me too," says Lana. "We had so much fun this year!"

After all the tearful goodbyes I walk out of the gym and off of Gosnell campus for the very last time. I walk all the way home from school that day through the green grass near the base fence. All the school buses are packed full of kids and lined up on the road beside me.

"Jessica!" Kids scream. I smile.

"I love Jessica!" Another yells.

"Wooooo! Pretty lady," someone else shouts.

I'm smiling so big. I turn and wave. And then I trip over a telephone wire and fall flat on my face. I can't tell who's laughing harder, me or all the kids hanging out of the school bus windows.

~

Jason and I meet at the park one last time. The light remains longer now and wisps of pink and orange illuminate the evening sky.

I watch him skate towards me. I have a dreadful feeling in my stomach as soon as I see his face.

"I'm going to St. Louis," he says.

"No!" I fall into his arms sobbing. I beat his chest with my fists. He squeezes me real tight.

"Oh God, Jason. How am I supposed to live without you? I can't. I just can't."

"Jess—shhhh." He holds me tight and rocks me back and forth. We stay until it is dark. He lays me down on the grass. We say goodbye in every possible way that we can.

~

The moving truck has already taken all our stuff to Nebraska. My father has the car loaded.

"Time to go, Jess," he says.

We pile into the K-mart car. My father actually turns on the radio for us to listen to as we drive. Boyz to Men sings, "End of the Road."

I don't care what my family thinks. I just sob. As we drive past Jason's house I put my hands on the window. My father lets me keep them there.

"Bye," I whisper. "Oh my God, goodbye."

We three kids have all grown so much. Now our knees press into the front seats, our eyes wider and wiser. We drive through the metal gate for the very last time, leaving behind the ignited prickly little spears that poke into the sky. I never would have imagined I could feel like this three years ago: that love could find me in a place I wanted to die. And how I must leave it all behind.

We turn right at the Sonic and drive down highway 181, past Gosnell High School, and back to the land from which we came.

Take me back to the garden
To the place of innocence.
Let me gaze at the stars again,
And watch the colors melt across the sky.
Take me back to the cave,
To the dark from which I came,
To the arms that once held me
Through the screaming nights.
Mother medicine:
Heal the pain of the world
And all her murderous sorrows.

> *Jung saw a transformation chamber in which the traumatized ego was broken down into its basic elements, dissolved, so to speak, in the nectar of the gods, for the purpose of later rebirth.*
>
> -Donald Kalsched

HIGH PRIESTESS

My father's family tree is filled with Bohemian gypsies. I am told the gypsies are the outcasts of society. The musicians. The artists. The storytellers. The truth bearers and tricksters. Growing up in the military is its own kind of Gypsy life. We are always strangers to the land; we say the wrong things, we break the unspoken rules, we carry incredible stories. I often wonder what it's like to belong to the land, to have the privilege of calling a place—or a body—home.

I imagine a great ancestor, an old woman with my Great Grandma Madison's twinkling eyes, moving from town to town wielding a boxy suitcase with old postage stuck to the sides, making a living from the simple wisdom she carries in her heart. Whatever wisdom I bring with me to Nebraska, much of it is still inaccessible, buried beneath a cement of pain, locked behind a forbidden door.

~

The name Nebraska comes from an Indian word meaning flat water. The Platte River is the central channel that runs through the area. Glaciers used to cover this land that once was an inland sea bed. Now the land is decorated with corn. The University of Nebraska's state football team is called the Cornhuskers.

~

The Goddess Demeter is also known as the Corn Goddess. She is the one who blesses the harvests, except when she loses her daughter Persephone in the underworld, then she allows nothing to grow upon the earth until her daughter is found.

~

I am driving our new Ford Aerostar past my old school, Ft. Crook Elementary in Bellevue, Nebraska. Peter sits in the passenger seat.

Now we call him Dave because apparently a 'peter' is another word for penis and he's tired of getting teased at school. We listen to the latest hits on the radio trying as hard as we can to be cool in our parents' brand new minivan. We drive by our old house and take a trip down memory lane.

"Remember how we used to climb up on the carport and hide behind the trees and shout, *Ice cream man sucks!* as he drove by?"

"We were so lame," I say. "All cuz our parents wouldn't give us any money."

I look at the carport longingly and remember Paul's arms around me, that feeling of new love. I feel so old now. I stare at the spot where it happened as if I could look through time and see the innocent girl standing there. I wonder who I am now. It seems like I am waiting for the world to define me again.

We pull up to the school playground. We play tether ball. Dave kills me on the court. We visit the old sledding hill, drive past our friends' houses who've likely moved on by now. Dave puts his feet on the dash and rolls down the windows. I turn up the radio so I can hear The Red Hot Chili Peppers sing, "Under the Bridge."

Dave's eyes are wide and full of life. His hair hangs down to his chin. He's almost as tall as me now. At least we have each other. He'll be a freshman; I'll be a junior. We can do this new kid thing together.

I look right then left and drive across a busy street. I see the streak of color out of the corner of my right eye. I hear a sound like I am underwater. Time slows down. My head slams into the left side of the window. Dave falls toward me. I hold the wheel as the back end of the car swings around. I hear the sound again.

"Are you okay?" Dave sits up.

"Yeah," he says.

I open the driver side door. I'm horrified by the sight of three smashed up cars, and the elderly couple emerging from the one in front of me.

A young girl about my age jumps out of the other car and starts screaming.

"You stupid bitch! What the hell were you thinking pulling out in front of me like that?" The elderly man from the other car walks over to us.

"Now, now," he says. "Look, no one is hurt too bad, that is the most important thing."

Dave and I stand like zombies not sure what to say or do, or if we should even move at all. My father arrives in the K-Mart car right away. When he sees us he smiles.

"It's okay," he says. "It's just a car. We can fix a car." He hugs us both.

~

I learn something new about my father that day. He may lose his temper over small things like lights and curling irons left on, but when it comes to really big things—he can be a hero. I think across the years and wonder again how he would have reacted if I ever had the guts to tell him what happened to me behind the high school. But at thirty-six years old—I still don't have the guts. I still live by the social rules of silence.

Silence encourages the tormentor, never the tormented.
-Elie Wiesel, Night

Colonel Peter Sarpy is a French Creole who supplies expeditions for the early settlers, helping plot and organize the land which is open to settlement after the Treaty of 1854 where the United States gained cession—that sounds so nice in the history books doesn't it? *They gained cession*—it means they forcefully stole the land and drove off the Natives. The name Bellevue is French for "beautiful view" after the bluffs that look over the Missouri River, the river that runs to St. Louis and makes fur traders prosperous and increases the number of settlers. Known as the oldest city in Nebraska, Bellevue's population dwindles until the military establishes Ft. Crook in the area, later named Offutt Air Force Base. After World War II, Offutt becomes home to the Strategic Air Command or SAC, which is where my father is now stationed doing top secret work.

He often joked, "I could tell you what I do, but then I'd have to kill you."

I had a sense that strange things went on here. When I grew up I learned that Offutt was rumored to house an MKUltra program. Omaha was also home to a suspicious elitist pedophile ring that despite tons of incriminating evidence, no one got prosecuted; kids who stood up to their abusers ended up dead or called unreliable witnesses of their lives.

~

Turns out the girl who hit me is in my grade and she goes to the same high school I'll go to in the fall. She was driving without a driver's license and got a ticket for it. I start to worry about the rumors that will spread. If all the girls will hate me before I even show up for my first day of class. History so often repeats itself, especially if the wounds of the past are unhealed.

My face has broken out in the worst case of acne I have ever had in my life. I try out for the cheerleading team that summer, but I don't make the cut. I try out for the dance squad and I don't make it either. I sit in my room alone. I listen to sad songs and cry. I look over all my old photographs. My entire life feels behind me. I can't put my sadness into words. I cry for everything that has been lost. Things unspoken. Things that have gone elsewhere, maybe never to incarnate my skin. My confidence is shot. My vision, blinded. My parents start to worry.

I hear my father tell his new friends, "Please keep her in your prayers."

~

Some of my father's work is now declassified. At a recent Thanksgiving dinner he tells me he worked with the National Security Agency at SAC and was responsible for two satellites that cost three billion dollars each.

"I was stressed out," my father says, "these satellites cost a ton of money and I was responsible for optimizing their performance. They can take a picture of you smoking a cigarette from outer space and report what brand you're smoking. We took pictures of all the bad guys."

Edward Snowden risked his life to let us know that our government is also taking pictures of us.

"Before I began working there, the satellite pictures had 90% cloud cover."

His weather unit forecasted the best times to take a picture.

"By the time I left, the pictures only had 10% cloud cover."

My father would assure me, "There are evil people out there, Jessica. We must kill them before they kill us. It's us or them."

I wonder: do they wear name tags that say *Bad Guy*?

"You know what else I can tell you now? I ordered a thermal maize expander for our unit. That means the government funded a popcorn popper for the office. I also ordered a Noise Suppression System, which means I ordered more speakers for our offices because one team liked country, another rock, and another liked eclectic stuff. One Master Sergeant used to put on 'Una Paloma Blanca' and we would all polka."

I guess if you can't have world peace, you can at least have popcorn and polka.

~

A boy named RJ lives down the street from me. He's a lot shorter than I am with white blonde hair and big blue eyes. His father owns all of these classic Rabbit cars that they fix up together. My mother asks his mother if her son can introduce me to some of his friends at the high school. RJ comes over to my house one night and asks me if I want to go for a drive in his convertible Rabbit.

"I guess," I say.

I look down, shy about all the pimples on my face. He takes me around the block. He tells me jokes and tries to cheer me up.

"Listen—tomorrow me and my friends are getting together—wanna come?"

"I dunno," I say. "I'll have to ask my parents."

"They already said you were free," he smiles. "Come on—it'll be fun!"

~

"But Mom, I don't want to leave the house! I don't want to meet anyone new!"

Her eyes soften.

"Let me take you shopping," she says. "Let's buy you some new clothes."

I sniff, "And shoes?"

"Sure, and shoes," she smiles.

She spoils me. I get more new clothes than I have ever had in my life. And two pairs of new shoes too—including these cute cowgirl boots that stop at my ankle.

RJ picks me up around dinnertime. At least I feel comfortable in what I'm wearing. I put a blue jean shirt (buttoned all the way to the top) over leggings and finish it off with my cowgirl shoes. I spend nearly two hours getting ready, trying to cover up of all my pimples, trying to smile in the mirror, and practice saying, "Nice to meet you."

We drive downtown Bellevue, past houses way bigger than mine. My father's new job has different requirements for living. We can reside off base now. My parents find a brown split entry way home in a clean suburban area which is mixed with other military and civilian residents. Dave and I get the two rooms in the finished basement and the downstairs bathroom all to ourselves.

As soon as we arrive at RJ's friend's house, I want to go straight home. All the girls here are on the cheer and pom squads, including the girl who looked at me with her cheery calloused eyes as she told me, "Sorry, maybe next year!"

One girl asks, "Are you from the south?" as she eyes my shoes.

"I lived in Arkansas," I say.

"Oooo, listen to that thick accent," another says.

"I hate country music," another girl says.

"Yeah, me too," several others chime in.

"Come on," RJ says. "Where's the food, I'm hungry!" We move into the kitchen, towards the chips and dip. The conversation is totally exclusive. I don't know the people they talk about or the things they are interested in. I keep eyeing RJ nervously. He gets my drift and finally he excuses himself to drive me home.

"Sorry about that," he says.

"It's okay," I say putting my head back against the seat and letting the wind blow away all my thoughts. He pulls into his driveway.

"Do you wanna look at all the stars in my backyard?"

"Why not," I say.

We walk around back. It's a beautiful summer evening. The insects and frogs are making music together. The stars are as bright as the hope that once lived in me. We both lie on our backs and take it all in. I enjoy just being there in all this nature. Then RJ rolls over on top of me and starts kissing me. *Fuck.* I just wanted to gaze at the stars. I don't know what to do. *If I reject him, will he tell all the popular people that I'm lame?* I let him kiss me and rub himself against me. And then, oh my God, he ejaculates and somehow it shoots up out of his pants and squirts me right in the eye.

"I gotta go," I jump up and run home. RJ never talks to me again. Or looks at me. Not in three years. Not once. I still don't understand how some girls are seen as just for sex, how I am seen just for that. Because I know I'm more than an object. Still, I have lost sense of my dignity along the way.

"Oh my word, Jessica! What happened to your eye?" My mother rushes towards me and tries to pry open my eyelid.

"Nothing, Mom! It's nothing!"

"It is certainly not nothing," she says. "It's so red and horrible looking! Did you get injured?"

Yeah you could say that.

"No, Mom! I just uh…I got some dirt it or something that's all."

"Well let's rinse this out as quickly as possible."

She leans my head over the sink and runs the facet water all over my face. Repeat traumatization.

"We're going to keep a watch on this. If it doesn't clear up by tomorrow, I'm taking you to an optometrist."

"Mom! It's nothing. Really."

I escape downstairs, lock myself in my bedroom and pull the covers all the way over my head. I just want to crawl into a cave and sleep until the nightmare is over.

~

Marissa calls me on the phone one night. She's worried about a bad relationship she's in. I can't hear her very well. She sounds so distant. Much sadder than the Marissa I remember. When I call her again, the number is disconnected. I miss her terribly. I worry about her. I miss the squad. Jenny Lee. And most of all, I miss Jason.

~

Pearl Jam's album, Ten is released. Every single song reminds me of Jason. I listen to "Black" over and over again. I call Jason on the phone in the evenings. He loves the album too. His favorite track is "Release Me." We talk almost every night. I hug the phone close to my ear, imagining that he is with me, that his arms are around me.

"What do you miss most about me?" I ask.

"Your crooked mouth," he whispers. "And your thighs."

"I miss your arms around me." I listen to his heavy breathing.

"Jessica?"

It's my mother's voice. Oh God. How long has she been on the line?

"It's time for bed. Say goodnight."

~

The Bellevue West High School mascot is a Native American Thunderbird. The Lakota word for Thunderbird means "sacred" and "wings". It reminds me of the Holy Spirit, but I like their badass bird a lot better than our white Christian pigeon. Our culture assimilated so many of these ancient powerful symbols to use to push our own agenda which included the oppression of indigenous people and the pollution of the earth for profit. The Thunderbird reminds me of the silver wings pinned on my father's Air Force uniform. It reminds me of the wings of the Egyptian Goddess Isis who flies around the world in search of her dismembered beloved. In our fear and ignorance of so many things which we do not understand, we hurt beautiful people, we hurt Mother Earth, and we felt justified because our ignorance was shroud in blind allegiance and unquestioning faith.

~

I don't fit into the jocks or the preps. I don't ever sit in the middle of the commons like I would have in Gosnell last year. Here I find my place among the fringes. There are a few familiar faces here from seventh grade and elementary school. But for the most part, people could care less if I was a nerd back then. I forgot, time keeps going and everyone else grows up too. Some folks say hi to me. Others pretend I don't exist. I am actually relieved to discover that I don't have to work so hard to escape the Queendom of Nerddom or the trenches of the notorious School Slut. But I discover that I am just as anxious about being nobody in particular at all.

The Journalism teacher invites me to join their staff. She looks at my writing samples and she likes what she sees. Now I write articles for the high school newspaper. I eventually get my own opinion column where I rail on the evils of feminism and liberal politics, all the things I have learned from my parents, church, and Rush Limbaugh who is always on the radio in our home. My writing upsets many of the strong girls and women at my school, including my dear Journalism and English teachers. Backed by blazon freedom of speech values and mixed with the essential callousness required to claim worldly power, I make my family and my church community proud with each dramatic piece designed to prove: I win by not feeling more than you do. I win by being tough like military soldiers. I win by disassociating from all the weak and disgusting vulnerable parts of myself. This is survival. I have a place now and a voice, a voice not yet my own.

~

A common theme in Native American spirituality is a fascination with the circle and unity. The earth is often revered as a Great Mother who sustains life. Earth based religions keep the teachings of harmonious living with the natural world. In the west we have been taught to conquer nature. I remember feeling as little girl the belief that saturated the headspaces I grew up in, that science was smarter than mother nature, that some white men in lab coats were smarter than my body. That someone outside of me knew better for me than the someone inside of me. That some wonder drug would fix everything nature got wrong. I remember believing in this religion for a time, as my father was a scientist. I remember searching for the most powerful laboratory medicines to kill my acne, even if it killed my liver. In Christian spirituality, people have been taught that matter or mother or Eve (which means the source of all that is living) is full of sin. We have been taught that nature is fallen. That women are less persons, less divine than men. We have inherited a dualistic vision of the world that pits the opposites against one another to war rather than learning how to dance the infinite dance of creation that circles on and on.

~

The last time we lived here we went to another Lutheran Church which was a part of the Evangelical Lutheran Church in America, the more progressive liberal branch where my mother's family tree is rooted. Now we are a part of a more conservative Lutheran church where feminists and gay issues are pushed to the fringes, maybe to keep the sexually repressed congregation more comfortable. I compromise my deep off limit instincts on these issues in order to fit in. I write an article on how women need to shut up and deal with sexual harassment. *Not feminists*, I quote Rush Limbaugh, *feminazis* I call my dear sisters. I decide that I hate the radical, angry women who bemoan our so-called purely theoretical patriarchal society. I hate how emotionally sensitive they are. I hate hearing about their pain. Why can't they just shut up and deal with it like I do?

It's really hard to offer empathy to another, especially when you haven't learned how to have compassion on yourself. You end up treating other people just as badly as you treat your own split off shadow.

~

I make the JV volleyball team. I meet a girl named Kara. She is tall like me with blonde wavy hair that hangs down her back. She drives a blue Skylark and picks me up before school. We smoke cigarettes on the way.

"Let's ditch school today," she says one chilly morning.

I look at her with wild eyes. "Let's!"

We drive downtown Omaha. We hang out at the mall. Buy more cigarettes. We get old guys to buy us liquor. We park in a forest preserve and get slap stick drunk.

At the end of the day, after we've sobered up, we drive back to campus to say hi to our friends before we head home. When we walk in the building a huge crowd runs gathers around us.

"Oh, my God! They're alive!" people yell.

Kara and I look at each other confused.

"The cops are here looking for you! Didn't you hear? Some girls across town were found dead before school today—everyone thought you were dead too!"

People give us hugs. Many have tears in their eyes. This is not good. Not good at all. We are so busted.

The vice principal walks up to us and puts his arms over our shoulders. "Your parents are going to be very relieved to see you," he says.

Not likely, I think.

A policeman drives me home. He sits next to me on the couch while I tell my parents what I did that day (leaving out plenty of details of course). My father is so angry that he doesn't even speak to me. I get grounded for a month and now my mother drives me to school.

~

Kara's in love with the school druggie, Andy. We go over to his house and drink Jack Daniels until we puke. She slips off into rooms with him while I pour myself more drinks.

I try pot. It doesn't work. I smoke like ten times and nothing happens. Until one day it finally does work and I get totally stoned.

"Yeah, you're feelin' it now, aren't ya?" Andy says. He leans back and laughs with his buddies. "Look at her eyes!"

"I feel like I'm floating," I smile.

All the sadness and anxiety inside dissipates. For the first time in a really long time, I feel at ease in my body.

~

The Native American peace pipe ceremony creates a sacred relationship between the Creator and the people of the land, connecting the realms of the spirit to the planes of the earth. There is a place in southern Minnesota called Pipestone where Native Americans dig for the red rock to create a peace pipe. Legend says that the Great Mother told the earth people to come here and take of her body and create a pipe that unites all the warring tribes. The land at this national monument is covered in ancient rocks, waterfalls and nature spirits. To this day Native Americans come and dig here. They believe sharing the peace pipe strengthens peace on earth. The U.S.

government exploited the rituals of the peace pipe ceremony by acting as Native guests at sacred rituals and making sacred promises which they broke when they got greedy for more land.

~

On a cold night close to winter, Kara and I race across an old country road in her blue Skylark. With the windows rolled down and the radio turned up we sing together, REM's song, "Man on the Moon." Cigarettes in our hands, colorful beanies on our heads, we look at each other and laugh wildly.

"Oh shit!" Kara screams as we hit a bump.

She turns the wheel hard. The Skylark does a 180 degree turn and slams into the ditch on the side of the road. We end up in a snow-covered cornfield facing the other direction.

"Holy Fuck!" She laughs until she snorts.

"Are you okay?" She's in shock.

We crawl out of the car and move our necks around and shake our arms and legs. Our breath makes little clouds in front of our mouths. The night is quiet. We look up at the big black sky and the tiny twinkling stars.

"Now what?" I ask.

Kara points to a glowing farmhouse.

"We walk there and hope they don't murder us."

"And if they don't—our parents will."

We march through the cut down corn stalks to the little house ahead like we are walking into a dark fairytale.

~

In one myth of the Corn Woman an old mother feeds her family, but no one knows where the food comes from. One day her sons secretly follow her. Different versions of the story say the corn comes from her scabs, the dirt on her feet, her fingernails or even her own feces. Whatever the origin, her magic life-making abilities come from a vile place and upon this recognition her sons refuse to accept her gift of corn any more. In order to feed her family, the Corn Woman tells her sons to chop up her body and sprinkle her blood upon the earth. Wherever her blood lands is where the corn will continue to grow.

Is the sacrifice of the feminine required for life to continue? Or is this just another tale twisted by power that justifies the sacrifice of women in a patriarchal age? The ancient women knew their blood fed the land. They knew they didn't need to die inside or otherwise to feed their families; they fed the land with their menstrual blood. When we remember how to honor our life-making abilities and our blood again, our disconnected madness will be healed, when the restoration of our crowns takes place the veils will be torn in two and we shall return face to face seeing of Akasha and Divine Essence. Our wild Medusa snakes will enter our bodies again as Kundalini energy for healing and awakening. And we will be restored and remembered as Sacred Women.

~

Kara calls her Dad from an old rotary phone while scary people eyeball us. But what is the most frightening is our reckless abandonment of ourselves. I am forever grateful for the development of a frontal lobe and for the life graced to me after a winter of adolescence.

~

Jason and I commit to a long distance relationship. We promise each other that we won't date anyone else. I tell him a little about the partying; he doesn't like it. He doesn't want me smoking pot. I can't help it though, it's like anti-anxiety medicine. It helps me relax and feel so much calmer in my body.

Jason's parents say he can visit for Thanksgiving. I spend my time obsessing and preparing to see him so that our time together will be perfect. When he arrives at my front door I can hardly stand up. I am so weak with joy. He kisses me and he holds me tight as I melt into his old familiar smell. We go to see the new movie, *The Body Guard* together. When Whitney Houston sings, "I will always love you," I do the ugly cry. We make out in a photo booth and split the pictures. He tucks his into a wallet and keeps it there for years. I put mine on my mirror at home, where I see it every morning. I feel I have always been searched for my beloved, out there. Something in him awakens something in me. And it's like the inhale and the exhale of oxygen.

The time goes by too fast. My emotions are out of control. When he leaves I fall to the floor and sob. Thor comes and licks the tears off of my face. He cuddles next to me in bed and he cries when I cry. My parents don't know how to help me. They are frightened by my emotions. They are not logical. We argue more. I don't know how to contain myself. I don't know who I am without Jason. Classic co-dependent behavior. I'm still so much a child searching for love's nourishment, unsure of who I am or what I am capable of, and wildly distracted by the long term effects of trauma.

We make plans for prom. I do better if I have something to look forward to with Jason. Our parents agree that it is okay for me to fly to St. Louis and go to Jason's prom in May. I cross off the days on my calendar. My thoughts are filled with daydreams of all the wonderful things that will happen when we are together. The present moment is too much to bear with its roots that reach into my dark fragmented past. I need the glitter of a future fantasy world to cover up all the pain.

I begin tanning. I start to obsess over my looks. I want to be the most beautiful girl in the world for Jason. My love for him is turning into a scary sort of desperation. I wonder what pretty girls he eyes at school and what details he leaves untold when we speak. I worry he may not be telling me the whole truth, just like I don't tell him the whole truth.

When prom comes, I throw myself at him hoping that he will love me and need me even more. I can't get close enough to him, and yet I just feel emptier and emptier.

I sob the entire plane ride home. The people sitting next to me are concerned. One man tries to calm me down. He talks to me about love and loss and encourages me to chase my dreams. Jason is my only dream. When I get back home Jason distances himself. He says we should play the field while we're young.

~

I delve deeper into drugs. It's the only thing that soothes the pain. I find friends on the fringes—I give up on being popular. I wear lots of dark colors. I shop at Goodwill. I buy old flannel shirts and ripped jeans. I give up on name brands. Fuck that shit.

I have a new posse of girlfriends: Kara, Paula, Katrina, and we dress to kill on the weekends. We all have long wavy blonde hair. Paula is short and athletic; she knows the most about boys and sex and teaches us many things and keeps us laughing all the time. Katrina is a little taller than Paula, with gorgeous ringlets that drop down the middle of her back.

"Do you want to know how to give the best blow job?" Paula says smiling ear to ear.

All of us lean in.

"Don't keep secrets, Paula, tell us all you know!" Kara says.

"You don't just blow on it?" Katrina says. I laugh.

"That's what I thought too!"

"No, you don't blow."

Paula grabs a beer bottle and proceeds to teach us all of her mysterious skills.

When we hit the town, we party like there is no tomorrow. This is not a small town. I don't know if it's better or worse that nobody cares. I get so drunk. I keep falling over people, mumbling about Jason. I drink so much alcohol and smoke so much pot. I want so much distraction. I need it to drown out all the self-hatred and pain inside.

~

Senior year, Jason invites me to go to his homecoming. He begins to call and writes me letters again. I stop messing around with other boys and give my full attention to him. I buy another pass to the tanning booth so my skin can look perfectly golden for him. I practice doing my hair in all these different ways. I spend months picking out each outfit I will wear for each day that I am there. My mother sews me another dress. This one is red. It has two small spaghetti straps that lay over my shoulders. It's skin tight and hits the floor. My favorite part: a slit that runs all the way up to the top of my thigh. Watch out world, this insatiably hungry tigress is about to prowl.

~

As soon as we are alone my clothes come off. I push him down on the bed. I ravage him like a seven course meal after 40 days lost in the wilderness. I pull out all the new tricks I've learned. I try to be everything he could ever want and more.

We make out to The Police, "You'll Be Wrapped Around My Finger."

It's so ecstatic. He enjoys me, but something's missing. My heart is an empty tomb. He's quieter, more reserved. It makes me reach for him even more.

"I'm going to Carbondale College," he says.

It's the one school my father will not let me attend because he went there and,

"It's a party school. Absolutely No."

"Jason—let's go anywhere else. Let's be together," I plead. "I'll go anywhere you want me to."

"I'm going to Carbondale," he insists.

By the end of the weekend he tells me he wants to put things on hold again. When I leave, I'm free to be with whomever I choose. I don't descend as far into the darkness now. It's just a numb return. I know this place of rejection, of lost hope. I know it well. The more I try to escape it, the more it draws me in.

~~

I can't remember how we meet.

Aaron has dark hair and wild blue eyes. He's tall and skinny like me. He wears flannel shirts and likes to challenge the absurdities he sees in society, and, most importantly, he likes to make me smile.

The first time he comes over to my house he wears his Charles Manson t-shirt.

"Good choice," I whisper.

"Just trying to be the respectable boyfriend."

I try not to laugh as my parents lay eyes on him. All the blood drains from their faces and their mouths hang open.

"9 p.m. sharp," my father says.

~

Aaron drives me to a playground in some neighborhood. We hot box the car.

"I don't think you made a good impression on my Dad," I laugh.

"I don't care," he says as he packs another bowl. "Christians are so stupid."

"Why?" I laugh.

"Because they believe lies."

"How can you be like that—so sure, so fearless?"

"Because I have nothing to lose," he exhales.

"Unless God is real," I say.

"But he's not," Aaron smiles. "You can't prove it. No one can."

"Who cares," I say. "None of it really matters anyway."

"What exactly do you do on the computers?" I ask him as I light up a cigarette.

"Well…I've erased an entire school district's grades."

"What? You didn't!"

"I did. I hacked into Benson High School and erased everyone's grades."

"No! Did you get caught?"

He laughs. "Yeah, but they said they wouldn't press charges if I could bring it all back."

"Stop it. Did you?"

"Of course I did!"

I admire his confidence. I eye him wantonly. "Wow. You're amazing."

He leans over to kiss me. "Smokers are disgusting," he says.

"You want me to quit?" I whisper.

"Yes please."

"Fine," I throw the butt out the window. "Then you'll have to buy me more weed to smoke."

"Fine," he says.

He pulls me closer. The weed heightens all of our senses. Every touch is magical.

I escape into the backseat. "Come here," I say. I take my shirt off.

He follows.

"Jess," he says. "This is my first time."

~

Aaron says I remember a few things differently than he does. Still, he gives me his permission to exercise my creative writing license.

Besides, when you consider the circumstances, it won't be hard to see how things started to blend together for me.

~

I am in the bathroom for the entire performance of the opening band. I throw up all over the floor. Like three times. It is hard for me to stand up. Or walk. I don't even know how I make it back to the auditorium. Or how I find my friends again. I put my head in Aaron's lap for most of the Nirvana concert. Which is a bummer since it is their last tour.
Billy Corgan is cool though. When I am riding the crowd at his Smashing Pumpkins concert someone rips my shirt off. He stops the song and tells the guys to cut it out. For Stone Temple Pilots, I am in the back of the show for most of the concert. I don't remember what I take that night. I just keep my head down and try to stop the room from spinning. Tool is the scariest though. The energy is dark. I fall on the floor and am almost trampled. The boys at the show frighten me. They have wide black eyes filled with hunger and a rage seems to search for the weakest link. I know I am a walking bullseye: I'm the girliest girl in the room.

~

Late at night when I'm alone and sober in my room, I begin to journal. I realize that I'm losing a self I never fully had. I think if I write down my whole story, it will help me figure out what is happening. I start to tell the pages my truth.

~

Katrina comes to live with us for a while. Her parents got orders in the middle of her senior year. We become like two sisters all tangled up in each other's insecurities. One night we get in a really bad fight. She rips up my favorite picture and I punch her.

I remember my father's reaction. He was actually proud of me for being violent. He gave me the sort of high five that a son might receive for winning a fight. It confuses me because I feel ashamed for what I have done and I know it was wrong. Katrina moves with her parents out west. And I harden my heart again.

For years I dream of finding Katrina so I can apologize. I am thirty seven years old when I finally have the chance. We sit down and have drinks together. We share our stories. We realize that both of us had to work hard to face our wounds and find the courage to stand up to abusers in our lives. When she forgives me, my heart heals even more.

~

"Jessica!" My mother holds a letter in her hands. "You got into St. Olaf!"

She looks so surprised. I am not surprised by her surprise; I feared my stupidity every day—because I didn't know how awesome I was in other things yet and my roundness just wouldn't fit in the square hole. I am relieved that I have a shot to explore the world and find my way out of the mess of my childhood. I assumed I would attend St. Olaf my whole life—well, that is before Jason says he will never go there—and before we ever thought that a college education could land you unemployed and in a lot of debt. Many of my maternal relatives went there. If I can't be with Jason then this is where I belong. It's a place I have visited many times as a child. I've watched aunts and uncles graduate there. My grandmother lives in town. It's a bittersweet future. I begin to dream of the day I am free. Free from my parents. Free from all this heartache. Free to explore. It's only a few months away.

~

"I don't want you dating that boy," my father says.

"You can't tell me who I can and cannot date!"

"As long as you live under the roof of my house, you will abide by my rules! He's a loser, Jessica and I don't want you with him."

"No he's not! And you can't control me!"

"Oh, you bet I can!" My father's puts his red face inches from mine. I am backed up against a wall.

"This is my house! I pay the bills! I put food on the table!"

I close my eyes as words and saliva fly onto my face.

I push back, "That's what parents are supposed to do!"

"Stop talking back! You don't know how much you need us. You better turn this around."

"I don't need you!"

"Oh really? Who's going to help you pay for St. Olaf?"

He wouldn't.

"That's right. Turn this around or you will not be going there in the fall—do you understand me?"

~

Aaron lands some acid and one night we drop together. We sit in a dark closet. He brings some glow sticks. He holds me close and we talk about the meaning of life. His eyes are filled with wide curiosity. I thought this would never happen again. The rush of butterflies. The sense of being fully alive. This journey breaks my obsession with Jason and solidifies my full on rebellion against my family. This feels so devilishly wonderful.

~

Jason calls one night. He says he misses me. Last year we agreed that he would come to my Senior Prom even if we were dating other people. He wants to see me again.

My mother is concerned.

"I don't think this is a good idea, Jessica," she says.

"Oh, Mom—we can be friends. I've known him since eighth grade. Besides, a guy like Aaron would never go to prom."

Maybe my mother and father hope Jason can save me from Aaron. They agree to let him come.

~

"Let's do seven," Aaron says.

"Seven?"

"Do you even know anyone who's done seven?"

"No," I say. I do not yet know any other psychonauts. I don't even know that entheogenic explorers of the soul are even a thing.

"Only certain kinds of people can drop acid," he says.

It's as if we are remembering an ancient practice together. He cuts the little squares and hands them to me.

~

Everything comes to the surface on entheogens. You face the light and the shadows of everything. Life-long problems that seemed illusive bubble up to the surface to be sorted out. This is a dangerous initiation. Sometimes it involves a lot of purging and working through super intense energies as you face your deepest fears and allow the illusions in your life to dissolve completely into the truth of being. It's an initiation of shaking you right to your very core, so you know who you are and what is most important, and what step to take next. It's an initiation of seeing how everything in life is connected. Sometimes it's shocking to return to the madness of the unawakened world. And sometimes it's easier to see the beauty and the connectedness of all things. Sometimes you can hear more clearly how we are so tenderly and wonderfully loved beyond measure.

~

We become like care-free children and run off to a park to play at night. He pushes me on the merry-go-round. I watch all the colors from the spinning disk streak into a brilliant rainbow. A giant circle of color surrounds me. I look up at the dark sky and lose myself in a black iris that stares into the depths of my soul. Suddenly I know that the universe is intelligent. I know it in my body. I feel it all around me. And I remember feeling like this. Something tugs at my heart.

I swing on the swings. The tracers make it look like my feet are still up in the air by the time I've swung all the way back. I giggle. Aaron's smile is so big. He can't stop grinning from ear to ear. He takes me in his arms. We fall on the grass. He kisses me.

"Jess," he says. "You're the most amazing girl in the entire universe!"

I'm not sure how this could possibly be true, but in that moment it feels as if I am potentially every girl that has ever existed and we are all amazing (and terrifying) and so it must be true. We kiss like we are kissing for all of creation, reaching for one another like all the opposites yearn to be reconciled in the cosmos. Our bodies are beautifully alive and this feels like the most incredible realization.

On entheogens, all superficialities are stripped away. One experiences God inside the body. Filled with wonder and awe, one tastes the nectar of heaven that has always flowed from the center of being.

Is it wrong to know to this innate cosmic beauty? To know as God knows? To eat of this fruit? It certainly would be hard to train people to kill one another when humanity saw more clearly our inherent connectedness. I wave to the watching universe. *Hello. I am here. I am alive!* It is both an amazing and terrifying thing.

In ancient times priestesses used ritual, dance, movement, meditation, and entheogens to access expanded states of consciousness in order to receive messages from the divine realms to assist humanity. My Christian roots have largely forgotten or condemned this ancient holy tradition, belonging at first to women, with its over valuing of the more rational Apollonian mind over the taboo ridden Underworld energies that belong to the feminine Goddesses who fell from the heights of heaven into our unconsciousness during the age of patriarchy. These are the energies and wisdom streams that flow through Sophia, Shekinah, Mary, Ereshkigal, Innana, Ishtar, Aphrodite, and Persephone. When the oracle priestess temples were taken over by religions that honored warring male energies, Christianity (and it's central message of love self and service to others) was co-opted and used to created a more militarized religious state. The earth-based prophetesses were demonized and forbidden to tune into nature and the Goddesses and forced to channel only Apollo, sort of like modern Christian girls are only given male names for the divine in Sunday School. I suspect this split is at the root of unconscious substance abuse, for a spirituality that only honors the mind makes the body mad. I also suspect that these seemingly opposing energies are integrated in the person of Christ who played so well the ancient sacred role of the Good King who pledges his allegiance to love creation and defend the vulnerable. The story of Christ's descent and resurrection repeats the most ancient sacred feminine myths from around the world.

With the loss of humanity's nature based spirituality, we've also lost the value of honoring the full human experience. Youth crave this wholeness, and without a proper place in society, drugs are used dangerously and without the wise guides and healers who know the ancient ways to apply these medicinal practices to help humanity integrate, heal and grow. The village needs its shamans and wise sacred oracle women again. She whom you most feared holds the key to integration.

~

"Aaron! Stop!"

"Why?" he says. "This is fun!"

He drives straight into each trash can like they are targets on the curb side. Garbage explodes everywhere. Old papers and diapers fly into the windshield. I don't like his destructive tendencies or the pollution of the earth. Aaron turns up the music. We listen to Pink Floyd's album, Dark Side of the Moon. The hysterical laughter, the ticking clocks. I look at Aaron, his smile, the way he drives his car. He's so confident. So adolescent. So dangerous. He terrifies me. He enchants me. I slide closer to him, pushing aside my fears as we drive off into the black night.

~

A younger girl sits behind me in Spanish class picking hair off of my sweater.

"You shed so much!" she says. I'm ready to tell her to knock it off. I turn around and before I say something rude I am pulled into her dreamy blue eyes.

"Soy Ema," she says.

"Soy Hessica," I say.

"Queires venir a mi casa hoy?"

"Do you want me to eat your house today?" I got my worst grades in Spanish.

She laughs.

"Come over to my house?"

"Si," I say.

Ema lives in a simple house on the other side of town. I curl up in her bed and pet her happy gray Schnauzer, Chevis.

"Have you ever read Wuthering Heights?" she says.

"I love that book."

"What about Romeo and Juliette?"

"So tragic."

She climbs into bed with me and we watch the light dance in each other's eyes.

"What do you want to be when you grow up, Jessica?"

"I don't know, Ema—I just want to be happy."

"I want to be the president of the United States of America!"

I am in love.

Ema dates Noah who's good friends with Aaron. The four of us end up on a beach at a state park one night. The guys put two little tents together. Ema and Noah zip themselves in one and Aaron and I squeeze in the other.

"Could you moan a little quieter, Jessica?" Noah says.

"How about you cum a little faster?" Aaron shouts back.

"Jessica—how big is Aaron?" Ema says.

"At least 8 inches," I say. "And Noah?"

"We're still working on it!" she giggles.

"That's it!" Noah yells. "You're getting tackled right now!"

Aaron's legs tangle up with mine. His dark hair falls into his face. He kisses my mouth, my neck, my ears.

"Is this okay?" he asks.

"Please," I say.

The four of us eventually emerge from our tents to walk on the beach in the moonlight.

"What a night!" Noah says.

The lake is peaceful.

"Let's get in!"

Ema takes her clothes off. Her curvy body is so beautifully different from my straight lined frame. She smiles at me. I remove my clothes. She takes my hand and the two of us run into the water.

"Come on!" We yell to the boys.

The boys strip down and chase us into the water where we splash and kiss and howl at the moon together.

~

In some ancient tradition of baptism the priest took the Paschal candle above his head, said some prayers and then plunged it deeply into the waters below. I don't know how liturgical theologians explain it, but the movement is obviously filled with wonderful sexual imagery.

~

"There's an amazing party downtown—can you spend the night?" Paula asks.

It's New Year's Eve and my mother wants me to stay in.

"It's just a sleepover," I tell her. "We won't leave Paula's house." I have learned to survive by lying to my parents for so long now, it hardly phases me. My mother lets me go. I arrive at Paula's house and the two of us dress to kill. We both put on little black dresses and bright red lipstick.

"First, we have to check out this party down the street."

Paula drives us to the party in her old Firebird. The music blasts through the entire neighborhood. The house is so packed there are literally arms and legs hanging outside of the widows.

"Come on!"

I follow her into the house. She hands me a beer.

"Happy New Year!" she yells.

Everyone cheers, clanks drinks and chugs.

The house music is bumping and I watch Paula start to sway her hips. Soon a whole crowd of people are dancing with her. I am not comfortable dancing, but I pretend as best I can. People are grinding their hips against us. Beer is spilling all over the floor. People keep handing me more to drink. The lights are flickering on and off. And then we hear the sirens.

"Police!" someone yells.

Unified swears go up like prayers and everyone runs.

"Come on Jess," Paula grabs my arm and we run out the back door together. We hide in the bushes and watch the crowd disperse. We watch a few kids get handcuffed.

"Good thing I parked one street over," she winks.

"Let's go!"

We make a break for it, jump in her car and squeal off. With the radio on full blast, we listen to The Breeders sing "Cannonball" as Paula beelines for downtown Omaha.

"I know this great club," she says.

It's an eighteen and older club only, but they let us in anyway. The room is red hot and glowing. Men keep handing me things to drink. I dance on the floor, feeling the beats in my bones. I dance like I don't care if anyone is watching. I watch Paula dance. Her skin is wet, her mouth half open, her eyes filled with desire. *She's so sexy*, I think. *How does she do that?*

I dance closer to her, she comes closer to me. The men back away and begin to cheer us on. We flirt. The men are going wild. One guy pulls Paula aside. I sit down and watch the two of them dance. The room is spinning and I put my head down on a table. When I wake up the room is empty.

"Let's go," Paula says with her black mascara smudged around her eyes.

The two of us pile into her car. I lay down in the back seat next to all the empty and unopened beer bottles. We are almost back to her house when I hear sirens again.

"Oh, shit!" Paula says.

I sit straight up. "What?"

"Don't talk," she says. "Get down."

She pulls the car over to the side of the road.

"What seems to be the problem officer," she says flirtatiously as possible.

"Young lady, please step out of the car."

Paula can charm anyone. But not tonight.

"You too, missy," He says to me.

He makes us walk the line. Follow his finger. Paula has to take a breathalyzer test.

"Girls, you are being charged with Minors in Possession of Alcohol and you little lady," he turns to Paula, "are facing a serious charge of drunk driving."

"Oh God!" Paula puts her face in her hands and starts to cry.

"Both of you will need to call your parents."

The officer hands us his phone. I ring my house. As soon as my father answers he knows I'm in deep.

"I'll be right there," he says.

When he arrives he doesn't say a word. This is the worst punishment ever. I just want him to yell at me and get it all over with. But we drive home in complete silence. By the time I'm in bed the sun is rising.

"Sleep," he says. "When you wake up we are going to have a very long talk."

I don't sleep a wink. I lie in my bed wide awake facing years of regret and shame and consider all the potential nightmares that may unfold from here.

~

"I told your father I was done raising you then. You were his responsibility now," my mother locks her eyes on me.

Someone gives my parents a book called *Tough Love* by James Dobson from Focus on the Family. In the months that follow I lose whatever small emotional connections I had with my parents as they buckle down on punishing me in God's name. The book's main premise is that when a teen has problems it is the teen's choice to act in inappropriate ways that affect the entire family. The parents are never to blame. Neither are any other societal, mental, or physical factors either, I guess. It's a behavior modification program that ignores the root problems of behavior and places responsibility squarely upon the child who is forced to conform (and especially not be gay or feminist) all in the name of God.

~

It's a month before I can hang out with anyone again. And I am banned from hanging out with Paula. I live in total isolation, only seeing my friends at school and talking to them on the phone in the evenings.

"Jess—" Jason says, "I'm worried about you. I think you're partying too much." I assure him that since my punishments were put in place I have not been able to party.

"When are you coming?" I ask.

"In three months and four days."

"You know me and Aaron are still dating," I say.

"I know," he says. He sounds impenetrable. *Come and fight for me*, I think. *Let the best man win*. Or maybe I want revenge. Maybe I want to hurt him, like he hurt me. I can't decide.

~

Aaron walks into my house wearing a black t-shirt with Jerry Falwell's face on it that says, "God is Dead."

My father takes one look at him and says, "Do not ever wear that shirt in my house again, understand?"

Aaron flashes a cheerful smile, "Sure thing, sir."

I am wearing a skin tight maroon dress that reveals most of my legs, black hose and black high heels. Jason stands shoulders above me in his black tux and matching bow tie. When I first see him, I have a little flitter in my heart. But I recognize that it's just that old time nostalgia. I'm onto other adventures he couldn't possibly understand.

Ema and Noah are here too, both dressed to the nines. Ema looks like a Greek goddess in her long creamy dress. My brother stands with us and his mysterious hippy girlfriend Rachael, whose dark hair falls all the way down her back. Dave is just as tall as Jason now. The seven of us pose for pictures in front of Mom's baby grand piano in our living room. We intertwine our arms. Ema looks at me and winks. Aaron has a cabin reserved for us at a state park. I don't even think we make it to the dance. (Aaron says we did!) We get so wasted that I can't remember one thing about it.

I do remember driving in the dark through the woods. Wild sounds echo through the forest as the wind bends the branches and shakes off the blooming flowers.

Jason hangs with my brother. He gets high for the first time. I can't imagine how he survived the night or how he coped when he realized his visit here was in vain. I was not to be won back.

~

There's a girl in the mirror that I don't recognize. Her eyes frighten me. They are wild like a cat's. Deceitful, hard, and cruel.

"Where is the real me?" I ask the girl. Her smile curls up around the edges.

"You can't see her anymore," the girl says. "She belongs to me. I keep her safe."

My hands begin to shake. A cold chill runs up my spine. I don't want anyone to see this dark girl in the mirror, I think. I don't want to be her. But she is a part of me. She is my shadow.

~

The Peyote religion stems from the ancient cultures of the Native American people of Mexico. A community gathers in a hut and drinks the psychedelic juices of the Peyote cactus in order to converse with the Great Spirit. In the 1800s, when morale is low and the Natives in the United States are suffering under military rule from loss of their land and their tribes, they begin incorporating psychedelics into their religion, as was done by ancient peoples around the world. Now the sacred rites include Christian language and imagery, though the official church rejects this practice. During the all night prayer meeting the community discerns "The Peyote Road" or the way of learning to live life well.

~

Grandpa Erling sits at my parents' kitchen table. He looks at me with kind, weary eyes.

"We pray for you every day," he says. "Ever since you were a little girl, we've prayed for you, Jessie."

I feel him trying to reach me. I'm almost 18.

"I got my bellybutton pierced," I tell him. I even lift up my shirt to show him. I am too defended to be truly vulnerable with anyone.

~

I am lying in my back yard tanning in a bikini. A new song "Crucify" by Tori Amos comes on the radio. I feel I know these words deep in my bones. But, I've never heard this song before. My heart starts to burn. Maybe it's the hunger for ancient truth, for feminine passion, and music.

Yes! I think. *This woman gets it!* Over the years I buy all her albums. She helps me reconnect and awaken lost pieces of myself. I keep up my writing and poetry. I put more time into making songs on our piano.

~

"Dad, PLEASE can I drive the new car tonight?" My father just bought a gray Ford Escort.

He looks at me sternly.

"Why don't you want to drive your Volvo?"

I am ashamed of that car because it is a classic and not a flashy new sports car.

"Cause it's old and this car is new and it's Dave's birthday! I'll be so super safe, I PROMISE."

"Just remember, I could leave the car safe in the garage all night. I expect it to return there in mint condition."

"Yes, sir!"

We turn the music up loud and head to Omaha's downtown area called The Old Market. The sun is shining bright on the slick brick streets. Rows of stop lights dot the sky like pretty party lights. The Missouri River is ahead and the bridge to Council Bluffs, Iowa, where we like to go cruising.

I don't even see the car. But I know the sound, the slowing of time, the pulse that turns my veins cold.

This time, my parents are not so kind. I am standing in the circle of a growing crowd. A woman is screaming at me for running a red light. When my mother arrives, she joins in yelling at me too. I remember stomping my feet into the ground like a two year old having a total meltdown. I apologize a million times but there is no way I can shake the shame of the crowd. I am lucky no one is hurt. But nothing can restore me. My dignity is lost. No one trusts me anymore. I don't even trust myself.

"I'm so sorry I ruined your birthday, Dave."

"Nah, it'd be ruined if I was dead," he laughs.

My father had to say it.

"I told you so, Jessica. I should have kept the car safe in the garage."

He was so right.

~

A 2007 study, by Russell A. Barkley of the Medical University of South Carolina and Daniel J. Cox of the University of Virginia Health System, concluded that young drivers with A.D.H.D. are two to four times as likely as those without the condition to have an accident — meaning that they are at a higher risk of wrecking the car than an adult who is legally drunk.

-John O'Neil in *The New York Times*

I spend more time at the piano but my music brings stress into the house. My parents hate it. Stay silent is the message. But how will I work through all these emotions? How will I heal?

~

"Jess—don't go home," my brother's eyes narrow. He stands behind the Subway counter making a sandwich.

"Why?" I laugh. He removes his apron and walks over to me handing me the sub.

"Come here, Jess," he pulls me into a booth. "Mom found your journal," he says.

"Oh God," I whisper.

"It's over," he says. "They're kicking you out. All your stuff is being bagged up right now. Go out tonight and have the time of your life. It may be the last night you have fun for a really long time."

How did I end up like this?

"What am I going to do?" I ask him.

"I don't know," he says. "Just have fun tonight, okay?" He pulls me into his arms and hugs me.

~

"Those assholes," Aaron takes me for a drive. We park on a hill where we can overlook the city lights. We listen to Pink Floyd's Delicate Sound of Thunder. The sky is so thick and black above. My heart is missing. The place where it used to be is cavernous. It's almost summer, but the world is so cold. I can't see a place for myself in it at all.

~

"Here's the plan, Jessica," my father looks across the living room at me. "You have two options. St. Olaf is no longer an option. Option A: you can join the military. This is what I would prefer. You would make enough money per month to pay for your housing and food and you would learn the important skills of obedience and discipline. The conditions are: you live here all summer and you stop using drugs, you stop seeing Aaron, and you have a 9 p.m. curfew. Option B: you move out and figure out how to live life on your own."

My mother's eyes are red. She looks at her hands. I can't reach her, just like I couldn't reach her when I was in third grade and my father was giving me the hyper technical sex talk after I watched the movie, Purple Rain.

"I am not joining the military," I say.

"Okay, then. What is your plan, young lady?"

I look up at the dead Indian warrior and his speared horse.

"I am moving in with Aaron. His parents said I could."

I stand up and walk down to my bedroom one last time. Thor follows me. He won't stop whining.

"Come here boy," I lie on my bed and hold him while I cry. He licks my tears.

"I'll always love you, Thor. Always. I'm so sorry I have to go, but I just have to."

I look around my room one last time. I look at the cheerleading pictures from Gosnell. The picture of Jason and me kissing on my mirror. *I tried so hard.* I tried to not let the pain drown me out. I tried to shut down my feelings like my parents wanted me to. As I walk out the front door, I think I have messed up my life beyond repair.

While Christian Roberts is now charming his way into the world and working his way up the ladder of success, I am fading away from it all. You don't just think your way out of this stuff. You can't just forget about it. Drugs will numb for a while, but then what? Punishing the behaviors that stem from it won't heal the root of it either. The wound must be brought into the light of consciousness and healed with love. But where are our wise healers and compassionate places of recovery?

~

The K-mart car is in pretty bad shape. The cloth covering of the interior roof falls down when we are playing punch bug causing all this yellow foam to randomly snow on our heads. We open the driver's door in the grocery store parking lot and it just falls off. Still, we drive it to the very end, even as it breaks apart. I am like that stupid car. When I move out my father finally gets rid of it and buys a red sports car and gives it to Dave to drive.

~

Very truly, I tell you, unless a grain of wheat falls into the earth and dies, it remains just a single grain; but if it dies, it bears much fruit.
-Jesus, John 12:24

Emily doesn't understand what's happening to our family. She feels in her body the tensions in our home. The secrets kept. Her tummy always hurts. She stops eating. My mother takes her to the doctor.

"She has anorexia," he explains.

~

"Walk!" I blow my whistle.

"Go fuck yourself!" the man shouts.

"Okay! Thank you," I reply.

He runs anyway. I don't blow my whistle anymore. I'm getting an $800.00 bonus for working as a lifeguard in gang territory in downtown Omaha because I could be shot or killed on the job.

I sit in the chair and twirl my whistle around my finger.

"Oh shit, he's going off the diving board," I mumble.

"Do it, man! Do it! Do it!" His friends chant. I sit up straight and watch.

"Naw, man, I can't do it. I can't," he says.

"Chicken! Bok, bok, bok!" The crowd shouts.

"Shut up. Alright. " He steps onto the board and walks slowly to the end.

"Jump! Jump! Jump!" the crowd yells. I lay the whistle down on my chair. I watch him bounce up and down. He jumps. He screams in the air and sinks under water. I watch his flaying hands reach up to the surface and move rapidly.

"Fuck."

I jump off my chair and swim over to him. I go under and find his arm. I twist it so the front of his body turns towards the surface of the water when we emerge. He's a little overweight so he floats so much easier than my last save.

"Oh, my Lord," he says when we get to the side of the pool. "You're an angel, you saved my life!"

"That's my job," I say and smile.

He hugs me tight.

"Thank you pretty lady. Thank you so much."

At the pool I save people all the time. If only I could figure out how to save myself.

~

"If we buy an ounce then we can break it up into dime bags—sell nine of them and smoke a dime for free. And—we make enough money to buy our next ounce so we can do it all over again and never pay for weed!"

"Does that make us drug dealers?" I say.

"Think of it this way: we are providing a service for our friends in need. And we are able to provide for ourselves."

"Free weed?" I kiss him. "Let's be drug dealers."

~

One night I ignore an important rule of tripping: never look too close at your face in the mirror. I get real close. God I never knew my pores were so big. Under the surface there are so many blackheads. My face looks terrible. It always breaks out when I move. I have large cystic bumps on my cheeks that hurt. My heart falls into my feet. I'm hideous. Completely disgusting. An ancient fear grows in my stomach: *If you're not beautiful, then who will love you?*

"Jessica!" Aaron pounds on the bathroom door. "Get out of there right now!"

"No!" I cry. "I don't want you to see me."

He unlocks the door and runs over to me. He wraps his arms around me and pulls me into his chest.

"Shhhh. It's okay."

He runs his fingers through my hair.

"That's not you. Whatever you saw, that's not you."

"How do you know?"

"Because, you're beautiful. Look at me," he grabs my chin. "You'll always be beautiful because the beauty is in your heart."

"Aaron!" his father shouts. "Come here now." Both his father and my father are good at the military tactic of I-can-scare-the-shit-out-of-you-drill.

"Stay in my bedroom," he says.

I wait for what feels like forever. Aaron returns with wide eyes.

"Just deny everything," he says.

"Oh my God," I put my hand over my mouth. "He knows."

"He doesn't know shit. He thinks he knows. He has no proof. Deny it Jessica. He wants to talk to you now."

I walk down the hallway to his parent's bedroom. It feels like I am walking back in time. The thick brown carpet and old war photos hanging on the walls remind me of things my parents would have in their house too. Our parents must have done drugs. How could they not have? Aaron's father is much shorter than Aaron. He looks exactly like Aaron's brother, Jonathan. I stand about a foot taller than him, which helps a little.

"I know what you're up to," he says. "Just admit it. You two are on acid."

"No, we're not," I say innocently.

He puts his face closer to mine. His eyes are pointed and hard.

"Don't lie to me in my house!" he says.

I put my head in my hands and sob.

I run all the way back to Aaron's room.

"Let's get out of here," he says. I grab my purse and we escape.

We drive to downtown Omaha. To the Old Market, to the brick laid streets. The cars look like shiny plastic toys with lights. We go to a record store. I lose myself looking at the posters.

"I want this one," I say to Aaron.

"Why?" he laughs. "I can't even tell what it is."

"Me neither. That's why I want it."

I look at the light blue colors. It's so detailed. Filled with so many people and pictures inside of pictures.

"It's yours," he says. He pulls out his wallet and pays for it.

~

Aaron's mother sits across from me at the breakfast table. She wears a white night gown. Her face is young and beautiful. I am envious of her perfect skin. She has curly auburn hair and deep brown. I am intimidated as she watches me eat my oatmeal.

"Have you talked to your parents recently?" she asks.

"No," I say. "They don't seem particularly interested in my life."

"I'm worried for you," she says. "What are your plans for fall?"

"Oh, Mom, don't pressure us," Aaron runs his fingers through his disheveled hair.

"I found a house in downtown Omaha that only costs $400 a month, Mom. And I bet I can make bank fixing people's computers." And he does.

She sighs and gets up from the table.

"I love you son," she kisses him on the forehead. His parents never mention the LSD again. I am confused by their calm and their kindness.

~

I hear Enya's song, "How Can I Keep from Singing," and I curl up into a little ball. This trip is different. It's not all beautiful and sparkly. Instead all of these old feelings come up inside me. My mind floods with memories of my early childhood. Enya's voice is so much like my mother's. I am four. Unable to sleep. My mother brings me warm milk and tickles my back. I miss my mother. I spend the rest of the night nursing a great sorrow about our broken relationship.

I decide to return home for her birthday with some expensive perfume wrapped cheaply in tinfoil.

"I miss you, Mom."

I hand her the pathetic looking gift. I listen to the crinkling aluminum unfold.

"Thanks."

She gets up from the table and walks away. She can't even look at me. *She hates me*, I think. And there is nothing I can do to make her love me. Her rejection is almost too hard to accept. And I've had much practice of hating myself and my needs in order to keep a connection to her. I decide this will be the last time I return home.

~

"Weed's like the miracle drug man."

Our dealer, Josh sits across the glowing room looking like white 70s Jesus in his tie-dyed shirt, his long curly blonde hair and his Birkenstocks. I look at the tattoos on his calf. The big cross. The blue flames. I want the ease he has in his body. And I want a tattoo.

"The government just doesn't want us to feel this good," he says. "Cause nobody would do their shady work anymore. Cause we'd all want world peace, man. And we'd take down the money making war machine."

Aaron gives Josh a wad of cash and Josh gives him a big bag of weed.

"You won't regret this, man," he says. "This is the life, I promise you."

We light up a bowl together to celebrate our new status as drug dealers. The acid we took earlier in the day is still kicking. The weed takes us to another level. The dark room is illuminated by candles and a red lava lamp. Josh turns up Pink Floyd's, "Adam Heart Mother."

"This is one of their best albums," he says.

We put our heads back and watch the street lights float across the ceiling from the cars passing by on the street below. Aaron holds my hand. Something in the air is stirring. I go to the bathroom. When I am alone, the room begins to fill with light. I start to become afraid to be alone. When I'm alone, the light always grows brighter around me, like some big realization is dawning, like a holy presence is drawing near. Like angels might suddenly appear. I scramble out of the bathroom as fast as possible. I don't want people to think I'm crazy.

~

We sell and smoke everything within a week.

"Shit, Aaron—I need something now. How am I going to make it through the next few days?"

Marijuana is also considered to be an entheogen with roots in other sacred religions. It has many healing properties, and I have discovered it helps me manage my anxiety and depression. Plus, I haven't worked through my issues with a counselor, so I'm still putting a lot of energy into repressing pain. All of the disassociated stuff that I am afraid to feel is trying to break through and I haven't been taught how to integrate and heal. I have only been taught to suppress and ignore and not talk about things that are uncomfortable.

"It sucks that Omaha is dry right now," he says. "I know, we could go to the grocery store and get some whipped cream in a can!"

He drives me over to the nearest grocery store and carefully picks up two cans of Reddi Wip.

"What is this?"

I roll my eyes and grab a can out of his hand.

"No, no, no!"

He grabs it back and returns it to the shelf.

"You can't shake them, then they won't work."

He gently picks out another one. He drives me to a dark area of the parking lot and turns up the music of Ween.

"Just suck in the gas at the top."

He shows me how to hold the can straight, he puts his mouth over the top and squeezes until a little whip cream comes out.

"This is lame," I say.

"Just try it," he says.

I put my mouth over the nozzle and press it back. I lean my head against the window.

"God, this is like sniffing rubber cement, Aaron."

"So what," he says. "Pretty cool buzz, huh?"

"No, not really," I say.

"You're so grumpy," he says with a smile. "Let me make you happy," he whispers as he leans in to kiss me.

~

"Are you sure you want a tattoo there?"

The big guy holds a needle that buzzes.

"Yep, right there." I point at my middle toe on my right foot.

"It's going to hurt," he warns.

"I don't care," I say. "I'm tough."

He draws a small flower on my toe with six little circle petals on the outside. He colors them in with blue and purple. It's perfectly symmetrical. I'm impressed.

"Now that is cute," he says. "And you're right, you are a tough girl."

~

"If you're that desperate for a fix, just ask around. I mean this is gang territory after all. Everyone has drugs here!"

Brittany is a rich girl from the suburbs who chose to work here just to piss her parents off. She tosses her short brown hair back and puts her sunglasses on.

"Brittany, God, really? I can't do that."

"What are you, chicken?"

"Yes. Yes I am."

"Come here," she grabs my arm and walks me over to the security guard.

"Jessica is in desperate need of weed, and she's annoying the hell out of us complaining about how no one has any. Will you please hook her up?"

The big black security guard has a kind face. He lifts the brim of his hat.

"Naw, you smoke the green girl?"

"Yeah," I say. "But Omaha is dry."

He laughs.

"It ain't dry girlfriend," he smiles. "It just ain't on the streets now. After work, I'll take you to get some, sweetheart." He winks at me.

"Wuss," Brittany says. "Told you."

She turns on her perfect legs and walks back to her lifeguard chair.

I shout, "Thank you!" She flashes me a gorgeous smile and waves me away.

~

"What's your name," I ask the security guard. We're cruising in his big old Cadillac riding low to the ground. He's got the windows rolled down and Slaughtahouse booming on the speakers.

"You can call me Lucky," he says. I smile at him.

"Must be nice to be Lucky," I say trying to act cool.

"Damn nice," he says.

I watch the neighborhood change. The farther we drive, the more ragged the houses appear. Yards are decorated with trash and old washing machines. I think of how proud my father was to have won the military base's award of the best manicured lawn and I chuckle. I don't think anyone here cares about that kind of stuff. There is a part of me that enjoys, or maybe feels obligated, to hold the opposite energy of my parents.

He probably carries a gun, I think. I'm going to a gangster's house. This is very opposite.

Aaron may kill me though. That is if I survive to tell him. Maybe Lucky isn't getting me weed. Maybe he's just going to cut me into a million pieces and put me in the freezer. I take comfort in knowing that at least Brittany knows I left work with him. If anything happens to me, she will know. Unless he kills her too.

"You ain't chillin,'" Lucky says.

"Ha, ha, ha," I laugh my fake laugh. "I just really need some weed," I smile and wink at him. He pulls into a drive way and turns to look at me.

"Stay here, girlfriend. Don't even think about steppin' out of this car."

He slams the door. I watch him walk into the small worn down yellow house. I have no idea where I am. The light shifts in the sky and the colors of the sunset light up the concrete.

How did you get here, Jess? A little voice inside me asks.

I pretend I don't hear it. *Just picking up some weed. That's all I'm doing. With my friendly security guard from work. Yeah. It's cool.* I put my arm on the car door and my hand on my forehead. I look at the broken tricycle in the lawn. *Who grows up here*, I wonder. *What kind of a life do they have?* I bet they know all about generational trauma.

I watch two children run across the grass. I admire their innocence and wonder. One stops to look at me. She has the saddest eyes. She's probably wondering why I am here too.

Cause I like weed, I think.

How did you get here, Jess?

Shut up, I think. I am not ready to face what's behind that door of suffering.

How long has he been in there? I look at my watch. It's been nearly 40 minutes. What if he doesn't come back? The children leave. Cars drive past. People watch me from a distance. It dawns on me: I stick out real bad. I slide down the seat and put my head in my lap.

"You fall asleep?" Lucky says as he slams the door.

"God, I thought you were never going to come back."

"Sweetheart, remember, I'm Lucky. Ain't nobody scoring weed in town but me. Here," he hands me a joint. "Rolled it just for you and me."

"You wanna smoke it now?"

"Hell yeah I wanna smoke it now, wich you."

I don't like driving stoned. Especially when I have to drive all the way from downtown Omaha back to the suburb of Bellevue. Lucky opens up a forty.

"Want some?"

"Naw," I say.

I just want to go home. But more than that, I don't want to offend Lucky. The two of us sit in the driveway and get as lit as I've ever been.

"This is really good stuff," I say.

"Fuck yeah it is. Lucky gets the best, baby," he talks smooth like Barry White.

After he drinks his forty, after we smoked a hell of a lot of good weed I should be nervous as he drives me back to Aaron's car parked outside the pool. But I'm so high I can't even think about being nervous. I put my hands in the air and move to the rap music.

"You alright, girl," he says. "Stay safe. See you tomorrow."

I put the bag of weed he hands me in my purse and turn on the radio. I dance to Dr. Dre's, "Nuthin' but a 'G' Thang" with my Volvo windows rolled down, my hair flying up into the air, and my guardian angels working overtime.

~

My mother and I remember this part differently. I recall her reaching out to me and asking me to reconsider. But she says I went to our pastor and asked him to help me convince my parents to help me get into a local college. She said she was done raising me. I remember going back home to live. My mother had all the paper work filled out and spread over our dining room table. All I had to do was sign. This is how I recall it.

"I want to talk to you," my mother's voice pierces my ears. I pull the phone away from my head.

"Did you hear me?" she says.

"I don't want to see you anymore," I say. (Do I internalize my mother saying this to me? Maybe I can't quite bear the fact that she would say this to me, so I remember saying it to her.)

"Jessica Jean."

I sigh.

"You are about to throw your life away. Do you want to end up living in some trailer park having Aaron's babies and living in poverty? How will you pay the bills? How will you put food on the table?"

How did she put food on the table? She got married and surrendered her dreams of the opera house for my father's career. Isn't that what I'm supposed to do too? I just want to be loved. I want to escape all the pain inside. Why is she so intense? Can't she just live in the moment? Must I too become an angry woman who is split off from the depths of her soul? I'm trying not to, but fate has me by the ankles. I feel I am being asked to surrender to the patriarchy—but not like that.

"I don't know, Mom. We'll figure it out. Aaron's good at computers..."

"Jessica, I don't care what he's good at. What are you good at?"

She hits a deep nerve. I despise the answer. *Nothing. I am just a stupid girl, remember? Aren't I doing a great job of fulfilling your incredibly low expectations of me? I couldn't kill my pain to succeed in life like you did. I hate myself because, I just can't bear hating you.*

"Come over," she says. "Please just give me one hour. I have a plan C that I would like you to consider."

"Okay, Mom. I'll come."

Maybe I am the one saying her words to me. Maybe I am becoming the mother I needed.

~

"It's just two hours away," she says. "I've already filled out the paper work. I am taking out loans for you. All you need to do is sign." She hands me the pen.

"What's in Maryville, Missouri anyway? It's like in the middle of nowhere."

"You can still have the college experience. And they have an amazing journalism program. I was thinking you could major in that since you love to write."

The loss of St. Olaf still stings.

"But, I've never been there."

"Neither have I," my mother says. "But we can go together. You can still make a life for yourself. You can learn new skills. You'll be able to land a much better job with a college degree."

Her blue eyes have softened. I look into them. I don't know the woman who is looking back at me. Maybe it is an aspect of my higher myself.

"Okay, Mom," I take the pen from her hand and I sign the paper.

"Come home," she says. "Come home and help me pack all your things."

~

Settlers have difficulty staying off the sacred sites of the Pottawatomi because their land surrounds the Missouri River in the north eastern part of the state. An appeal to the authorities is made so the settlers can access the river too. Congress then makes a law to remove the Natives from their land.

~

"What about us, Jess?"

Aaron's eyes search my face for some kind of answer.

"We'll still be together," I say. "You can come visit on the weekends—it's only two hours away."

"What are you going to study there?"

"I dunno. I'll take the Gen Eds I guess and see what I like. I think I might try journalism."

"But why do you have to leave now?"

"I have a lot of boxes to sort through with my Mom."

He holds me in his arms.

"Dance with me," he says.

We sway in his room together. He puts his chest against mine and I feel the sadness in his heart.

"I love you, Jess," he says. "I don't want to lose you."

"You won't," I whisper. "You are always right here," I point at my own heart.

~

My dorm room is on the seventh floor of Millikan Hall. I look out at the sunset sky that glows over fields of farm and tiny people below buzzing with excitement. My sweet roommate Jane is off flirting with boys. I put the new Sarah McLaughlin CD in my boom box and decorate my room. When I am finished, I put a towel under the crack of my door and light up a bowl to celebrate this new chapter in my life. I'm free. Now I can become whoever I want to be as I listen to the song, "Fear."

~

Maryville, Missouri is located in Nodaway County, named after Mrs. Mary Graham, the first white woman to live in the town. Nodaway is an Native American word for "placid" or "snake."

Nodaway County has a violent past. The first hanging occurs in the town in 1881 when two brothers are charged with murdering their father—an author and town founder. Men are regularly shot at the local bars, dragged out into the streets, and their bodies are thrown into the river. Some are hung over the bridge. One man kills an entire family including two young children after a bad poker game by burning their house to the ground.

In 1931 a black man named Raymond Gunn is accused of raping and murdering a young white school teacher. A mob of over 10,000 men show up at the jail and demand his release. The mob carries Mr. Gunn to the Maryville school house and burns him alive on the rooftop.

If any town needs the healing energy of Mother Mary, this town certainly does.

~

"You have to know the most important element in your story."

My professor tells us to call him Mark.

"You can't just blab on indefinitely for no reason."

He looks at me with a funny smile. I separate the red and orange skittles on my desk and pop the red ones into my mouth.

"You have to have a point and you have to state it clearly. This part of the story is called the climax—" He draws a line with a hill at the end.

I copy the image of the hill on my paper and scribble down the word: climax. My elbow bumps the uneaten pile of skittles sitting on the corner of my desk. One by one they each fall in slow motion. Mark turns from the chalk board and glares at me as each skittle bounces loudly upon the tile floor. The sound echoes across the silent classroom. I look out the window and watch birds ascend in the sky.

"This is college, now," he says to me in a low voice. "Get it together or you will never make it."

Getting anything together always feels absurdly impossible. All I want to do is fly away.

~

"Aw, Mark's cool," Gaia says.

She hands the blunt to me.

"He's an ass," I say.

"He gets high with us."

"No."

"Yes! Trust me, you'll be fine."

We sit together with thirty other folks on the second floor of the coffee shop her parents own in town. The room fills with smoke and someone turns on the Grateful Dead.

"I think we rolled an entire dime bag into this joint!" She laughs. Soon everyone is up dancing, laughing, coupling and making out in the corners of the room.

~

"She really likes you," Luke says standing almost seven feet tall with white blonde hair. He has Viking blood like me.

"What do you mean she really likes me?"

He holds the dumbbell over my chest.

"Two more," he says. "You can do it."

"Why am I doing this again?"

"One more."

"Fuck!"

"Great job! Give me a month and you'll see," he smiles.

"Gaia thinks you're hot," he says. "Have you ever been with a girl?"

"No," I say.

"Well, have you ever thought about it?"

My face turns red.

"Of course," I laugh.

"Then this is your chance. She wants to hang out with you sometime. All you need to do is call her," he hands me her phone number.

My stomach fills with knots and butterflies. This is college, I tell myself. A time to get it together.

~

"Would you mind?" I press the phone into my cheek. I want to hear every detail of his reply.

"Would I mind?" He laughs. "I think it would be fucking cool!" Aaron says. "I only wish I was there to watch."

"God." I say.

"Hey, I scored an ounce," he says. "You think you can it there?"

"Oh, yeah," I said. "Everybody here smokes."

~

Aaron arrives the following weekend. We split up the ounce and roll it into dime bags.

"And one for you," he hands me mine.

"Look what I brought," Aaron pulls out a sheet of acid from his wallet.

"A whole sheet?!"

"Yeah, I'm selling this too and it makes us enough to buy larger amounts of weed and make more cash."

Aaron pulls out a huge bong from his bag, "To college!"

I put the towel under the door and open the windows. It's a breezy day. I light a stick of incense too. We get stoned out of our minds. And I hear a loud knock on my door.

"RA! Open up please!"

I put my eye to the peek hole. There are three of them standing outside my door, the hall RA, and two executive staff.

"Shit," I whisper. "Clean it up fast!"

"Hold on!" I say. Aaron lights a cigarette—he carries them for emergencies like this only. I throw the bagged weed into a cup in my cabinet. Aaron slides the bong under the bed.

I take a deep breath and open the door.

"What is going on in here?" The tall guy demands. They begin looking around the room nervously.

"Oh, I'm sorry, I smoked a cigarette in here. I know it's against the rules," Aaron says.

"And I lit incense to cover it up. I'm sorry. I know that's not allowed here."

The guys open my cabinet where I tossed the weed. It's over, I think. I'm going to jail. Then he closes it.

I spot a big bud on the carpet and kick it under the bed. My RA gets on her hands and knees and looks under the bed.

Fuck. The bong. Fuck. Fuck. Fuck.

She stands back up. All of them seem suddenly at ease.

"We're going to have to write you up for this."

"Okay. I say. "I'm so sorry."

"No more cigarettes or incense."

"Yes," we say. The three of them walk out of my room and close the door.

"Oh my God!" I say as I drop to my knees. "My whole life just flashed before me."

"If they would have called the cops and searched us, we'd be in for at least ten years," Aaron says.

"That is not helping."

"So we need a new place to smoke weed," Aaron says. "Want to go for a drive?"

We meander down the country roads hot boxing Aaron's car, listening to Pink Floyd's album, *Obscured By Clouds*, as we consider the cost of freedom among the cows and corn fields.

~

A college friend of ours is busted later that year for having two ounces of weed in his dorm room. He spends several weeks in jail and gets kicked out of school. They want to lock him up for 11 years—make an example out of him for all the other college kids. We never hear if he gets out of it.

~

Gaia and I end up back at my dorm room. The moonlight pours in through the window. She's so easy to talk to. I am lost in her big brown eyes. Her dark hair is cut short and artsy and she wears funky plastic glasses. We lay down on my bed. I unbutton her shirt. She has a dolphin tattoo above her left breast.

"Cute," I say.

She unhooks her bra and lays naked before me. Her body is so different than mine. Her breasts are large and soft. Her hips are curvy and wide. She lets me explore her body. I know just what to do. I enjoy making her feel good.

Afterwards, I lay my head on her chest and we fall asleep together. It's so different than lying with a man. Instead of being held by him and feeling needy and weak, I hold her, feeling confident and strong. Holding her helps me hold a part of myself that I thought I had lost a long time ago.

~

Gaia brings a new energy into my life. She helps me incarnate myself. Instead of lovers, she and I become friends. My relationship with her helps me fall more in love with life. And with Aaron.

He spends the following weekend with me and brings mushrooms. We lie around naked in my room for hours, completely comfortable in our skin. I watch him sleeping. His body is beautiful, not in a traditional way, but because of all the light that radiates underneath his skin, the symmetry of his bone structure, his unique markings, muscles and mane. It's so much easier to love someone else besides myself.

In the evening we take a walk around the pond in the center of campus.

"It's so quiet," he pulls me down to the grass and we look up at the moon. I take off my shoes and dig my toes into the damp earth.

"Look at all those stars!" he says.

Something is stirring in me. Some new revelation. Something profound. I can't find the words for it, for anything really. A thought comes, *I am an earth creature.* It repeats like a mantra in my mind sending peace throughout my body. I realize I have been trying so hard to find myself for years. I was trying to escape the Christian goodie-two-shoes, the nerd, be cool, be the cheerleader, be the alternative girl. I have all these labels floating around in me causing tension, all these fragmented parts of myself. I realize suddenly that I transcend them all. None of the images can hold the largeness of my being. I am an ancient earth creature that has come into the world to live in this space and time. Oh the wonder of it! I feel a dissonance resolve within as all the categories melt away. I don't want to ever worry about what I wear or what I look like or who I am. Who am I to label myself? Who is anyone to put constricting labels on others? I want to honor this simple, mysterious existence.

"What is it?" Aaron looks at me quizzically.

"Everything," I say.

"These are good shrooms, huh?"

"It's more than the shrooms. It's something bigger. Something divine."

He pulls away from me.

"Don't go all God on me now."

"I'm not," I protest. "I'm just happy."

But a seed of darkness is planted. I hold my joy close to my heart where I think I can keep it safe.

~

"Mondays are ten cent draws!"

Amber bounces up and down. "And most of the time, they refill the ladies drinks for free!"

I join a bunch a freshman at the local bar where the football game is blasting and cigarette smoke fills the air.

"This is awesome!"

Amber's brown hair hangs down her back. She talks more like a guy than a girl.

"Fuckin' A, man, fill us up!" she yells to the bartender. We're drunk within the hour, on the dance floor and spinning around in circles.

"Ninety dollars to the girl who gets the loudest cheers on stage," he says to her.

"Jessica—you have to do it!"

"Do what? Just walk up there?"

"Work it. You got it. Just sway your hips a little."

"I really don't know how to sway my hips."

"If you win, you can spend it all on weed!"

"Fine."

Three of us are chosen for the final round. We stand on the stage under the hot lights.

"Take it off!" the men beg.

"I'm not taking it off," I laugh and twirl and try to move my hips. The girl next to me flashes the crowd. She wins.

"Chug! Chug! Chug! Chug!"

People begin to chant. We end up dancing on tables. And that's where my memory ends.

I wake up the next morning with Amber's high school friend in my bed.

"What the hell are you doing here?" I say.

He rubs the sleep out of his eyes.

"What? Oh, no you don't! Don't be like that."

"How did I get here? Why are you in my room? You know I have a boyfriend! I don't even like you! Why are my clothes off?"

"Damn, bitch, what is your problem. You liked it last night."

"Liked what? I don't even remember a thing! I didn't want this. What happened? Tell me what happened!"

The guy jumps out of my bed and pulls on his pants.

"I can't believe you, you crazy bitch. Leave me the fuck alone."

And he runs out the door.

That's three. I spend the day crying in bed, thinking there's nothing I can do about it. I can just imagine trying to explain the whole night to a police officer that I was drunk on a stage at a bar swinging my hips for the crowd to cheer—everyone would think I deserved this.

Aaron is pissed. "I'm enrolling," he says. "I want to be there. This would have never happened if I was there."

He'll protect me. And then I think, *I have thought this before.*

~

"Oh God girl, give the boy a break. You were drunk. What did you think would happen to you?" Amber rolls her eyes. "Boys will be boys. You can't just get drunk at a bar and not expect that to happen."

Still. It doesn't feel fair. I consented to party at college. I did not consent to sex with a stranger.

The risk of sexual re-victimization, according to the Center for Disease Control, is based on vulnerability factors. One of these is the pre-existence of PTSD from a previous assault. Being the victim of child sexual abuse doubles the likelihood of adult sexual victimization. PTSD levels are actually higher in those who have been previously victimized than in survivors of only one assault. PTSD could give the victim the appearance of vulnerability in dangerous situations and affect the ability of the victim to defend themselves.
-Rape Crisis Information Website

My English professor returns the poems we wrote a few weeks ago. Mine has an A+ written in red pen at the top with a note by it, "Keep at this—you're onto something."

"Hey," the guy behind me pokes me in the back.

"Weren't you the one at the bar dancing on stage last weekend?"

Somehow the image of that girl doesn't mesh with the one who is here now holding this poem in her hands.

"No," I say honestly. "That wasn't me."

~

My time at the gym is paying off. I have abs for the first time in my life and my stick-like arms are round with muscles. But more than physical signs, something is coming into definition within. I am reminded of warm summer nights in Rome, New York, when I am a five year old girl with white tangled hair and wild blue eyes. Of a time when the space between my body and the earth seem naturally connected. When I run through the grass with bare feet clenching frogs in my hands, enchanted by the white moon and the lavender sky above. I am remembering the magic I carry within.

~

"But I have a speech to give tomorrow!"

"Write it while you're tripping. It will be awesome!"

We each take two tabs—a small amount compared to what we normally drop. We lay down on the floor in my dorm, cuddle up and watch some new Nickelodeon cartoons.

Something is not right. I cling to Aaron's arm and bury my face in his red shirt.

"I can't watch this anymore."

"It's funny," he says laughing as the characters explode and blood drips all over the screen. But my muscles tighten and my entire body begins to shake.

"Jess! Jess. Look at me."

But I can't. He jumps up and turns off the television.

"This acid is no good," I say. "I want this trip to stop. It has to stop now."

"Jess—here, take this," he hands me some niacin which is supposed to take the edge off. But, unknown to us, it has the effect of turning your skin red—which wouldn't be so frightening if I wasn't tripping balls.

"Do I look funny to you?" I stretch out my arms to him.

"No," Aaron lies. "It's just…the lighting."

His squished up eyebrows reveal his doubt.

"What's happening to me?"

I turn my fiery arms over and stare at my palms. I begin to see boils all over my body which is severely shaking now. I throw up. And then I throw up again and again until I am dry heaving uncontrollably, unable to make the reflex stop.

"Jess, you need to take some deep breaths."

Aaron puts his hands on my shoulders and pulls my chin up so I can look into his eyes.

"Your body thinks you're sick. It's trying to expel the bad stuff from your system. But you can't get rid of the acid. The only way out is through. You have to ride this out. I want you to tell yourself that you feel better. You're not sick, Jess. Your mind is making your body do this. Take control of your thoughts. You can do this, Jess."

"I'm having fun," I dry heave again. Aaron laughs at me. I laugh a little too.

"Come here."

He holds me and rocks me back and forth.

"Shhhhh, you're going to be okay. This trip is going to change. It's going to have a happy ending. You are going to feel better as soon as we walk outside."

He takes my hand which still looks bright red and we slip out into the cool night. I take off my shoes and walk on the grass. I breathe in the crisp air. I look at the moon. As soon as I connect with nature, I return to myself.

"I had no idea how powerful our thoughts are. How healing nature is. How did you know that would work?"

"I had a hunch." He looks at me mysteriously.

"I love you," I say as I lean in to kiss him. "Thank you for saving me."

"I love you too. Hey, now you got a great topic for your speech tomorrow," he pulls my hat down over my eyes.

My thoughts race with possibilities. Phrases like, *the power of the mind, belief shapes reality,* and *next level of human consciousness* convince me that this speech will be like a drop of water in the ocean that ripples out and awakens humanity.

"You know Einstein's brain is on display somewhere," Aaron says. "And they discovered that there are more connections between the right and left sides, which is very similar to how your brain functions when on acid—the thoughts move faster across the nerves, like there are no breaks, nothing is lost. You can actually think better on LSD. In regular brains the nerves are like this," he shapes a ball out of his two hands and shows me the space between the ends of his fingers. "The messages have to leap across here. But Einstein's brain was different," he puts his fingers on top of one another. "This is how we make the world a better place," he says prophetically. "Wisdom is born in the mind."

I much prefer the Tantric idea that wisdom is found in a woman's body, particularly in her heart.

We talk about our government's fear of people's free thoughts. Of illegal drug use and how we can work to make therapeutic drugs available to heal others and live in the utopia that is meant to be.

~

I make a ball of my hands like Aaron did last night.

"And Einstein's brain was like this."

The entire class is speechless. The grandfatherly teacher's mouth hangs open. I have just, not so subtly, announced to everyone that I drop acid and I'm pretty sure it's obvious that I haven't slept all night and that I may still be tripping right now. I walk back to my seat with a sudden panicky fear racing through my body. There is a lot of wisdom to be found in the ancient tradition of mystery schools. Many people are not ready for these teachings. I have just committed treason against the social norms. I try to push the racing thoughts away. My mind returns to Gosnell, to the taunting faces. My stomach turns to lead. I can't bear the realization. I race out of the classroom and hunker down in my dorm room.

Fuck it, I think. *I don't need anyone but Aaron.* But that's not true. We all need connections to the larger human family.

~

Aaron enrolls for the second semester at Northwest Missouri State and we smoke up every single day of January.

"I'm worried we have an addiction," I say as we sit on his bed listening to Pink Floyd's album, *Meddle*. This album has become the soundtrack of our relationship.

"You can't be addicted to pot," Aaron says as he blows all the smoke through a toilet paper roll stuffed with dryer sheets to cover up the smell.

"I wonder what it's like to not be stoned. Do you remember?"

"Yes. It sucks." He packs another bowl and hands it to me.

"Did you hear about Becca and Tom? They spent last night in jail because the campus police found their pipes. They didn't even have any weed on them!"

"Those pigs," Aaron says.

"I'm worried," I say as I take the pipe. "We're like the only ones who haven't been caught yet."

"We're not getting caught," Aaron says. "I have the best hiding place ever," he pats a bulge behind a poster.

I'm not convinced.

"And the duct tape is fool-proof," I eye the doorway with the gray tape sealing all the cracks to insulate the smoke.

"To the smartest drug dealers ever."

He lifts the bowl to me and smiles. I don't feel so smart.

"I have to go the bathroom."

Aaron walks over to the door, puts both hands on the knob and leans back with all his strength. I watch his face turn red. It takes a minute but then it finally gives. The noise of the duct tape popping off the doorway echoes all the way down the hall.

~

It's cold outside, but the woods are warm as we huddle together in a tight circle passing the pipe. Our faces shine when it's our turn to smoke and many of us sport singed eyelashes and eyebrows.

We are on a mission. I can't remember what the mission is, but we end up in the Old Market, giggling over fantastic Italian food. There are eight of us—no, four—well, I just stick with Aaron, he's my ride. I like when he smiles. He looks so happy. Not a care in the world. I like being near him when he's happy.

"More weed!" Someone says and it turns into a chant.

We're on the bridge now. The big one over the Missouri River that goes into Council Bluffs. It's really dark out. I can see the lights on the shore. We hang on the metal beams dangling our feet over the water way below.

Someone is moving up high in the rafters.

"Look!" I point. All of us stare at the kid on the top of the bridge.

"Hey, man, you alright?" Aaron says.

"I'm gonna jump tonight," the kid replies.

"Bad day?"

"I gotta gun," the kid says. "If I don't jump, I'll just shoot myself."

"Dude, man, not tonight. Look at that moon!"

What was the guy's name with the afro? I can't remember.

"Come down and smoke up with us," Aaron says.

"Seriously?"

The kid makes his way down. "Why the hell not—better to go stoned if you're gonna go."

"That's what I'm talking about," the guy with the afro says. *Kevin, that's right, his name is Kevin.*

It doesn't take long before we're all giggling again. We take the kid down and back to our car. We drive back to the woods because someone left our bag of weed there. We actually walk into the woods in the middle of the night and we find the weed using road flares! Idiots. We all smoke up to celebrate.

I don't know what happens to that kid. But I know he didn't jump that night. Who knew stoners could be such heroes?

Aaron drives us back to Maryville.

"It's like the clouds have come down to earth," I say.

"That's called fog," someone says.

"Oh, yeah. That's right. Fog," I say.

~

Aaron and I are sitting at Roy's house. Roy looks to me like Jesus with long red hair. He doesn't speak much. He looks zoned out most of the time. There is something strangely spiritual and dark about him. He told me once that he was God. He also says he's Mormon. He hands me a towel coated in some fumes from a few cleaning bottles stashed under his kitchen sink.

"Inhale it," he says. "It's out of this world."

I feel invincible, because I'm nineteen and full of self-hatred. So I do it.

My view of his living room closes in. The "I" in me is now far away, in the back on my mind, down a long narrow tunnel where I can only make out a little light at the end. Seas of people surround me. I think they are the saints of heaven. Or the angels. They are chanting like solemn monks in a gothic cathedral. I think I am going to be with them now. To stand in the circle. To face my judgment. The monks are not happy with me.

I reach down to earth and search for Aaron's hand. I want to touch him. I find his fingers, but they are very cold, like all of the life has gone out from them. Then I realize that it is my body that is cold. I am the one who is leaving. *No!* I tell the chorus of monks. *I want to stay! I want to be inside my warm skin again! I want to be human a little longer. Please, please don't take me yet!* Someone says it's not my time. I wake up the next morning in Aaron's bed, unsure of where the night had gone.

~

Ice covers the sidewalks and at least a foot of snow is plowed earlier today. I walk over to Aaron's dorm room to spend the night. He's driving back from Omaha and will be here later tonight. I pick up his room for him and prepare for another journey. As I'm cleaning off his desk I find the rolled up poster we bought a few months ago. I remove the plastic and unroll it. I decide tonight's the night I spend some time with these intriguing images. When the room is in order, I light some candles, turn on Floyd and put two tabs of acid on my tongue. I wash it down with orange juice, light a bowl, and hover over the poster on the floor holding my chin in my hands.

Little creatures fill the spaces, some demonic looking, some angelic, some human. Huddled masses gather around little orbs of light. From their heads sprout future generations. Most grow into tree like appendages that lean to the right where I see a lake, mountains, and a bright blue sky. But shadows tug at the edges, red flames and broken bones mar the black earth.

"The wide way is an illusion," says a voice in my mind.

On the left, familiar faces come into focus. Holy men with long beards, the patriarchs, Moses, Abraham, and this one must be Jesus. I put my finger over his heart where a small ray of light beams out of a space shaped like the eye of a needle. Through the center a small wizard like creature walks on a tightrope juggling atoms.

"This must be God the creator of life," I think.

I trace the ray of light across the poster. It falls upon a little girl in the center. Her body is full of white light. Her arms are flung joyfully in the air. Suddenly I am reminded of myself when I was five.

Oh, that little girl pierces my heart. She's the one who experienced divine love. *Remember her?*

I feel a trickling sensation in my heart, like water leaking through a crack. I am afraid of it. I have kept it locked up for so many years. The room fills with light. I close my eyes. But I can't escape the growing presence of light. I run out of the room and into the bathroom to hide from the light. But even here it finds me. The light is within me. The tiles glow brighter. I hear water dripping from the faucet. I put my fingers on the handles and try to turn them tight. But the water keeps dripping. I am frightened to look at my face in the mirror, but I do it anyway. The scary cat-eyed girl is not there. Instead I see a dignified woman with a strong chin and cheekbones. My blue eyes are large and full of honor and strength. My face shifts into my father's, then my mother's. I see my grandmothers, my grandfathers. I see all of my ancestors and how they live on in me, all of their lifetimes flowing into this form. I notice how my hair curls around my face and my skin turns gold. Then I look and I see that I am actually a lion, a bold and beautiful lion from the tribe of Judah.

I step back from the mirror. I am afraid of my own strength. I have always been afraid of my own strength. Maybe I have internalized others' fear of my own strength. I leave the bathroom and run back to Aaron's room. I curl into a ball on his bed. It's early evening and the sun is setting. It begins to pour in through the windows. I still try to resist what is happening. The little crack inside of my chest widens like the statues of Jesus and Mary that open and reveal their flaming hearts. The trickle of energy soon becomes a flood. My body fills with a gentle peace. As the light increases, so does a very old feeling. Suddenly I am sitting in the dark movie theater again. An ocean of joy bubbles up within me. *How could I have forgotten?*

I bury my head in my hands. "I'm sorry," I whisper. "Oh, God, I am so sorry!"

I have walked away from my one true love, from the most important thing in life.

The light continues to increase.

"Stop," I beg. "Stop loving me so much. I can't handle it."

I think of the Ark of the Covenant and how those who came too close to the presence of God instantly died.

"I can't be so close to you. I want to be, but I can't handle it."

Shadows make a cross on the wall. I don't understand the meaning of it. But I hear the chorus of my ancestors calling me home.

"This is grace," I think. "I have tasted the grace of God and now I know that it is true."

As I watch the cross stretch across the room I think of the church I have left behind. The one that seemed irrelevant to me for so many years. *People need to know this*, I think. *People need to know God's love is so real. People need to know that it is beyond the small categories the church has created for us.* Are these my words? They feel like they flow from the divine realms. *Yes*, I vow, *I will tell people. I will make my way back to the church, and to God, to tell everyone of this wondrous love.*

Part III
The Tree of Life

I believe in things unseen
Like feelings
Hiding
Beneath the skin
Somewhere near the cliffs of hell
Down the dark long tunnel
The girl is locked away
Screaming
And sometimes—
When you come to look for her,
She sings.

The woman who is a virgin, is one-in-herself, she does what she does—not because of any desire to please, not to be liked, or to be approved, even by herself; not because of any desire to gain power over another...but because what she does is true.

-Ester Harding

PADAWAN

Ancient Shamanic practices require young initiates to undergo death and rebirth to mark the transition from child to adult. Some drink psychotropic substances before they are sent out into the wild to experience a sort of disembodiment. The journey calls the initiate to face the annihilating demons within and without. These experiences send them to the edges of reality and push them to discover the integrating principle—the healer within—before they are allowed to return home.

~

"What the hell is going on here," Aaron says when he returns to his room and finds me on my knees praying.

I show him the poster, the little girl and the light. I try to explain the spiritual awakening I am having.

"No, Jess. No. Not this. How can this be happening? You can't really believe this?"

I tell him about the great love of God. I try to hug him. But the energy has shifted between us. The magnetic force that once pulled us together is now pushing us apart.

"I have to go," I whisper. I run down the hallway. He chases after me.

"No! Jess! No!" he screams in the stairwell.

It's about six in the morning. I run out of the building into the icy winter morning. I watch my breath make clouds in front of my face. I feel the presence of angels all around me. I hear their gentle whispers like prayers and songs in the air as I wonder how I could possibly walk away from Aaron.

I climb the seven flights of stairs and bundle up in warm sweaters in my cold dorm room. I haven't been here in ages. It doesn't look like Jane has either. I hear the sound of a rattle snake. I look out the window and see Aaron running into the building. I am suddenly afraid. I randomly open my Bible and begin to read:

Let those who fear the LORD say: "His love endures forever." In my anguish I cried to the LORD, and he answered by setting me free. The LORD is with me; I will not be afraid. What can man do to me? The LORD is with me; he is my helper.

Aaron knocks on my door. He runs to me and puts his arms around me. His face is filled with darkness. I cannot see the light underneath his skin anymore.
  "Why are you doing this to us?" His eyes are hollow and empty.
  "I can't help it," I say. "It's in my blood."
  I show him the Bible verse I was reading. I try to make him see.
  "I know God isn't real," he says. "Because I just prayed that if he was you would kiss me."
  "God doesn't work like that, Aaron," I try to explain, but I don't know how. We hold each other with heavy arms and sorrowful sighs. I can feel a group of gentle of angels circling us, assuring me with their mournful whispers that destiny is calling us apart.

~

I end up in ER before I am finally able to let go of Aaron. We continue to try to connect, but we just don't fit together like we used to. The energy has shifted and it is impossible to put the Genie back in the bottle now. I try to teach Aaron like a child, the things I learned in Sunday School; I try to catch him up with where I am at, but I come across as condescending and disrespectful of our different paths.
  Aaron and I begin to fight a lot. Our fights escalate quickly. He punches out one of the windows in his dorm room. He throws a trashcan down the hallway. His rage reminds me of my father's. I have never seen this side of him before. Or maybe the light triggers the darkness. I don't know how to diffuse his anger, but one day he accidentally slams the door that my hand is holding.

I don't want Aaron to come to ER with me. One of the RA's carries me down the stairs. I cry while everyone watches in silence. I don't care what they think because my heart is broken and it hurts more than my finger split wide open and bleeding.

~

I get one of those Christian fishes tattooed around the flower on my toe. I mark myself as Christ's own forever. When people start putting that Christian fish all over the bumpers of their cars, I am so embarrassed. I realize in a moment of horror that my tattoo is now like having the K from the K-Mart car permanently inked on my toe. *What was I thinking?!* Shame has such a tight hold on me. Years later I learn that the fish symbol predates Christianity and was used first to celebrate the ancient fertility goddess. When stood straight up it is a symbol of the vagina, the door of life. I can certainly live with that one.

~

I pray now when I trip. Each time is a spiritual adventure, a chance to learn and reform my mind. I look at all my baggage. I ask for guidance. One time I neglect to pray and I have a full blown bad trip. Large shadows come to life on the walls. I realize I can sense the energy in everyone around me and their darkness can see me. That old feeling of being unprotected in a dangerous world is triggered again. I am so frightened that large vessels break on my leg from clenching my muscles too tight. I decide to refrain from LSD.

That night I have a vision. I am told that my mission is to share divine love with the world through stories and music. I vow to follow the call. But I develop panic attacks when I try to speak with others about God—or just anything at all. I am so afraid to do it wrong and disappoint God. I don't know how to begin. I fall back into the old unhealthy forms of Christianity that devalue women and our ways of being in the world. Pastors and people on the radio compel me to talk to strangers. To ask them if they are saved. I find myself stuck in a lot of awkward situations trying to "save" people in the conventional evangelical way. I bring homeless people to church.

The pastors and congregants look at me strangely as if they were thinking, "We really didn't mean for you to welcome the outcasts here!"

One guy has a mental illness and he can't stay seated. He decides to get up in the middle of the sermon and give a little mini-sermon himself.

I start going to the Assemblies of God church down the road from my college. People speak in tongues. One night I am called up and asked to pray and lay hands on people. When I put my hands on the girl's head, she falls over.

"You are filled with the Holy Spirit!" she says when she wakes up.

But other people tell me I am not filled with the Holy Spirit, and I shouldn't pray for others because I cannot speak in tongues like I used to as a child, or because I am a woman I cannot teach or pray for others.

~

My first Sunday home after my freshman year of college, I sit in the back row of our Lutheran church. I haven't been here much during my high school years. Soft light illuminates the circular window carved out of the front wall. The pastor is preaching on the prodigal son. I don't care who sees me. I can't hold back my emotions any more. I do the ugly cry. My mascara runs everywhere. I have to sit down because my body is so heavy with sorrow. My father sees me in the back row. He walks over to me and embraces me. I've come home, I've returned to the faith of my family. I bury my face in his warm sweater and know beyond a doubt that he still loves me. My mother leads the music with the band up front. She sings, "How Deep the Father's Love for Us." I cannot contain how big God's love is for me, for all of us.

~

The mind abhors a vacuum. Symbol systems cannot simply be rejected, they must be replaced. Where there is not any replacement, the mind will revert to familiar structures at times of crisis, bafflement, or defeat.

-Carol P. Christ

I return to the faith of my parents because it provides a familiar shape for my religious experiences; these forms have structured the fibers of my family lineage since before I was born. As I return to my parents' way of practicing religion, I lose something vital as I try to fit my experiences into ancient patriarchal structures that have chopped up and dismissed women's bodies, voices, and wisdom for centuries. I fear my experiences will be dismissed if I share it with others since I had so many while I was on LSD. I fear the rejection of the truth of my being because it colors outside of the lines of orthodoxy. I do not yet know how to contain myself in the world or my faith in the church. I tone down the light of my own soul lest I offend anyone. This seems to be an unspoken code in my Lutheran Norwegian lineage. I am still trying to please others. Giving my life away feels too natural. I serve at the expense of my own soul rather than in service to my soul's interior truth. I bumped up against the ancient taboo: *How arrogant for you to think you would have something unique and important to offer? Who do you think you are?*

People don't really teach you how to tune into your soul at church. They just teach you how to follow someone else's rules. Get involved. Stay busy. Don't question. Don't feel the range of human emotion. Don't color outside of the lines. Don't backslide in your faith.

~

Because I don't yet know how to be alone, I begin dating the Youth Minister at my parent's church. He writes me love songs about my blue eyes. He takes me on dates and out to dinner. Again, I have another man coming to my rescue. I don't understand why men fall so easily in love with me. Years later a therapist helps me see that I am what Carl Jung calls, an anima woman; I reflect for men the projections of their own soul. I am a mirror. I am a shapeshifter, especially when I am afraid to reveal my own thoughts and feelings and risk breaking the dazzling projections. I am afraid of being alone and unloved. I am baffled at my ability to become what someone else needs, but not what I need. I am scared to know all of this, because now I must do something different and I don't know what to do. I have not been raised to value my own needs because that was considered selfish and 'navel gazing' in the churches I grew up in. It is drilled into me at a young age that caring for self is being selfish and selfish equates to evil. Having no-self is good and holy. This feels less spiritually enlightened and more like justification for being a slave to someone else's needs and desires that don't necessarily serve the divine or the greater common good. Maybe this is exactly the sort of twist of the Christian message that suits the military industrial complex and corporate America and anyone else who fears humans hearing the messages of their own soul and participating in the spiritual revolution that is bubbling up from the depths of our being.

Within six months my new boyfriend is talking about marriage. My parents are thrilled and ready to marry me off. But I am already mindful of history's pull. My mother dropped out of college and married my father after her sophomore year. She still regrets that she never finished. I feel how it gnaws at her confidence and I cannot ignore her regret.

I return to Northwest Missouri State. My youth minister comes to visit. I meet his parents. We begin making plans. I vow to remain pure until our wedding night (because now that I'm a Christian, my sexual purity is of the utmost importance). And then I discover he has cheated on me with his old girlfriend who has been stalking him and slashing his tires.

After a painful breakup I feel the heavy disappointment of my family and my new found church community for letting him go.

I overhear my mother speaking with my father, "Who will take care of her now?"

I am still seen as a child. I want to learn how to take care of myself. I still feel the desperation to grow up and be a woman.

~

Aaron calls one night. He misses me.

"Guess what! Remember that security guard at the pool who gave you weed?

"Lucky?"

"Yeah, that guy. He was Omaha's distributer! It was all over the news today. He's in jail. So is Josh. It's all gone. Can you believe it?"

No. I cannot believe how close I was to throwing my life away.

Aaron comes to visit one last time. We try to kiss like we used to, to hold each other in the old embraces, but our energy doesn't mesh anymore. He leaves with heavy shoulders and sunken eyes. This is the last time I see him for many, many years.

~

I don't want to date Jude. My instincts are dead on. But I silence them when he comes over to my apartment and curls up in a fetal position on my dining room floor and begs me to love him and help him. He tells me he wants to become a seeker, to also find God. He tells me he needs my help. How can I refuse? I hold him in my arms and kiss his forehead and I fall in love with his heartache—which mirrors my own—I fall in love with the little boy I see in those deep brown eyes, the young one lost in a man's skin who still hopes to find redemption. *Shhhh, there, there...* I comb my fingers through his hair and I rock away his fear, probably like he always wanted his mother to do. I promise to love him, to try and reach him.

I am a tantrika. I am remembering that I have innate skills to help men (especially) heal. But there is no sacred role for this work in my present world-view, only my intuition to guide me. So I continue to confuse my clients and my boyfriends.

Jude comes from a strict Christian home. He left his Nazarene faith that didn't let him dance—and he's a wonderful dancer. He told me one day he came home from school and couldn't find his parents. He was convinced they had been raptured and that he had been left behind... for dancing.

I'm enchanted by the way he moves his hips and his long curly hair that hangs down his back. He plays in a rock band around town and we share melodies and begin to write songs together. I sing for him. We make a cute hippy couple.

But Gaia warns me that Jude is a compulsive liar. That he only pretends to be on a spiritual journey with me. I deny it. I understand that he is confused and unintegrated. I do not understand how dangerous that is for my heart to navigate.

~

I return home for winter break. I am invited to a TEC (Teens Encounter Christ) retreat at my parents' church. It's three days of games, junk food, and discerning the things in our lives that keep us from God.

"This brick," says the girl holding a red cardboard box, "is alcohol." Her hair is dyed black and she wears a lot of makeup. "This brick," she continues, "is drugs." She tells us of her attempted suicides. Of driving on the opposite side of the road and playing chicken with her friends in the car.

"Wow," I think, "We are really speaking the truth! Really being honest!"

I can't wait for my turn. I listen to several more confessions. I watch everyone thank those who have shared.

"This brick," I say, "Is boys." I intuitively know that the church would frown upon this area of my life. That lump returns to the back of my throat. I release the flood.

"I thought me and my youth minister boyfriend were going to get married! I thought he loved me! He was the first Christian guy I have dated. I was working on turning my life around. And, then he cheated on me with his ex-girlfriend!" I sob into a Kleenex.

"And now…" I sniff, "Now I'm dating an agnostic!"

Several people suck all the air out of the room. The pastor—a very kind and gentle soul—stands up and raises his open hands.

"Thank you for sharing, Jessica. If anyone else has any sensitive information to share about our church staff, please talk to us in private."

I return to my seat disappointed and think, *I guess you can't really be honest here either*. I seem to be a little clueless about social situations sometimes or overly tuned in. Or I am repeating my karma—I'm humiliating someone else about their sexual mishaps in a public way, as that happened to me, and I've not worked through that yet and so the cycle of unconsciousness repeats.

As an adult I wonder if I am also on the spectrum like my son. Like him, there are times I have no filters or I am all filter. I want my inner and outer worlds to balance and have that authentic connection. But my inner world is a pretty magical place, and for many centuries women were killed for sharing their wisdom with the world.

~

I return to Northwest Missouri State.

"You paint great pictures with your words," my English professor says.

I get good grades on my projects. It feels like a far off dream, but I work towards that someday when I will be able to translate my experiences into pictures and words.

~

"I got orders," my father says.

"Where?"

"We're moving to the St. Louis area—O'Fallon, Illinois—where Jason lives. We actually found a house just a few blocks away from his."

I put a hand to my face and think, "Now? After all these years? After all the incredible loss? Now I will live close to him?" The irony is painful.

~

I bring a new focus to my studies and work to get my grades up. I reapply to St. Olaf my junior year and against all odds I am accepted.

~

Jason calls me out of the blue one day, "I miss you," he says.

He reads me the lyrics to the Indigo Girl's song, Ghost. "I'm in love with your ghost," he tells me. "Can we give it one more try?"

"Oh, Jason," I say. "I've been through so much. You would hardly recognize me. You don't know me at all."

"I know the real you," he says. "I should have gone to school with you. We could have been together. I heard your folks are moving here—like in the same neighborhood."

"Yeah, can you believe it?"

"I would have given anything to know this is how the story would go all those years ago."

"Jason, I'm seeing someone now," I say. "I'm sorry."

~

I spend the summer working as a Christian Camp Counselor in the northern woods of Minnesota, determined to share the love of God with kids. My brother and his best friend Russ become counselors with me. I'm hardly in St. Louis at all this summer, and when I am, Jason has already left for school.

I lead engaging Bible studies and learn how to sing and play the guitar a little. Russ and Dave sneak their groups of campers into my Bible studies because Dave says I have some sort of a pipeline straight to God when I talk.

I write lyrics in my free time and put them to the tunes I have been playing for years. Whenever I sing in public though, my throat tightens, I sing off key. I can't yet bring into the world what I can do when I'm all alone.

~

One night Simon, the director who grew up at this camp, returns from the canoe trip and pulls me into a room alone.

"What did you accomplish today?" His face is red with frustration.

"I mowed the lawn, cleaned up the cabins, swept the attics..."

"Why didn't you clean out the fireplaces? I told you to clean out the fireplaces! Is that so hard?"

"Simon—I was working all day! I didn't get to them yet."

"You're pathetic. Pathetic and lazy!"

He shouts. I curl up in a ball and lay on the couch while he yells at me. I am pathetic because that's the projection he's sending out and I somehow just become what others think of me. I show him how pathetic I am by lying there and crying while he treats me like garbage. It's strange how defenseless I am. I used to be too hard—no one could get in. Now I'm too soft. How do I hold my dignity as a good Christian girl who is not supposed to get angry, talk back, or question authority? I have been taught to lay down my life for others and letting them walk all over me in Jesus' name. In order to stand up for myself I need a sense of self. I need access to my anger when that self gets disrespected—but I think anger is sinful and I'm trying to be as good as possible now.

~

Dave, Russ, and I begin our lives at St. Olaf together. They are incoming freshmen and I am a junior. The three of us sit on a couch nervously filling out forms, shaking hands with guidance counselors and our Resident Assistants. I look around at the sea of strangers and dread the familiarity of the unknown.

"Come over," Dave says. "We're having a party tonight." I'm a little shy about hanging out in a freshman dorm, but when my parents leave I experience a strange vertigo, like I am drifting into outer space.

Who are you? I ask myself. The answer to the question eludes me. The dread grows into a black hole that starts to suck me in. It is a question I am invited to consider over and over again during my time upon the hill. Through the fiery tree tops, the limestone rocks and quiet snow, I wrestle with anxiety attacks and bursts of insight. Piece by piece, in philosophy and psychology, in religion and in my solitude, I am sorting the seeds of possibilities.

I walk over to Dave's dorm. There's a slight chill in the air and the moon is big in the navy sky.

I follow the sound of The New Kids on the Block singing, "The Right Stuff," until I am standing in front of my brother's room. He's hooked up Dad's old speakers and has the volume turned up to eleven. He and Russ and a few other kids are dancing like we did in the early nineties, like totally unrestrained nerds.

I lean against the doorway and laugh. Russ walks over to me, "Jessie!"

He gives me a big hug and hands me a red Solo cup of beer.

"We're going to have a lot of fun here," he promises. I find comfort in his smile and I trust the light in his eyes.

~

Shortly after the Dakotas are fought off of the land in southern Minnesota, Mr. North and his wife Anne move into the area in 1855. They gather like-minded people who believe in abolition, women's rights, and helping your neighbor. Northfield is quickly known as a place that educates farmers, teachers, and pastors. Before many women attend college in the United States, St. Olaf welcomes women, including my great grandmother, my grandmother and my mother who quits college early to marry my father.

Who benefits from the removal of the Natives? My family does. Most Americans do. But we benefit for only a short time. Until the consequences of our actions catch up with us. Until we begin to experience the cost of our disconnection from the land, of broken and superficial relationships, until the time that the prophets have warned us about: when justice returns to her rightful place on the earth. The time is now.

~

Before Philosophy class I think I might throw up all over my desk. I remember that I was remedial in high school. I am convinced I am too stupid for St. Olaf College. I don't yet know how essential foolishness is to find wisdom. How there are many streams of wisdom. How I am different and I have an untapped well of gifts to share with the world.

I pull out the thick textbook from my back. It taunts me. I push it aside.

Professor Polson sneaks in the back of the room, mysteriously eyeing us as he crouches by the black board poised with a piece of chalk in his hand.

"What can we know?"

He greets us with wide eyes and a secretive smile.

"How do we know what we know? Do we even know what we know?"

He prances around with a wild look in his eyes.

"We can agree upon certain facts, one plus one is two. This is a color we call blue. I was born on this date. But are there boundaries to what we know? What lies beyond the boundaries of scientific reason and mathematical equations? How do we know experience? Can we? Is it something we can share? How does this mysterious realm of subjectivity and intuitive knowing shape our perception and our world? What is it made of? Who is the ghost in the machine? And what constitutes all that lies beyond our rational reach?"

"Is it God?" I ask. "That is beyond what we know?"

The entire class looks at me. I can't believe those words just flew out of my mouth.

"Great question, Jessica," his smiling face beams at me. "I appreciate you speaking up. Class take note, this is to be a philosophical discussion—not a lecture."

"You can't prove God," a guy replies.

"Ah, but can we prove that there is an order to existence? Is there any criteria by which we can determine and agree upon the greatest good? How do we know what is a good action, even the best action to take in any given situation? Is there anything we can agree on?"

"That the world is not as it should be," I say.

"And how should it be?" Polson pushes me.

"People should be kinder," I finally say.

"Insightful, Jessica. Does the class agree with this?"

I listen to the silence and watch them nod their heads. Dr. Polson writes my response on the board. I take the thick book off my desk and return to my dorm room. I make some tea and read Kant, fascinated to discover a world where people ask the most important questions about the meaning of life.

Yes, let's explore the rules by which we make up a society and consider again our presuppositions of "The Truth." I feel the budding of a new kind of love. The love of wisdom.

~

Jude and I date until Christmas. He visits me at St. Olaf a few times. I draw boundaries around our relationship and how far I will go since I'm trying so hard to be a good Christian girl now.

Jude is obsessed with my body.

"You're perfect," he says. "Like a goddess."

"Shut up." I say. "Liar."

"Jessica—I only date beautiful girls. You should feel honored."

I feel anxious that he attaches his love for me to things that will inevitably fade. His obsession is contagious and I start to look more closely at my body too, as do many women who get lost in the male gaze. I notice all these new flaws about myself. I worry my looks are the only thing that makes me lovable. I have not yet been initiated into the beauty of the heart. I play oppressive message in my mind, *If I get old he won't love me—maybe no one will.* I make an appointment with a dermatologist to have some work done. My face gets all bruised up after the treatment. I think Jude will like that I am working on all my flaws. Instead, he tells me that his stomach hurts when he looks at me.

"You're not perfect anymore," he bemoans.

"Did you know you have a little white hair growing on your upper lip?"

He looks out my window trying to hide the sadness in his eyes. He needs a perfect Goddess to counter his imperfect mother. I am not perfect. I am a real, live, bleeding, aging, human, woman. I am no longer able to hold his projections.

He cuts his visit short. When he leaves that winter day, it will be the last time I ever see him again. He doesn't even call me to break up. Gaia does.

"He's dating this new young teacher—she wears short leather skirts and drives a red convertible," she tries to tell me gently. "Jess, he never loved you—he would rearrange his house before you came, he'd put out his Bible and his religious books for YOU—he never cared about any of that."

I thank her for her honesty.

"Are you OK?" she asks.

"I'm totally fine," I lie.

When I hang up the phone I crawl into my closet, pull my legs into my chest and pound my fist in the floor. *You stupid girl! Never again, will I be so foolish to love…NEVER!*

What a foolish, Faustian promise.

~

The question I have for myself today is: why did I agree to hold his perfect projections of a woman? I think his projections helped me feel connected to a bigger sense of myself. I was hungry to know myself more and to love myself as passionately as men seemed to love me. Healthy relationships allow for the process of ongoing human transformation, for the revealing of the soul and everlasting love. Any illusions that keep us from that will not last forever. Relationships can reveal parts of ourselves to us; it's our job to discover and love ourselves completely.

~

Money promised to the Dakotas for their land arrives too little too late. In 1862 desperate hurting Natives begin to band together against the settlers. As punishment, the largest hanging in US history ensues.

A memorial of the Native American men who were hung stands in Mankato, Minnesota today.

Mass executions of the Native people happened in many places. Listen to an elder tell you their horrific stories of running for their lives and having their children taken from them or killed. Men, women and children were rounded up, shot and thrown in mass graves.

I asked one of the locals how the river got its name. I was told it was named the Red River because it used to run with Indian blood.

Today, some of our grandparents may even remember this. This is not ancient history. These are the collective traumatic wounds that we have all inherited. These are the collective wounds of injustice that cry out to be witnessed with compassion so that we can all be healed.

~

One of the many problems with the theology of original sin is that it attempts to answer simply the problem of evil. But overcoming evil demands that we understand the history and the forces that compel people to act and react in horrific ways to unresolved traumatic events and forces that have shaped our lives. What is required in the healthy spiritual life is right compassion, not right doctrine. Compassion allows the suffering a space to breathe and heal. Trauma needs a compassionate witness in order to be released. Ignored, the shadow only grows more powerful in the unconscious. Doctrine is void of compassion. It judges others indiscriminately based on a monolithic world view disconnected from creation—most often, a view that primarily serves power, not love.

~

"Just open up your mouth and speak," the kind indigenous woman puts her hands on both my cheeks. "The Holy Spirit is here, I can see it resting upon you."

I look at the Monterrey Mountains, the little white cottages nestled within the clefts of rock. A homeless dog runs past me down a nameless ally in Mexico.

"I feel silly," I say.

"The Lord wants you to be baptized in the Spirit," she says. "You need to learn to be vulnerable again. Vulnerable to the Lord."

"But I was baptized as a child."

"You need the second baptism," she says. "And it's here. All you need to do is receive it."

The air grows warm. I hear the wind circling around my head. I open my thirsty mouth and my tongue utters words without meaning or definition.

"There it is," she says like a proud nurse who's just delivered a baby. "Good girl."

I speak in tongues again, just like when I was five.

~

"Holy God, Father, oh, Father God, we love you Father God. We praise you Father God. We ask you to bring your Holy Spirit to this mountain, Father God, that the city of Monterrey will see and know you Father God."

Their prayers sound so sensual, so ecstatic, so…erotic.

Our mission group links arms and huddles together in a circle. "The Lord wants you all to speak in your prayer languages," the youth leader says. Everyone begins moaning and sighing and babbling their strange words.

One of the boys says, "Look at the cloud around us!"

We open our eyes and see a thick fog rolling into our midst.

"God has come to be with us!" One begins to prophesy, "Go to the lost, heal the sick, bind up the broken, and let every tongue confess that Jesus is Lord!"

~

I walk down impoverished streets of Monterrey, knocking on doors and passing out tracts printed in Spanish. With a translator by my side, I ask to pray with the residents. I ask them to accept Jesus as their Lord and Savior. The Young Life group is so proud of how many people I bring to Christ.

"But they are Catholic," I protest. "They all have crucifixes hanging in their living rooms!"

"Catholics are not Christians," one of the leaders explains to me. "It is a dead religion and they need to be saved from it and brought to the living hope of Jesus Christ."

I don't buy it. I don't believe in salvation that requires the reciting of a few magic words so that one gets into heaven at the end of their life. As I look into the yearning eyes and bare homes, I think I haven't saved anyone from anything. Salvation would be bread. Money to pay the bills. I keep these thoughts to myself.

~

"This is God's word!"

The fiery preacher slams his hand on top of the Bible.

"God doesn't make mistakes. You can either take God at His word, or you can follow the world to hell. We are in dark times. These are the last days, when the saints of God will be tested. We see Satan at work in the world—destroying families through the lies of feminism. God knew what he was doing when he created and ordained man to be the head of the family. Wives, you are to submit to your husband. You are not to teach a man in church. These are God's laws. And I'm afraid for you women who have gotten so mixed up in the world—the devil is prowling around like a lion ready to devour you. You need to be in the Word every day ladies. Learning to put a bridle on your tongue. Let the Lord lead you through your husband."

I'm starting to feel very uncomfortable at church. I feel lost in the Christian confusion of my childhood again.

~

I dream my mother shows me how to perform a crucifixion. She takes the little baby girl's arms and pins them to a tiny cross. I tell her: we're not supposed to crucify the baby! We're supposed to die to sin! But she looks at me and says, "Children are born in sin."

I awake feeling heavy and lost in a thick fog.

~

Young Life meets on St. Olaf campus for weekly Bible studies. One night the fiery pastor from the local non-denominational church joins us. He wants to pray and prophesy over all of the students here this evening. He puts his hands on each of the students' heads. He squeezes his eyes shut and speaks in tongues. He recites his visions, Bible verses that cross his mind, he offers warnings and blessings for each person. I am so excited for him to put his hands on my head and hear what he has to say to me. But when he gets to me he looks at me blankly and simply moves on to the next person. I am the only person he doesn't pray for. I return to my dorm room and crawl into my bed and into a dark space.

"What is wrong with me?" I cry into a pillow.

I dream of a sword coming out of my mouth.

~

When I grow up and spend some time studying the meanings of my dreams I learn that the sword can represent a phallic symbol, the masculine energy able to quickly discern what to penetrate in order to protect. Now I understand this dream as an invitation to speak, to penetrate these men and these ideas that want to have power over me, who want me to remain silent and submissive. Now I claim my co-creative power with my living word.

~

At the next gathering I tell the leaders about my confusion and hurt. Two men turn to each other with knowing looks. They are both short; one is skinny with ashy hair and acne, the other is obese with jet black hair and a voice that he plans to use as the next big televangelist.

"He was afraid to catch your demons," the heavy one says. "They come out of the head, the most spiritual part of the body. And you have no male head of protection over you right now. You would do well to find a man to marry as soon as possible."

Great. Just what my mother thinks.

"We need to cast the demons out of you," the thin one says, "so you can be pure."

"Ok," I submit to their authority as my heart sinks into my toes. I realize my mysterious life-long problem has been, apparently, demon possession.

"With two of us praying for you, we can stand strong together and do the spiritual battle. Sit here," they pull out a chair for me. I put my hands in my lap and my head down.

They begin praying with their hands over their heart. They pray prayers of protection over themselves. They lay hands on one another and their words become filled with passion and longing. Then they both lay hands on my head and start to speak in tongues.

"You have many demons in you, daughter," the future TV preacher says. "Satan, release your hold on her in the name of Jesus!" His loud voice frightens me. Tears begin to roll down my cheeks.

They babble louder. "The enemy has a strong hold here," the other says. "Demon of Confusion, leave in the name of Jesus!"

"Wow!" the other says. "I just saw this hippy demon flying around you!"

"In the name of Jesus, Hippy Demon you must leave!"

"There's a Demon of Witchcraft I see. Have you ever played with the Ouija board?"

"Only once when I was little."

"You opened a doorway to a dangerous world."

He prays extra fervently for this one. "All Demons of Sorcery, Witchcraft, and Feminism flee in the name of Jesus!"

"You are bound to the world of flesh," the other says. "The flesh is set against the Spirit of God. You must renounce your flesh. Say, I renounce it."

It doesn't feel right. But what do I know? "I renounce it." I say.

They continue on like this for an hour. I have every conceivable demon cast from me. After it is finished, I sit hunched over, sobbing.

The two of them stand a little taller, proud of the work they have done in the name of Jesus. They embrace and bless each other as they depart. Afterwards, the male leaders of the church are still careful not to touch me or pray over me. Possibly my beauty tempts them. Or my unconscious feminine power frightens them. I must have some demons in me still, as you can't quite cast the mystical girl out of my skin.

"Go and sin no more," the heavy one says. They leave me trembling and crying under the flickering fluorescent lights.

~

The way others talk about God doesn't match my experience of the love and grace I knew as a little girl. I remember feeling this a long time ago. This is the process of discerning. Of sorting small seeds. This one goes here, and this one goes here. This is how we build a self and become whole. In my life, I have learned to give away my power, my voice, to others, to men, now to men who rule the church who worship a male God and all the unconscious female hating projections that are allowed to flow from that image. I realize the only way forward is to take back what belongs to me and receive who I am, and let nothing other than that possess me. It's like I've been reliving the rape story over and over, allowing other people to define me.

~

Grandpa looks like a ghost. His skin and hair has become so white, like he is filled with light. He looks very small, like he is returning to infancy. He is curled up in the fetal position. The man in the hospital bed is a stranger to me. But somewhere deep in that unfamiliar body is the person we all know and love: the peaceful pastor, the powerful preacher, the man who smells of a pipe, the one who gazes at the stars for hours with his telescope, the one who always wears a thin smile and sparkles in his eyes: that man is still here somewhere.

I must look worried because a nurse with kind eyes turns to me and puts her hand on my shoulder and says, "He's dying honey."

Suddenly I realize that I never had the chance to tell him about my return to faith. I want to thank him for all his prayers and tell him that I am okay now (kind of—at least I'm trying to be ok now) so that he doesn't need to worry about me anymore. But the time for telling has already passed.

When he leaves us my grandmother and all five of their children are gathered around him. Before he passes, he is drifting in and out of consciousness.

At one point he wakes up, his eyes widen and he says, "Did you see him? Jesus was here. He says he loves us all. He loves the whole world. And he's wondering why it's so hard for us to remember to love. It's all about love, nothing else matters."

Grandpa is in a lot of pain; his breathing is labored and it quietly slows. Uncle Tim says the benediction and makes the sign of the cross on my grandfather's forehead. My mother tells me the moment before he dies he opens his eyes one last time and smiles like he has just been surprised by something wonderful. And then he is gone. It is a Sunday afternoon, the last day of the year of 1995, and I remember people whispering about the newspaper that came out that morning. The front page article announced the birth of a new star.

That night I fall asleep heavy with regret. He is gone and I didn't get to tell him about that night at college when I remembered God's love. How I couldn't believe that I had forgotten it for so long. I wanted to tell him that. I wanted to tell him that I believed in Jesus' message of love too.

I am asleep, but then awake in a sort of twilight, and I smell his pipe in the room. I sit up in my bed. A rush of wind blows through me and I feel a deep love fill my body.

"I know," I hear his voice in my mind. "I know," he says. And my sorrow turns to joy.

His funeral is bitter sweet. When I behold his body I know he is not here. I know he has risen. I know that my grandfather lives on in the spirit world and with me in my heart forever. And from time to time he visits me in my dreams and he helps me here on my path.

He reminds me often: It's all about love.

Who let you in the door?
Is it me?
You're looking for?

Oh my Hades is it you?
Have you come to claim your bride?
Take me back to the other side?

Yes I can see
The leaves are falling
And I am fading
Should we grab a cup of Joe before we hit the road?

Oh my Hades is it you?
Have you come to claim your bride?
Take me back to the other side?

Take me
All the way
Back into the pain
Take me
Ravish me
Like you did on that summer day
When you stole my life away
Oh my Hades, is it you?
Have you come to claim your bride?
Take me back to the other side?

One more thing,
Don't you ever forget
Who's your queen—

I am
I am
I am
Persephone

As I understand the virgin archetype, it is that aspect of the feminine, in man or in woman, that has the courage to Be and the flexibility to be always Becoming. Rooted in the instincts, the virgin has a loving relationship to the Great Earth Mother...they have been through the joy and the agony of the daily sorting of the seeds of their own feeling values in order to find out who they authentically are, and they continue to do so. They are strong enough to surrender to the penetration of the Spirit and to bring the fruit of that union into consciousness.

-Marion Woodman

Virgin

"We have been raised as objects for men!"

The large black student in my Women Studies class slams her hand on the table and I catch the fire in her eyes.

"Have we lost a sense of who we are without a man in our life to define us? Why are we still underpaid compared to men? Society values us for our looks and not our substance and certainly not our voice! The power of a woman's authentic voice terrifies the establishment."

The teacher redirects our focus to the articles in front of us. She tries to keep the passionate conversation grounded in the readings. We look at numerous psychological studies that show how a woman's self-esteem is shaped by the patriarchy's male gaze. We learn about the mistreatment of women around the world. About female castration. About how women are stoned after they are raped because the family believes her honor and the honor of her family has been destroyed by someone else's wrongful action. We behold She, the scapegoat.

As we gather around this table week after week, a heat grows in my belly.

"We need to reclaim our bodies," one woman says.

I love her strength and her passion.

"We are the ones who define ourselves, not men. We speak for ourselves, for our deepest feelings. And we use our anger to fight for justice!"

There's a knock at the door. The handle turns and I am horrified to see my father and mother standing there.

"We just got here and we were too excited to wait to see you!" my mother says.

"What class is this?" My father asks.

"Women Studies 301." My professor smiles.

"Well, I study women every night," my father laughs and leans in to plant one on my mother.

I feel the electricity rise in the room. I am not sure if they will put my father in his place or if I will die any second. Finally my parents wave goodbye and shut the door.

The strong black woman shakes her head says, "I'm so sorry honey. It's so good that you are here. You are going to learn how to be powerful."

~

"You can't listen to this music!" Leah confronts me in the commons. I look down at the Ani DiFranco CD in my hands.

"Why not?"

"Because it's demonic!" she insists.

"What? Why?"

"Women are to submit to the spiritual head of their husbands! These women hate men and God too."

"No they don't."

"Jessica, just ask the Young Life leaders. This music will pollute your mind and steal your soul."

~

I need to get away. My head hurts. My mother's sister, Pam invites me to her home in the country. She giggles a lot and lifts my serious mood. I spend my time curled up with hot mugs of coffee looking out the windows. I watch the clouds hang in the sky, the grass bend in the wind. Life is so simple here.

"I want to get my hair cut," I tell Pam.

"I know this great place," she says. She makes all the arrangements and drives me out to a hip salon.

"Cut it all off," I tell the woman.

"All of it?" She lifts my hair and measures it. "You've got about twelve inches here!"

"Give it to Locks of Love," I say. "Cut it as short as you can."

"Are you sure you don't want to work your way up to short?"

"Yes. I am sure. I just want it all to go away."

"Jess! You're so brave!" Pam squeals.

When she's finished she spins me around to the mirror. Pam gasps and claps.

"You are a brand new woman," the stylist says.

I look in the mirror and I know that it is true.

~

The girls in my Women's Studies class love my hair. The Young Life crowd, not so much.

"What have you done?" One of the male leaders frowns. "Your hair is the glory God has adorned you with!"

"It's just hair," I say. "It will grow back."

By now word has gotten around that I am listening to Ani Difranco and taking Women Studies classes.

"We're praying you don't lose your salvation," Leah says.

One of the exorcists joins her in the commons.

"Please come to church on Sunday. I'll pick you up."

The little mystic girl yearns for the spiritual connection. But the young woman in me who is trying to break free from the chains of patriarchy is nervous. I want both.

"Okay." I tug at my sleeves and bow my head.

~

The week is long and by Sunday I am yearning to rest in some heavenly peace, to pray and to hear some encouraging words. I wear my old jeans and grungy green sweater with holes around the thumbs. I sit in the front row and put my shaved head into my hands to pray.

The auditorium is packed with people and there is a restlessness in the air. I watch the preacher make his way to the stage, but before he gets there, someone steps up to one of the live microphones.

"I have a vision from the Lord!" the woman announces. "I was deep in prayer all week, and the Lord has told me that he wants his people to yell for His deliverance."

The Young Life leaders look at me knowingly.

"For such a time as this," the future TV evangelist whispers.

Everyone begins speaking in their prayer languages.

"My people, oh my people," the woman continues, "I want you to cry out to me as loud as you can!"

Shrilling voices echo off the white walls and pierce my ears. I hate the sound of the rising cacophony that inspires more than three hundred people to scream at the top of their lungs. I bury my face between my knees and vow never to return to this church.

~

Patriarchy has stolen much from me in my young life. But I've decided I'm not letting anyone steal my spirituality or my voice anymore.

~

"God is calling me elsewhere," I try to explain to the Young Life kids.

"Jessica! You are walking away from the Holy Spirit!"

I look away from the intensity of their gaze.

I don't know how to argue with them. But I am used to being an outcast and living with a community's unconscious shame. I will pick up my cross and carry on.

"I'm sorry," I say, "I'll still try to come to the Bible Studies."

But I can't bring myself to do it. They withdraw from me. When I see them around campus they look at me suspiciously. I have chosen to make peace with the demons they fear.

~

Professor Lunn distributes the Xeroxed papers and lays one in front of me. My eyes follow the little black line that moves from the words fundamentalism to liberalism.

"Christianity, Judaism, and Islam all contain various expressions that fall along this continuum."

I listen to the chalk moving upon the blackboard.

"Fundamentalists in each group demand a strict adherence to a literal interpretation of their sacred texts. There isn't a lot of room for debating meaning or various perspectives from other group members. There is a fear of thinking differently, a belief that any deviation from the held doctrine or creeds puts you outside of the group, and outside of the community's understanding of what is holy."

"Fundamentalists adhere to moral codes that restrict certain behaviors of their followers. Rules about dancing, eating, drinking, dress, and the diminished role of women are strictly enforced."

Light pulses in my head as he continues to speak. My heart begins to race. An ancient fog begins to lift. I can finally see the bird's eye view of the confusion I have grown up in: fundamentalism and the more conservative branch of evangelicalism. Now I see that if I walk away from this, I am not necessarily walking away from God. I put my finger on the beginning of the line and move it closer to mysticism. I want to go here. This is where I belong. This is the place where women are allowed to define God by their own experiences and in their own voices, in their own sacred bodies.

~

"I was so worried about the effects of fundamentalism on you."

My grandmother and I sit in rocking chairs on her screened in porch holding mugs of coffee. I sit in Grandpa's old chair.

"He prayed for you every day," she says.

"I know," I blink back the tears.

"Why do you think my mother raised me so differently than you raised her?"

"I could never figure it out," she says. "You know your mother hurt your grandfather very deeply when you were little," She pushes up her glasses and twirls the rings on her fingers.

"They were attending that charismatic church in New York and they came to visit us."

I remember this. Before we walked inside my mother sternly warned me not to tell my grandparents that I had been baptized a second time at our church when I was four.

"It would be like a slap in God's face," she said as she pointed her index finger at my nose. I didn't understand her fear or her anger. I still don't. But I want to.

"They carried their Bibles and highlighters with them around the house. They even took them into the bathrooms to read. They tried to convince your grandfather that he had gotten his faith all wrong. He was devastated."

"They didn't understand the value of the sacraments," she says and I think, *I don't understand either*. I look at my grandmother, the way her skin glows, the fire in her eyes. I know my journey entails so much more learning. That as we move forward on our healing paths, we also move backward in time and heal our ancestral lines. My path is forward, but it circles around the past, even as it spirals out into the unknown.

~

"Hey," he says.

"Hi,"

It's hard to look each other in the eyes. I nervously tug at the ends of my sleeves and he runs his fingers through his shaved head.

"You cut your hair," he says.

"Yeah," I say. "Kind of an 'I-hate-men' phase I guess."

He laughs. "I hope you don't hate me."

"Jason—how could I ever hate you?"

He takes me out to eat in downtown St. Louis. The mood lighting and wine helps us both relax. We giggle. We reminisce about the old times. Pearl Jam's song, "Elderly Woman Behind the Counter in a Small Town" comes on the radio.

"Wow," he says, "this song takes me back."

"Yeah," I agree. We both sigh.

"I miss you, Jess," he reaches his hands across the table.

"I miss you too, Jason." I put my hands inside of his.

Our clothes cling to our wet skin as we walk the hot sticky streets towards the river boats and the arch. We stand together watching the Mississippi waters crash upon the sidewalk.

"Remember when we rode that carriage through town for prom?" he says.

"Remember when I nearly passed out at the top of the arch?" I say.

"Jess," he runs his fingers through my short hair and looks at all the different parts of my face. He leans in and kisses me gently. "We can still make it work," he says.

I look down at my fingers.

"I don't know, Jason. I'm not the same girl anymore."

"I'm not the same boy either, Jess. But we're here after all these years. It's just what we've always wanted."

I watch a dusty crescent moon light up the river.

"I'm not sure what I want anymore," I say. "I've locked up my broken heart for safe keeping. I don't know if I can love anyone like I used to love you—not even you."

He pulls me into his chest.

"Oh, Jess. I'm so sorry for all the pain I caused."

I hug him back and sob.

"Sorry," I say as I pull away and wipe my face with my hands. "I snotted all over your shirt again."

We laugh.

"I'm never washing this one either."

~

I look at my parents with wide eyes, excited to share what I am learning in philosophy. I've made the honor roll at St. Olaf and I'm set to graduate cum laude next spring. I learned I'm really turned on by big ideas.

"Everything we know, according to Plato, is like shadows on the wall of the cave. The forms are the a-priori, and our journey out of the cave into the light of the sun is our movement towards consciousness—a greater vision of all the forms and how they fit together in the sacred symmetry of life!"

It's usually hard to get a word in edgewise in my family, but I want to be a person now. I want to have a place at the table. And a voice.

My father takes a bite of meatloaf. His face looks as red as the ketchup.

"It's amazing the kinds of degrees they offer you these days that let you all parade around like you're intelligent," He looks right through me. "In my days we had to learn the tough stuff of math and science. We earned our degrees with our hard work—not fanciful ideas."

I set my silverware on the table. I'm suddenly not hungry anymore.

"Philosophy and Women Studies!" He laughs and turns to my mother, "Can you believe they can actually major in that?"

"Dad, it's hard stuff too!" I protest. I'm so close to having a triple major in Philosophy, Religion and Psychology and a minor in Women's studies.

"I'll make this easy for you," my mother says. "I'm not financially supporting your education for those other majors. You choose one. But I'm only helping support you if it's the more practical major of Psychology."

I throw my napkin on the table and stand up.

"You are not excused," my father says.

I walk out the front door. Thor follows me, watching me with those compassionate eyes, whining and following at my heels. Together we lose ourselves in the canopy of trees awash in the colors of fall. I turn to Thor and ask him, "Why can't I explore ideas with them? What are they so afraid of?"

Thor jumps on my leg and lets his tongue hang out the side of his mouth and smiles the biggest most goofiest smile.

"Come here boy!"

I scratch him down and dash off through a pile of orange leaves. He chases after me making the leaves soar like falling stars around us.

~

I delve into Psychology by diagnosing myself with every disorder I study. I remember scheduling a meeting with the fairy godmotherly professor to confess to her that I may in fact be crazy, in case she had been wondering. Like a good religious confession I list off all my known disorders I have discovered about myself since we began the course.

Rather than expelling me from St. Olaf like I feared, she looks at me with tears in her eyes and reminds me what she told us at the beginning of the semester: that it was likely we would all do this, that all of these disorders are on the spectrum of normal human behavior.

It's also winter on the hill and I haven't seen a ray of sunshine in over twenty four days. I'm mildly relieved, but then I begin to wonder: where is that line between normal and crazy? And how close am I to crazy? I've unearthed another ancient taboo: intelligent intuitive women have long been labeled crazy.

My kind professor tells me how one day she was floating in a pool as a young girl and she asked herself that very thing.

"It's just not really a helpful question to spend your life on thoughts like that. It's not very joyful."

I watched her shake off the darkness and make a boundary for herself. I thought: *ah, we get to define our reality*. She just showed me how. I begin to see in my women's studies courses how our realities have been defined for us by a patriarchal society. How we are trained to look through the male gaze at ourselves and devalue our naturally feminine essence. How we have been perceived as crazy and hysterical, evil, witchy, all these things that society has collectively feared about the power of a woman. It is flipping my worldview on its head. I give myself permission to think through the forbidden thoughts. I take and eat the fruit of the Tree of Knowledge.

~

Now that I've had a taste of excelling, I pour all of my energy into school. I spend most of my free time curled over a book in my dorm room. My brother tries to pull me into their parties, but I usually stay in and read.

"I've already partied my life away," I tell them. "Now it's time to see what I'm made of."

Russ often comes up to my room to check on me. Sometimes we don't even talk. He makes all these goofy faces until I'm buckled over and begging him to stop so I can breathe again.

When I do steal time away, I sneak into the music department and lock myself in a practice room to play piano. I experiment playing and singing at the same time. Sometimes it works and my entire being lights up. I've never heard my real voice before. I think I can sing, but I don't know exactly how. I have so much fear about it. It feels completely vulnerable. I have to stay in the present moment, I have to practice relaxing and opening and allowing this river of inspiration to flow through me.

I sign up for a voice class with one of St. Olaf's world famous choir directors. When I sit in the bright room and listen to his lectures my entire body goes stiff. He's like a legend in our family—practically a demigod. I need to figure out how to be calm in that room and show him what I can do in the practice room so he can help me. I lock myself in a practice room and belt out sounds from other dimensions. I nail the high notes. I improvise. I begin to write my own music. I am able to access my gifts hidden under my anxious protective layers.

When it's my turn to sing in front of the class, I think I am ready. But my body resists. My muscles tighten as I enter the room. My hands begin to shake. My heart races.

The formidable choir director looks at me like he has x-ray vision and can see into my darkest past and call my name to perform.

I walk to the front of the room. The small class stares at me with wide eyes. They represent the ominous group of peers waiting to laugh at me, the potential trauma wheel waiting to turn again. I cannot let that happen again. I clear my throat and begin. But only air is coming out of my mouth. I push harder. I squeak out a few sounds. The director walks up behind me and puts his hands around the back of my neck.

"You need to relax," he says as he pushes me down into a forward fold and I stare at the worn corduroy circles around my knees. He shakes me like a rag doll and commands, "Relax! Relax! Relax!"

But I only stiffen and dread coming up again and seeing the smirks on the faces of my classmates. When I do, my peers look like ghosts. Several have their hands covering their mouths. They look as mortified as I feel.

"Sing!" he commands.

"Sing what?"

Please, dear God, just let me wake up in my bed now, I pray.

"Ahhhh...." He belts out a bold beautiful sound.

"Ah..." I belt out a pathetic one.

"Sing! Louder!"

"Ahh…" F-A-I-L.

"Sing, Jessica, sing from the depths of your being! Don't look at them. Sing from your gut! Sing out all your pain! Throw it against that wall!"

"Ahhhhhhhhhhhhhhhh!"

I don't know whose voice suddenly fills the room. No one else knew either. The director gasps. The class gasps.

"You see," he says to me knowingly. "I knew you had a voice in there."

Deep down I knew I had one in there too. I just wanted to learn how to coax it out with a little less public humiliation.

~

I seem to have this invisible code in my energetic field where people are drawn in and compelled, almost unconsciously, to repeat the pattern of abuse that was stamped on me so many years ago. This is one reason I prefer to be alone. I have too many hooks for people's unconscious projections. I hold something archetypally dangerous. I hold the feminine aspect of the human spirit that so many are struggling to love and respect within themselves. For ages we have all been taught to abuse and neglect or control and suppress feminine aspects of ourselves. Men are taught this as a basic right of passage and the code is enforced as boys are told: don't be a girl! Anything but that. Here she sits at the very bottom of the hierarchy, like Sophia thrown from heaven with her broken crown, lost in the underworld that has been denied or painted into a hell where some people go simply when they die. But I know it as a realm to which I intrinsically belong as a woman. I know it as a dark sanctuary, as a deeply incarnated place in the body, the place where pain is transformed into new life, the place where resurrection happens. And until I learn to have compassion on myself and my place in the universe, I continue being stuck in the death cycle of grief, attracting everyone else's unconscious pain to me as well. This is the realm of the Dark Mother. She who sees every suffering of each of her children. She who feels it in her body, for all of life springs from her. I am not yet aware of how to be a priestess of this realm. But someday I will be.

~

"That's really beautiful, but you can't play that in public," says Chris, my earthy friend.

"Why not," I am afraid to ask.

"Well—it's just….that…. the song's not finished yet."

He's right. But still, I've played for so many years by myself. I think it's about time I try to put my music out in the world. I am motivated to share my gifts with the world, but I have not yet disciplined the self-sabotager or discovered my taboo gifts of channeling and improvisation.

I go to the weekly open mic on campus. All the music majors are there playing their Bach, their pop music perfectly from their song sheets. When it's my turn, I sit at the piano and stare at the black and white keys. My body stiffens. My heart races. I can't even remember what the first note is. I make something up. Hit a few wrong notes. Try to sing, but instantly forget the words. I mumble something and leave the stage as fast as I can. I decide being on stage is the most awful place in the entire world.

~

I don't know how to integrate my women's studies with my experiences of God's love. The telos of psychology leads me to a scientific world. But my soul hungers for colorful symbols and stories not cold facts. For art, not numbers. I'm made different. Differences ought to be celebrated not feared.

My greatest joy comes in writing, especially theological and philosophical papers. I love seeing the big picture and understanding the ideas that have shaped human history. I toy with the idea of becoming a counselor, but I haven't yet done my own deep work to know how I might truly help others. And I don't love myself enough yet to truly love another.

~

A beautiful, tall graceful woman sits in front of me at St. John's Lutheran Church in Northfield, Minnesota. After the service my grandmother introduces me to St. Olaf's new campus pastor. When Jennifer smiles at me I stand a little taller and my pounding heart quiets within. I recognize something of myself in her. She meets me on campus for coffee. We talk about the meaning of life, religion,

God, philosophy, love. I babysit her dog. She helps me make sense of my past and mentors me through valleys along the way during my time on the hill. She inspires me to consider the path of the pastor.

Years later, I discover how many people Jennifer inspired when I sat in Boe Chapel with hundreds mourning her death. Her husband and two children sit across the aisle from me. We have no theological answers to cancer; we have practical desires for a clean environment. We cling to the hope she preached. A hope in the love that embodies us while we are here. A love that is even stronger than death, and a love that lives beyond the grave.

The night she passes away, she appears to me in a dream. She confirms that I am deeply connected to the spiritual realms.

~

In May of 1998 I graduate with honors from St. Olaf College. My grandmother takes me out and buys me a beautiful dress. She tells waitresses, salesmen, even the stranger on the elevator how proud she is of me. I'm not used to this. She gives me what my parents, for whatever reason, could not. She mirrors something within me, something I almost lost many, many times.

After graduation, I sit on her couch and watch her beam at me from across the room. I realize that I have hungered for someone else's approval my whole life. Today, I know I have earned not only someone else's approval, but also my own. The person within my skin is different—confident, capable, intelligent, more self-reliant. I see myself as so much more than the bad rebellious girl now. I feel it in my bones, a sense of goodness knit in my innermost being, the joy of second chances, of hope and love. I wish for all beings to experience this grace. I will spend years moving into this temple of goodness and building a new foundation for myself. And the rebellious girl in me will not let me forget about her either. Eventually I will need to reconcile all parts of myself. We are all made of shadows and light. Any pretending otherwise is like building your house upon the sand; it will not stand when the storms come.

~

"Why won't you talk to me, Emily?"

My sister rarely makes eye contact and when she does she throws daggers.

I press, "Why do you hate me so much?"

"Because you ruined our family!" She unloads on me. "And my childhood!"

"Oh, Emily—I'm so sorry."

"I'm working on forgiving you—but I'm not ready yet."

One night I take her out for a drive. I tell her my story, how my life fell apart after we moved to Blytheville. How I didn't know how to deal with the pain. How Mom and Dad never knew—or asked. We talk about how none of us were raised to talk about our feelings. In fact there seemed to be a lot of influences on all of us to shut down our connection to our feelings and our bodies in order to survive. We had no way to navigate these storms, we did what was passed down to us through the generations or through the presence of the military in our lives: repress, silence, ignore. These are the consequences of corrupted power.

Emily's face turns white.

"I think I'm going to be sick," she says. "All this time, I blamed you. I had no idea what was really going on!"

She reaches over and hugs me. She tells me how she survived those years. Her eating disorder. Her ghostly anxiety. How she wrestled with things she couldn't see, but felt in her gut.

~

I return to St. Louis for the summer to help my parents pack and move to Asheville, North Carolina, my father's next military post. My father, now a Lieutenant Colonel, will serve as the co-commander of the Federal Building in Asheville where the United States houses the National Climatic Data Center—the world's largest active archive of weather data.

We are packing up the last boxes. My parents sell the picture of the dead Indian and his horse. They are growing too. My mother's good friend has a daughter that comes out of the closet.

"I hate how hard it is for the people to accept her at church," my mother says. "I mean, we're all God's children for Pete's sake."

"I know," I smile.

I wonder if she even remembers her old words. It doesn't really matter to me if she does. None of us can be caged in anything too small for our souls for long. Our true nature will eventually find a way to shine as bright as the stars.

My father is redecorating the house. He gets weepy at dinner prayers and gives me lots of big hugs. He is warmer now, more relaxed, more in touch with his emotions.

Rather than pinning one another to our mistakes, we would do better to support our ongoing growth. Somehow it has become taboo to see our inconsistencies as bad—when to be alive is to be constantly changing and evolving. Sure we stand on deep pillars of truth, but we also are also constantly expanding into the unknown too. This is the dance of the yin and the yang. The masculine contracts and protects the wisdom we have birthed, and the yin, the feminine, continues to creatively move into the unknown. We are never the same person on any given day.

~

Jason and I happen to be in St. Louis at the same time. I walk over to his house late one night to see him before we move. I am mindful of the longing in my chest that grows with every step. I miss his green eyes, the way he can see all the different girls in me. How he is one of the few friends that grew up with me. My mind returns to the river, to his plea to be together. Suddenly my heart is filled with joy. *I will tell him yes*, I think. I will marry Jason and we will be together forever. My walk turns into a run.

I find him holding a pile of rocks in his hand, tossing them one by one into the concrete sidewalk to see how many times they'll bounce. Shadows loom over his face in the dark evening.

"Well, look who it is," he says as I approach him. His eyes are wild tonight.

"Gosh, I've missed you," I say walking closer to him. He pulls his body away and tosses another rock.

"How ya been, Jess?" the sound of his voice travels in the opposite direction.

"Really good," I say, "for the first time in a long time, I am really well."

"Me too," he says.

"That's great," I look down at my toes sticking out of my Birkenstock sandals.

"I just got back from the going away party they threw for my Mom at church," I fill the heavy silence.

"I can't believe you even go to church," he says.

"Why?"

"Because God is a figment of people's imaginations."

"What if our imaginations are real?"

Jason laughs. We're getting nowhere fast. I grab his arm and turn his body towards me. We look closely at each other's faces, the nuances time has decorated upon us.

"I want to give it another try, Jason. I want us to work out. Forever this time."

I lean in to kiss him, but he pulls away from me.

"Jess—it's over. I found someone. She's the one."

His smile breaks the last hope I still have for us. His eyes have changed. They are hard and distant now. I know it is true. I know it is really over between us.

"Gosh Jason, that's great! I wish you all the best."

I drag myself home in the descending fog, not sure where my life will go from here.

~

Indian artifacts found in the western hills of North Carolina belonging to the Cherokee tribe are more than 11,000 years old. In 1540 Hernando DeSoto leads an expedition here bringing the first European people and infecting most of the Indian population with smallpox.

~

Six months later a card arrives at our new home in Asheville from Jason's mother. Inside Mom finds a web address.

"Oh look! Jessica!" She calls me into the computer room. "Jason got married! Look at all these adorable pictures!"

But I can't even look at the screen. I back out of the room and run down the basement stairs. I bury my face into a pillow and do the ugly cry.

~

In 1830 Congress passes the Indian Removal Act. The army sends troops who surround the Cherokees with bayonets. A few hundred escape to the hills. The others are driven from their homeland in the Blue Ridge Mountains, across the plains. Many die on the dusty roads to Oklahoma upon the Trail of Tears.

~

I spend the next year in Asheville working with two clients doing social work. In the mornings I meet with a young woman, Franny who had a baby at sixteen and has been diagnosed with borderline personality disorder. The young man, Matthew, lives with cerebral palsy and mild mental retardation. I take both clients out of their home and teach them life skills that I am learning too. We learn together. We drive on the enchanting Blue Ridge Parkway together. We grab coffees, lunches. We work on keeping calendars, doing volunteer work, exercising, and showing appropriate social behavior.

The preachers on the radio are teaching me that Christianity is all about thinking the right things. When I work with Matthew I try to teach him how to think about things the right way as I am instructed to do. I feel like I am becoming more like my father, like I am accessing his energy (even unconsciously) as I move into the world as an adult. But Matthew just won't think the right way about a lot of things, his brain just doesn't work like that. I begin to worry; I begin to project the ancient theological struggles onto him—*how can someone be saved if they can't think the right things?!* I have so much Christian deconstruction work to do. Isn't this why some churches don't allow children to have the bread and the wine until they rationally understand (in some way) the mystery of the Eucharist? After working with Matthew I begin to wonder: *what if spirituality isn't about thinking the right thoughts? What if thoughts are neither right nor wrong? What if it doesn't matter whether someone is sprinkled or dunked, or says the sinner's prayer? What if God's love is big enough for everyone, even for people who don't think the right way?*

These are rebellious thoughts that make me feel alive.

~

The one lane road is backed up for miles. I stick my head out the window to see what has everyone moving so slowly. The night is growing and I'm starving for dinner. I inch my way forward and soon see a painful situation.

One goose is standing by another goose who has been hit by a car. The goose friend is trying to help the other goose get up, but the other goose is not going anywhere. Half of its body is flat in the road, but it's not dead yet and it's waving its other wing at her friend. I feel compelled to do something to stop the bird's pain.

I'm watching the cars drive carefully around the pitiful scene and I start praying that someone will just put that bird out of its misery! It seems I am not able to witness pain yet (in myself or in the world) with compassion. I just want to make the pain to go away. But the true metabolizer of pain is compassionate witnessing. As I get closer and closer I realize it has to be me. *Oh. Dear. God.* I take a deep breath. I think I am being courageous. I am very careful to avoid the goose's friend. I slowly drive over the suffering half squished bird. Ug. The way it feels under my tires nearly kills me. But, this is the worst part. I do not kill it! I only made it suffer even more! Suddenly everyone who is stuck in traffic here is shooting daggers at me. *What have I done?* I watch the guy in the pickup truck behind me through my rear view mirror as he gets out of his vehicle and moves the poor suffering bird to the side of the road where, oh sweet Jesus, it continues to flap its wing!

It's official: I am the worst person on the planet.

I sob all the way home. I can hardly see out the windshield through my tears. I run through our front door.

"Oh my God! Jessica! What happened?"

I can't get any words out. Just these horrible moans. My mother runs to my side and pushes the hair back from my face.

"David! David! Come quick!"

"Breathe, Jessica, just breathe," she says.

"The goose!" I blubber.

"The what?" my father says.

"The goose! Oh God. I….ran… over…. the goose!"

"Wait. You hit a goose?" My father relaxes.

"Yes, but...." The moaning continues. "I didn't.... kill it!" My Mom tries to hide her smile.

"And...it's friend—oh God... that poor goose's friend..."

My parents cover up their faces with their hands. I wipe snot all over my arm.

"All those people! Oh, God. I'll never be able to show my face in town again!"

They give up.

"Goose Killer!" They wipe the tears from their eyes.

"But, I didn't kill it!"

My parents think this whole situation is hilarious. They buckle over. I lighten up a little. They get me laughing too. Because what are we taught to do with our deepest pain? We deny it. We ignore it. We laugh at it. How else would we go on? We would have to learn how to move through it. And that is the most dangerous and rewarding journey the soul can take.

~

Over the years, I have come to realize that the greatest trap in our life is not success, popularity, or power, but self-rejection. Success, popularity, and power can indeed present a great temptation, but their seductive quality often comes from the way they are part of the much larger temptation to self-rejection. When we have come to believe in the voices that call us worthless and unlovable, then success, popularity, and power are easily perceived as attractive solutions. The real trap, however, is self-rejection. As soon as someone accuses me or criticizes me, as soon as I am rejected, left alone, or abandoned, I find myself thinking, "Well, that proves once again that I am a nobody." ... [My dark side says,] I am no good... I deserve to be pushed aside, forgotten, rejected, and abandoned. Self-rejection is the greatest enemy of the spiritual life because it contradicts the sacred voice that calls us the "Beloved." Being the Beloved constitutes the core truth of our existence."

-Henri J.M. Nouwen

I have a dream. Matthew is walking towards a man in the sunset. It takes me a few moments to recognize the man is Jesus. Matthew is smiling as he walks closer and closer to Jesus. Then, I see the goose! Jesus is holding the goose in his hands! He releases it into the air and it comes flying towards me! My depression immediately lifts as the dream assures me that Matthew and the goose are just fine. Their lives and their suffering are known by forces beyond me, and they are deeply, deeply loved.

~

In the afternoons I work as an afterschool counselor for the Boys and Girls Club of America in downtown Asheville. Miss Daisy Mae leads us in devotions before we begin.

"Jessica—" her teeth are as white as snow, her skin as black as night, "You know there ain't nothin' but Jesus. No Jesus and. Just Jesus. She stands as tall as I do at six feet.

"People always be sayin' they like Jesus, but they got too many distractions in their life to make him a priority!"

She throws her head back and cackles at the absurdity.

At Christmas time we stand outside of K-Mart shaking in our coats and mittens, ringing bells and collecting coins. I meditate on the K-Mart sign and remember our K-Mart car and my old shame of being poor. I ring my bell louder and shake off those old taboos.

"Jessica—can you believe Paul, ridin' on his donkey, goin' to kill all of Jesus' friends, thinkin' he can stop God? God done knocked him off his horse, Jessica!" She buckles over in laughter. "Ain't nothing stopping God, Jessica—everyone gonna fall off their donkey if they even try!"

I slap my knees and clutch my stomach laughing with Miss Daisy Mae and her hilarious love of God.

"Jessica—if you become a mass murderer—I won't even be surprised."

"Daisy! What are you talking about?"

"Jessica—we all just humans. Each one of us is capable of doing awful things. I ain't gonna be surprised about none of your sins, ever," she says. "No matter what we do—God loves us anyways, and I gonna always love you no matter what."

"Jessica—all you need to do is love kids and pay them mind. That's all they need. Just Jesus' love, and you so good at givin' them Jesus."

~

Years later I learn all about the Black Madonna. Reflecting on my past I see that Daisy Mae was my Black Madonna. She taught me how to relate to children and how to trust my intuition as I practiced and honed my spirituality. She steered me away from the dangerous black and white certainties in fundamentalist Christianity and invited me to laugh instead at the absurdities with her, to extend love and grace to everyone without being a doormat.

I work to make her proud. I work to show the kids unconditional love. I set up a reward system with the kids and we play games and learn Bible stories. The ones that used to walk in here with heavy eyes and slumped over shoulders begin to stand a little taller. Their faces beam a little brighter. At the end of the year when it's time for me to go, crowds of kids circle around me, hugging me and begging me to stay.

~

I teach Sunday school at the church I attend with my parents. This time we are members of the Methodist Church. I sing backup with my mother and sister in the worship band she created. I am trying to integrate everything that I am learning and that I have experienced. But I am growing more confused. Living with my parents, I become enmeshed in their conservative religion again and I easily lose touch with my body and my instincts. I've pretty much shut down my sexuality and even my mannerisms are more masculine. It's hard to differentiate myself and my spirituality at home. I gain ten pounds. My face breaks out. There is a fog that enters my body every time I am in their house. I forget who I am and who I am supposed to be. I go unconscious. But I do want to mend our relationship.

My parents and the religious leaders all give me all sorts of different advice. I don't know who to trust anymore. I read through the whole Bible again, but I don't understand it. There are so many confusing passages within these pages. And how can I be a Christian if I find sections of "God's Word" particularly troubling? I don't want to give up on God again, but I can't find the path to growth. I don't hear teachers that can open up the texts. I hear a lot of suspicious overconfidence. I hear a lot of fear. I hear a lot of justification for violence in a gospel that clearly teaches peace. I hear a lot of critiques about women like me.

~

I look into a few schools. I fill out some applications. A letter arrives in the mail one day: I am accepted to Fuller Theological Seminary in Pasadena, California in the fall of 1999.

"There is no way you are going," my father says. "You are too young, too naïve and you'll never make it out in California all by yourself!"

His face is red. I curl up in a ball on the floor and cry like I did when the camp director yelled at me.

"Look at you!" My father continues and I back myself into my closet. "You are pathetic. You think you can make it in the world all by yourself? You're a slobbering mess."

He walks out of my room, slams the door and leaves me in pieces on the floor. I think I have to learn how to not be weak. But then I am confused because I'm trying to follow God's way of humility and the New Testament talks about Christ's power being perfected in weakness. I know what it feels like to be dominated, and I don't want to do that to others. But my father's world seems to be telling me that if I ever want to make it in life then I'd better learn fast how to dominate and control so I'm not the one dominated and controlled. I know I must find another way to live.

~

I save up all my money and I make up my mind that I am going to California. Daisy Mae thinks I should go too. But in the middle of summer, something happens that changes those plans.

"Do you accept Jesus Christ as your Lord and Savior?"

The nervous man stutters.

"Yes, yes, don't worry, I'm a Christian. Can you please just jump my car?"

"What kind of Christian are you? You know there lots of 'em them out there that ain't even saved. You say it first—Jesus Christ is my Lord and Savior."

I repeat his words as quickly as possible so we can get working on my dead car. The man's hands are shaking. He crosses the cables. I turn the key in the ignition and sparks fly out of the engine.

"Goddammit!" he says as he switches the cables. I turn the key again, but nothing happens.

It's crystal clear: this kind of Christianity will not serve as a vehicle for my soul. And I must learn how to make better boundaries.

~

"It must be God's will," my father says at the dinner table that night.

"You'll have to give us the money you have saved up to fix the car. God doesn't want you to go, Jessica—can't you see that?"

I write my father a check and clear out most of the money in my bank account. That was my plane ticket out of here.

~

In the next week two cards arrive in the mail. I open the one from Ema first. She writes:

> *Jess, I believe in you. You will rise like a phoenix out of these ashes. Follow your dream, no matter what! I love you!*
>
> *Always, Ema*

The second letter is from my Grandma:

> *Dearest Jessica, I believe God is calling you to the seminary. I have already contacted the associate pastor your grandfather used to work with and his wife—you remember the Jahnkes? They are wonderful people. They would love for you to live with them in Claremont while you get your feet on the ground at Fuller.*
>
> *Love, Gma*

Inside her letter is a check that covers the cost of repairs for the car. I am learning that when you follow the dream in your heart the universe conspires to give you just the help you need.

~

The land beneath me was taken from the Native people. Missionaries from the south converted and enslaved the Indians, killed the resisters, and infected the rest with small pox and other diseases. Humanity carries so much baggage. Too much. Still, I come to search for the gold among the rubble.

~

I begin the work of reconnecting with my childhood mystic and cultivating compassion upon the nerd who loved Jesus that I had left for dead. All these girls belong. They are connected to my ancestors and the spiritual legacy in our family line. My energy is heavy, like carrying around a new born baby that needs lots of attention. It feels like I am just beginning to live a real life and not a sealed-off fantasy. It's painful. But I am finally learning how to witness the pain that once was unbearable.

> *Hope is the thing with feathers that perches in the soul*
> *-Emily Dickinson*

I am on a plane, flying west into an unknown future. I am on my way to seminary and adulthood. I am terrified. I do not yet know who I am, but I am beginning to see. Unsure of where I will land, I am finally brave enough to leave the nest and spread my wings.

The creation of the world begins with a thought
Spoken
Day after day
Year after year
Images conceived
Squeezed into small words
Like old jeans
That don't fit after the babies come
Like tiny embers
That keep the whole house warm
A reality
Unseen
Unmeasured by mathematical equations
Or scientific studies
I simply am
I am who I say that I am
And I still am
Giving birth to myself.

Jesus said, 'If you bring forth what is within you, what you have will save you. If you do not have that within you, what you do not have within you will kill you.'

-The Gospel of Thomas

Mother

The airplane shudders with turbulence. The lights flicker on and off as the plane begins to nosedive. The door to the cockpit flies open and I can see some crazed man has taken over the plane. Several passengers rush forward and jump him as they wrestle for control of the plane. But it's too late. The end is near. I try to pray but all I can do is scream as we descend into the earth.

~

A terrorist organization steals me out of my bed at night. I am brought to a large warehouse where I witness factions of our government killing hundreds of people. My hands and feet are bound. I am squirming on the floor, crying and pleading for my life. On my stomach is an egg. This egg is my child, it is also somehow the egg of Mary Magdalene for it contains the lost secrets of the sacred feminine.

A cool headed detective (who looks like Kevin Bacon) finds me in the warehouse. He unties me and helps me escape the bloody scene. We are speeding away in his car and I notice the egg has cracked. I am worried that the embryo is too young to survive. He assures me that she can still survive. I do not want this man to leave me for I know that the terrorists are tracking me and they will find me again, but he must go. He takes me to my mother's house. I feel safe here and I leave my egg in the kitchen with my belongings while I take a shower. While I am away, my mother destroys the egg. She doesn't mean to. She's just trying to keep everything clean. And life is very messy.

~

I am looking up at the sky and I see millions of strange alien space craft invading our planet. Everyone in the world is watching the sky because this event is going to change reality as we know it. These alien machines have powers like none we have ever seen before. In an instant we all become enslaved. Creatures in space like suits infiltrate my home and point guns at me and my children. Behind me is a book with pictures of Christ on the cross. He is near us and he is communicating an important message through sign language to all of his followers: stay awake, the end is near.

~

There is a lot of blood on the white sheets wrapped around a woman's dead body. I can see her delicate hands and feet poking out the edges. Several men are hauling her body through the city trying to hide it. I follow them. I will not let them get away with this. They are in broad daylight and laughing as they parade her dead body around. I think they will be caught for sure, but the people on the streets drink their coffee, laugh, and walk their dogs. No one seems to notice the dead woman in their midst. Or if they do, they don't care. The men who are carrying her body around realize they are safe in public. No one cares about the dead Goddess. They turn to me and smirk. I watch them throw her body in a dumpster and laugh.

~

Someone is in my house. I hear the wood floors creaking. I hear the doors opening. I slide out of my bed and tip toe down the hallway. I freeze when I see the shadowy figure standing in my kitchen. He is nearly 8 feet tall. His eyes look demonic and they glow in the dark. He holds a long sharp blade in the air. At my feet a long vibrant green snake begins to coil around my leg. My body is suddenly frozen. I cannot move or get the scream to come out of my mouth.

~

"Jessica, Jessica!"

My husband shakes me awake. We have been married for almost three years now. At first I think he is going to be the one to finally save me from all the troubles of my childhood. He's smart and willing to deconstruct toxic Christianity with me. But the academic rigors of deconstruction turn out to be endless and higher education solidifies his heady rationality and his suspicion towards women's intuitions and my creative soul suffers. I have to keep reminding myself that I am responsible for carrying my dreams into the world. The only problem is that my dreams have become so terrifying not only to me, but also to my husband.

"Shhhh. It's okay. You had another nightmare.

The nightmares are waking us up several times a week. The intensity of them is steadily increasing. Currently they feel more real than the rest of my life. My eyes are regularly bloodshot and my face is dark. Everything is supposed to be okay now. I have been "clean" for about eight years. I have graduated from seminary. I am working as a Youth and Children's Minister in the Episcopal Church. My dashing brilliant husband has started his PhD program in religion and is studying with the Jesuits. Everything on the outside of my life is stable, but my Saturn is returning, my unconscious is erupting. And the underworld is calling.

~

When my ex-husband started studying with the Jesuits in Chicago, I started seeing tall reptilian creatures in my apartment at night who were very interested in my son. When I started working at a big Episcopal church in one of the wealthiest towns in the country, it was little grey aliens who surrounded our beds while we slept until I had the house blessed by a priest. About this same time I became aware of one of the most widely verified UFO sightings while I was working out at the gym. Five on-duty police officers and many others confirmed the sighting of a large triangle craft on their radios. I had just started working at a big prestigious church and was running on a treadmill when I saw the pictures of the flight pattern. I nearly fell down when I saw streets I recognized. The craft flew right by my parent's house near Scott Air Force Base. Sufjan Stevens wrote a beautiful song about this incident. I start to put the pieces of the puzzle together. I have a sense that my story fits into something much more mysterious than I can possibly comprehend.

~

Seminary teaches me to be historical and logical. Even as it frees me from fundamentalism, I experience this learning as another domination of my body and my instincts as I see how the game of logic can run right over things we know in our bones and things we feel in our hearts. My women's studies wisdom feels far away from this world. I don't know how to make them connect. One professor offers me a tip: it's about learning to play the game. Learning to act a part. I hear: you have to sell out to make it. You have to hide your true self. There is no place for the Maiden or the Goddess in this world. My inner rebel says: no way. I'm not about to abandon myself now.

It becomes harder for me to let the Biblical text speak without checking the Hebrew and Greek. I don't enjoy living my faith out in this particularly logical way. I'm not well suited for it either with my visions and creativity, even though I maintain high honors in my undergraduate and graduate studies. I don't know it at the time, but I eventually learn I am more suited for the ancient role of an oracle priestess, but that sacred path has been blocked for ages with taboos of witchcraft and all the social ostracization that goes with being an intuitive woman. In the 1970s women were finally allowed into the priesthood (in some congregations) so long as they performed the role according to patriarchy's logic and worshiped a male God.

Many of my images of God (or false gods) die at seminary. I'm glad they do, because for the divine to be truly alive, many of our images will have to break. New wine requires new wineskins. What dies is the white bearded, disappointed, zealous, jealous, fear mongering God. I'm left with a puddle of unknowing awaiting the lotus' bloom. This is what so many warned me of: they will destroy your faith at seminary. Seminary (or any spiritual path) is a place to unveil the illusions we have attributed with our conceptions of God. Yes it's uncomfortable when the veils part and we are left face to face with an incomprehensible mystery. But what is the spiritual path all about if not that? Ignorance is bliss only for a little while. Ongoing bliss requires change and growth, birth, death, resurrections, mysteries, and surprises. Too many liturgies lack the creative animating spirit that is the force of life itself. Because the Church lacks a healthy relationship with the divine feminine—the entire other half of God.

The remaining weeds of my early fundamentalism are finally pulled up and I am free from those who would quote scripture at me to try and control me. I am free from the power of others who say they know what God's plan is for my life. I am free from the heavy guilt that an angry old man up in heaven is always watching over my shoulder, looking down on me and judging me in a way that feels like a disapproving father, or like other men who perceive me as weak and weird or just a piece of meat for their entertainment. I am free from the pressures to talk to and convert everyone I meet—free from the 'dominate and control' programs that are not inherently Christian, not found in Jesus' teachings, but have somehow have invaded much of our modern day spirituality like a cancer. Studying theology and the strange marriage of colonialism and Christianity has helped me dissolve many illusions. But still, my spiritual life has become like one long Good Friday.

I have a few inklings of new life, like those first flutters of a growing baby in the womb. I hold onto these mystical encounters. I remember what my grandfather said before he died: It's all about love. This makes so much sense. But I have to get that love back inside my skin. I need less logic, and more embodied experience. I have to get this faith from my head down to my toes. Peering down the vast and dark terrain where my muscles are stiff and jittery, where shame and deep roots of sorrow hide—and passion, so much passion. There has to be a spiritual pathway to this embodiment. And I am going to find it.

~

One morning after another episode of especially gruesome night terrors, I pick up the phone and call the Jung Center in Evanston, Illinois. I studied Carl Jung a little in college and after seminary and I find his work is intriguing. I am drawn to the idea that dreams could be interpreted as living symbols, keys to unlock blocked energy and link us back to our Source and our true self. Jung's work challenged many 'civilized' people to reconnect with their wildness. He revived an ancient understanding of dreams, one that goes all the way back to Bible times and ancient Egypt. Someday I was going to get around to learning all about it. I guess that day is going to be today.

"Thank you," I say as I scribble down the phone number of a Jungian Analyst in my area, who also happens to be an Episcopal priest.

~

It's a fall day when I lift the latch on the metal gate and descend the concrete steps behind my analyst's house. I feel like a nervous initiate, consciously descending into my own personal hell. A cold wind whips my hair into the sky where the sun lights up the orange and red leaves and swirls them into the blue air.

The room where we meet is like a cave. It's warm and dark. The walls are lined with books. The lower shelves are filled with plastic toys: wizards, animals, swords, bones. There is a large tray filled with sand in the room. And a piano in the corner. My body relaxes. I wonder if this is how men feel before they enter a woman's body.

A metallic sign hangs at the entryway that reads: bidden or not bidden, God is present. This is reassuring. I need someone who understands the complexity of religion and mystical encounters—someone who won't prescribe me a large dose of lithium and send me off to the loony bin.

Steve is in his late forties, maybe early fifties. His hair is gray but his face is young. He has kind brown eyes that tend to light up with the joy of a child. When this happens I feel a flash of recognition and I am connected to my own little girl who once new that joy too. I have had two or three sessions before he finds the secret door that has been locked for years and marked: Never Open Again.

"Can you tell me about your eighth grade year?"

Those words make me feel like I'm being pulled into an annihilating black hole. I am twenty seven years old and I have still never told a professional what happened to me in the eighth grade. I open my mouth like a grave. My stomach is filled with ashes and bones. My head seems to detach from my body and looms near the ceiling somewhere like it is waiting to witness the destruction of earth. The ground is vibrating beneath my feet. I swear all of the lamps are flickering. And the furniture seems to be dancing around the room. Nothing is stable. Nothing but Steve. I keep my eyes on his kind face to guide me through this shamanic releasing.

"I was the new girl in a small southern town…"

I can hardly breathe. I think I might throw up all over myself. The air around me seems to be sparkling. My eyes are sharp. My tongue is dry. I don't know how I form the words. It's a labor. I take deep breaths and push the sound out of my body. I deliver the story from my body into the room and into his witnessing presence. I am afraid to look at him. When I do I am surprised to find his face wet with tears.

"That is one of the worst stories I have ever heard, Jessica—and trust me, I have heard a lot in here."

I can't believe he's crying. He's not looking at me with pity or judgment. His body is not stiff and his eyes are not hard. I am not used to being gazed upon like that. My body softens.

"You know it was rape, Jessica. That was rape."

"Well, I didn't really say no."

"Jessica, he was a sexual predator!"

"But I went along willingly!"

"You were a child! You were just a child, Jessica."

Then the water burst from the rock and years of repressed sorrow floods out of my body.

~

After I tell Steve my story, my dreams shift.

Christian Roberts lies on top of me, trapping me inside a school bus—trapping me inside my childhood. I can't find my voice to tell him to stop. Night after night he continues to appear, luring me into caves, dark houses, and graveyards. He is the one who has everything: all the power, all the friends, he even has my piano in his living room! He is charming and knows exactly what to say. But I am paralyzed by my own fear. I cannot move in my dreams or speak or stand up to him.

"It appears that your dreams are telling you that your work is to make boundaries in your life and express yourself more," Steve lifts his eyebrows and waits for my response.

I want to slide out of my chair and onto the floor. I tell him about all my troubles at work. About groups of women I experience as bullying, gossiping, just like in high school and I am struggling to find the right way to resolve these tensions. I have long since learned that just because people are in church, does not mean they are nice. Often people use the church to hide their shadows. And child sexual predators tend to target the church because there's usually a ton of kids around and people who are always looking for volunteers to work with them. Congregations can also be a little naïve when it comes to the reality that every community experiences sexual violence regardless of race, class, gender, or denomination. At a place that offers healing to the public, there's still so much silence, so many codes of not talking about it.

"They are like Christian," I say. "They are charming and they talk really fast and suddenly I'm all buttered up and eaten alive."

"So this pattern has been going on for quite a while then," he says calmly.

"Oh my God," my mind hurts. "Yes." I say. "Yes. It's like in so many ways, the rape keeps happening over and over again. People can be so mean and I don't know why I am continually targeted!"

"Maybe you give people permission—even unconsciously—to treat you poorly."

It's hard hear this, but it was true.

"Great, so it all boils down to being my fault after all."

I can hear those ancient self-destructive tapes begin to play: *Stupid girl. Stupid idiot! Why can't you figure this out already? Because you'll never figure it out. Never!*

"Maybe because I'm stupid and I deserve it," I mumble.

"Exactly," he jests. And then he gently says, "Jessica—you carry so much self-hatred towards yourself. You are lacking the abilities to be a good enough mother to yourself."

I look straight into his eyes. He is right.

"When you feel this way about yourself, it gives others permission to dump their unconscious hatred on you."

"Why can't people just be nice?" I moan.

"We need to work on building up your ego," he says.

"But I thought egos were bad?"

"If you are only a big ego who thinks you are God then yes, that can be bad. But if you have no ego than it is impossible to incarnate and birth the numinous energies," he explains. I must look confused because he continues to explain.

"The ego is essential, according to Jungian theory, because it holds the "I" in us together. It helps us negotiate healthy boundaries in the world. Jung believed that in order for the growth of an individual to happen, one needs to push up against boundaries."

Without sacred boundaries, an individual's sovereignty is lost. Their space is invaded by a culture that shrugs at rape as humanity is largely enslaved and forced to participate in the destruction of the earth. Then the human spirit, or the soul, isn't able to fully incarnate the body and the world. It becomes overwhelmed with numinous god-like energies—victimized by them or possessed by them. Our goal is to claim our sovereignty so that we can hold and embody our divine potential in the world—and this is the key—while maintaining a meaningful link—a golden thread—with Source. This is what frees the soul and our planet.

Steve returns to his bookshelf and pulls out Edward Edinger's book, *Ego and Archetype* and shows me a diagram.

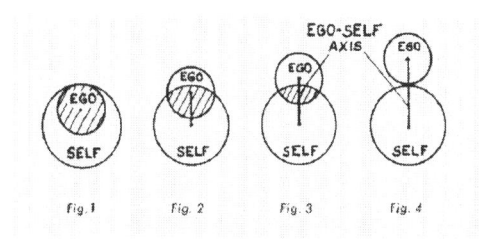

Edinger, E. F. (1992)

"Most of our modern neuroses arise because people have lost a meaningful connection to the numinous or the higher spiritual energies. You have very strong connections to those energies, Jessica."

The darkness also has its gifts. Rape victims and trauma survivors often have a deeper understanding of the inner dimensions, intuitive skills, channeling abilities, and keen insight to other's patterns of suffering—and the paths to healing. The challenge is to incarnate those gifts in a world that feels unsafe.

"So when I had those profound mystical experiences as a child and in college it was like I was here," I point at figure one.

"I believe," Steve says slowly, "That you have experienced so many traumas in your younger years that it was the energies of the Self that held you and protected your inviolable spirit against the unbearable pain. This is very necessary and helpful. But when you are strong enough to grow, the energies of the Self can turn dark and keep you enclosed because there is a force within you that is trying to protect you from being harmed like you were before. This may be at the roots of your depression. You have this incredible creative energy, but you're having trouble bringing it into the world."

"Because I'm terrified of repeating eighth grade," I say. "I'm terrified of being publically humiliated."

"So your next challenge is to step out into the world a bit and face that fear. Put your voice and energy out there and prove your fear wrong."

I feel my stomach lurch. I'm not so sure I can do that.

"So God has a dark side?"

"What do you think?"

"Well that certainly explains most of the Old Testament fire and brimstone thing," I say.

Steve laughs.

"So basically in order to save us, God has to become human and then commit suicide? That sounds like a terrorist's strategy to saving the world."

"The question with suicidal impulses," Steve raises his pen to the air, "is what symbolically needs to die in us in order to make room for new life to begin?"

We sit together in the thick energetic air and wonder.

"So I have to face my demons," I finally say.

"The image of Christian Roberts that you carry around holds a lot of negative power. When you project that image on others, you give them your power."

"So I need to confront my inner rapist?" I laugh.

Steve looks at me with eyes of steal. Suddenly I am frightened.

"It's time to cut those negative voices down to size," he says.

~

The following week I have the worst nightmares of my life. A huge powerful force is rebelling against the changes I want to make in my life. Rebel meets Inner Rebel. I am up at night screaming. The terrorists grow taller and wider. Their eyes fill with more demonic energy. Their knives are replaced with guns. I am shot, raped, and cut into pieces.

~

"Oh God. How do I even begin to turn this boat?"

I sob into the tissues that Steve hands me.

"I know I need a new script. I know I can't give my power away and play the victim. I am ready to learn. But you're right, the dreams fight back and I am so frightened. I actually had a dream last week that I had a new script, but I kept losing it. I am in a muddy field, pushing apart wild grasses in search of my lines, my voice."

"Yes, of course," says Steve thoughtfully. Sometimes I wish I could read his mind.

"Then I dreamt that my entire right arm was sliced in half! The gaping wound looked like a swelling vagina!"

"Indeed," he said. "That is a powerful image of the wounded feminine."

"See how wounded I am!"

I wipe the tears from my cheeks. "How am I supposed act all assertive when I'm walking around with this gaping thing?" I sit for a moment before I ask, "How will I ever heal?"

Steve looks at me with a twinkle in his eyes, "Can you see any good that could come from this big wound in your past?"

Suddenly I am enraged.

"How can you say that?" I retort. "You said yourself my story was awful!" My body is trembling again. "There is nothing good that can come of this! NOTHING!"

"Look how much energy there is in you! Listen to how strong your voice is!" I think of the choir director. *I knew you had a voice in there!*

"When you speak with that kind of power in your voice," he says, "isn't it hard to be depressed? Look, you've stopped crying."

"Yeah, because I'm angry."

"Good," he says. "You should be. You have every right to feel your own anger."

And then I hear the key drop to the floor.

"But I'm not allowed to be angry," I say slowly as I step into his dance.

"And why are you not allowed to be angry, Jessica?"

"Because girls are supposed to be nice," I begin. "Because Christian girls especially do not get angry. Because every time I got angry as a child I ruined everything and I got in so much trouble. Because my father's anger frightens me…"

Steve stands up and pulls a book off of the shelf. He thumbs through the pages and pauses on some pictures of old Minoan Snake Goddesses.

"Look at her power," he says.

I gasp. "I dreamt about one of those snakes wrapped around my leg! What does that mean?"

"Let's see…"

Steve pulls another thick book on symbols from his shelf.

"Snakes are symbols of renewal and resurrection because they shed their skin—often associated with female goddesses and feminine strength. A symbol for the Goddess of the Earth. Sometimes depicted in dual form as a Mother and Daughter—Persephone and Demeter in the Greek. Snakes symbolize protective power and healing power."

He shows me also the image of the snakes on a pole—the symbol used by hospitals—a reference I thought was based on the Moses story. But this symbol is even older. Later I learn that the snake is also a symbol for Kundalini the energy, or Shakti, the feminine form of God that coils around the base of the spine and spirals up through the chakras to spiritually awaken the body.

"The Goddess is making herself known to you. She will give you the strength to fight the terrorists," Steve says. "She can teach you how to mother yourself."

"So that's why I had the snake with me when I faced the terrorist in my kitchen!" I said excitedly.

"It's interesting that this terrorist is in your kitchen—the place of transforming foods into nourishment. The Divine Feminine is with you to help you get back in your own kitchen, so you can learn to feed and nourish yourself." The reptilians blocking access to my sacred space gotta go. I also wonder if secret military programs have anything to do with this.

~

Carl Jung believed that our outer world reflected our inner worlds. I found that statement to be especially profound as I began to face my inner terrorists in the wake of 9/11. As school shootings escalated I became acutely aware of how this problem was not simply "out there." My psyche was also tormented by visions of wounded masculine figures who went on shooting rampages. If the feminine is wounded, then so is the masculine.

According to Jungian theory, all of the figures in our dreams are reflections of ourselves and our bigger Self/God. If our work is to heal the world, then it must begin by confronting the figures and the energies expressed in our dreams and collective unconscious. If the antidote to the wounded masculine is the Divine Feminine, then this spiritual path is about more than my own personal healing. Seeking the Divine Feminine will also guide us to find the healing needed for our time.

~

Here is where much of American evangelical Christianity gets it wrong: theologies that claim that all is well if you just think the right way rob us of our real spiritual journey and the experience of our bodies. If Jesus already did everything for us by dying for our sins (atonement theology) then there is nothing more for us to do but simply think the right thoughts or assent to a doctrine or believe a certain way, or belong to a certain club. Much of Christian theology denies that any shadowy figures can exist in our own psyche once we are baptized and filled with the Holy Spirit. When this denial happens our psyches split and we project our shadows onto others rather than doing the lifelong work that Jesus asked us to do: to take the logs out of our own eyes. This is why some Christians have the reputation of being so judgmental and hypocritical: they have identified with the light while projecting their darkness outward rather than doing the spiritual work of becoming conscious of our shadows, relating to them, practicing hospitality towards them, witnessing their pain with compassion (which is our own pain), integrating self, and ultimately redeeming and healing self. Some New Age folks are guilty of this as well. It's an old (dare I say Satanic?) way of seeing the world that continues to fragment our spiritual life and wreak havoc in our culture.

Many of our religious practices teach us to see things separately—us and them, insiders and outsiders, good and evil—when ultimately we are all made of the same stuff. We are all intricately connected to each another and to the living universe. It's not that Jesus' message (or any of the great spiritual teachers) is intrinsically flawed; it's that for centuries the message of love has been exploited and retold by ruling powers. So much so that we have no idea who the real terrorists are. There are powers actively working to keep us from connecting to our true natures by continuing to inflict trauma upon the human family, spinning false flags to divide us from one another and the true source of life which exists as the most powerful free energy source: unconditional love for all of creation. All of our divisive spiritual practices need an upgrade. It is all actually very simple: just receive love from Source for self and neighbor.

~

The tiny sanctuary is closing in on me. The red carpet reminds me of blood. I am finding it difficult to breathe. I hold the little red Book of Common Prayer in my hands. I cannot bring myself to say the words with the congregation.

"Lord God, heavenly King, almighty God and Father, we worship you, we give you thanks, we praise you for your glory. Lord Jesus Christ, only Son of the Father, Lord God, Lamb of God, you take away the sins of the world...In the glory of God the Father...Amen."

How am I supposed to connect with the energy of the Goddess here? All these words of my religion describe a Divine Father who is ordered, logical, unmoved, full of power and might. It's no wonder I am reminded of the military when I worship: these images can be traced back to the Roman Emperor cult. Where did the Mother Goddesses go? Where are her sacred birth and menstruation practices? Why did she disappear? Was her cult also infiltrated and corrupted? Was her true power a threat to the rising military state? Why were her mysteries lost and marred with taboo? Where is she who spirals in circles, the one who loves the muddy earth, the mess and wonder of childbirth? Where is the celebration of the Divine Feminine aspects that Source expresses through our humanity? She has been silenced, raped, her children have been taken from her. Her body has been polluted, left raging in pain in a world that finds her inconvenient to the status quo. She exists as a part of the sacred geometry of life for she reigns over that dark space in the hologram, which also exists as frequencies in our bodies, waiting for us to notice her, to descend to her pain, so we may rise again whole, and clear the energy fields for others.

The Apostle Paul and the early church fathers steered Hellenistic Christianity away from the Pantheon of Greek Goddesses. It has been suggested that the earliest form of the Holy Trinity was derived from the Gnostics: Father (The Creator), Mother (Sophia/Wisdom) and Son (Christ). Later Christianity removed the Mother and replaced it with Holy Spirit, who is now officially a He in the Nicene Creed that is recited each week by millions around the world. The earliest trinity—the ancient triple Goddess—was replaced with triune maleness.

A major theological stumbling block to donning the female form with divinity in the church has been the historic vilification of the flesh which is said to war against the Holy Spirit. In Romans 7:18 the Apostle Paul writes, "I know that nothing good dwells within me, that is in my flesh," a statement that would be very difficult for many pregnant mothers to make. The 4th and 5th century theologian Augustine coined the term "original sin" (which does not appear in the Bible anywhere) and has gone on to shape the West's self-loathing—a move away from what is written in the book of Genesis, where it is asserted that God created male and female in "God's image" and called them "very good."

When the desires of the flesh were deemed sinful, so were women, sexuality and the simple joys of life itself. Nourishing food, comfortable clothes, a cozy home, a lover, a family—all appeared frivolous distractions to Christianity's growing asceticism.

(Church lady chimes in: Can you say, Satan?) The more nourishing spiritual values that Jesus taught likely stemmed from the Egyptian healer and mother Goddess, Isis.

It's also likely that many of our ancient spiritual practices of have been infiltrated with creation destroying practices—even the Goddess cults. It's likely that patriarchy may be a pendulum swing response to a long ago out of balance feminine power that desacralized the masculine essence of the divine. It's likely this deep (even unconscious) fear of dark feminine power is why we are so nervous about integrating the Goddess again. Everything has a shadow side. I'm not pretending the Goddess doesn't. I'm not pretending that I don't. And we can no longer afford to pretend that the Patriarchy doesn't. Post Trump election 2016, all the shadows have come out of hiding. Now we have the opportunity to consciously face our hell and return Eden to Earth. One who can guide us on this journey of healing and transformation is the Dark Goddess Herself, for she knows the most ancient ways of resurrection. Women know it in our bones and in our DNA. We just have to collectively remember.

It is likely that Jesus was connected to priestesses and secretly passed on the teachings of the Goddess in his counter cultural gospel message of love. Jesus' teachings addressed the growing violence and evaporating tenderness in the patriarchal Greco-Roman culture which was growing bloodier by the day. He reminded people at a pivotal time in history to recall what happened in ancient Egypt when another peaceful culture fell under a similar infestation that had turned an Eden people into a slave driving state back in the time of Moses.

Today we are facing similar infestation. The lore of Mary and Jesus easily flowed through the mother-son figures of Isis and Horus that had populated the land for thousands of years prior. Isis temples spread throughout the region from Egypt to Italy to Rome. The Goddess Isis cult was also invaded and the practices that once held the sacred balance between the earth and her people were usurped to serve the destruction of creation instead. Both Mary the mother of Jesus and Mary Magdalene were likely priestesses of Isis, as Mery-Isis means 'Beloved of Isis' and was an ordination title not just a popular name.

It may be no coincidence that the world's major terrorist group is called Isis—Her name and Her energy is still being riddled with taboo and terror—to keep people from remembering, to keep people traumatized.

Today the global infrastructures of our world run on a military industrial complex that makes money by creating wars. Wars are orchestrated by these ancient forces that run through every facet of our culture, even our very personalities. It's the energy of the ancient Set, (whose name we get the derivative Satan—which means 'adversary' in Hebrew) who appears in many disguises, always the wolf in sheep's clothing, the evil king who cuts Isis' husband Osiris to pieces scattering his body across the land. Set represents the ancient problem of evil we all face as we claim our sovereignty and draw upon the Sacred Mother's power to hold together all of our fragments under her wings, in her womb, so we can be born again. It is She who gathers all the lost pieces of self and holds the weave of life together, She Grandmother Spider who helped create this grand design, She who knows that all of her creation is connected. She who comes as a Dark Mother raging at every enemy who wishes harm to her husband and children, She purifies us in her fires of transformation and shows us how to walk through her sacred doorways into new life.

~

As I close the little red prayer book I realize that my search for the sacred feminine must lead beyond the doors of the traditional church and into the cosmos to find a way to weave my own warring fragments back together again.

~

I plunge myself into the literature, reading books like Elizabeth Johnson's *She Who Is* and Jean Bolen's *The Goddesses in Everywoman*. When I read the story of Demeter and Persephone, I weep. I had moved around so much as a military child that I had somehow missed Greek mythology in my early education. When I read about the earth cracking open, about Persephone's rape and abduction, about her descent into the underworld and her mother's impassioned search for her daughter, I realize I am reading my own story. I realize that the Mother Goddesses are also looking for me. I understand how these ancient myths are actually our human stories, archetypal patterns that have existed throughout time. I learn that many cultures have a Goddess that rises from the dead in the spring. Imperial Christianity took over popular Earth based Pagan celebrations with the story of Jesus' resurrection. Easter is no longer a celebration of the Anglo-Saxon moon Goddess Eostre, but now a story about a beloved son rising from the underworld. The earliest human story points us to the first recorded descent and resurrection in the myth of Ereshkigal and Inanna, Queens of the Underworld and of Heaven—but we don't really hear that story in school or seminary, at least I didn't. Persephone and Demeter are later expressions of that earlier story. I learn that Persephone's work is to transform herself from a victim into a queen and now I understand that this is my work too.

~

After years of studying about the Divine Feminine and working with Goddess energy, my dreams take a dramatic turn.

The ceiling fan is on high. I have a beautiful little blue bird in my hands. It begins to fly up to the spinning blades. *No! No!* I scream. *Not this time!* I punch my arm into the blades and stop the fan and save my bird.

"The dream shows your growth," Steve says. "Now you have the power to protect your bird—you know birds are often symbols of the soul, and the Holy Spirit."

And now I know that doves were also associated with the ancient oracle priestesses in a time when women were revered as the more natural prophets and seers than men.

~

Christian Roberts is lying on top of me again and taunting me, "You stupid little girl! You ruined your life! You'll never make anything of yourself! You'll never have a voice!"

I scream and push his heavy body off of me and stand up. I say in my most powerful voice, "You are never allowed to talk to me like that ever again!"

"Are you alright, Jess?" David shakes me awake.

"Yeah," I say wiping the sweat off of my face, "I think I am now."

I see Steve almost every week for five years. In time I am able to behold Christian as a wounded child—one who was probably sexually abused himself, possibly also a victim of a some kind of military mind control program. He too is one who never found his true voice. In a way we suffered from the same disempowerment. He was a boy afraid of being devoured by forces that overwhelmed him; he was attracted to the weak so he could feel again the power he thought he had lost when he was abused. It doesn't justify what he did to me, but it makes him human. And by seeing him like this, I am able to take back the power I once gave him. Then my nightmares about Christian Roberts and terrorists cease.

Compassionate witnessing heals. It just does.

~

"I think I have an answer to your question," I tell Steve near the end of our time together.

"What question?"

"A long time ago you asked me if anything good could come from my wound. Now I know the answer."

"I'm dying to know," he sits on the edge of his seat with wide eyes.

"My voice," I say. "Through these wounds I will give birth to my voice."

We sit at the piano and I play him the new songs I have been writing. He encourages me to bring my voice and my music into the world. I begin to write. *August, 1989. I lost my virginity on the concrete behind the high school.* I can't stop shaking. I have to leave it alone for a while. For a year or more. In resurrecting hope, I have also resurrected all the demons that raise every old fear that lives in me. During this time of my life, I have two miscarriages. I fight with everything I have to hold onto my dreams and birth them into the world.

~

I am inside a haunted castle. A zombie-like man is chasing me. My feet are suddenly too heavy to move. I make it beyond the moat but I fall on the ground near a stack of children's toy blocks. The zombie-man finds me there, but he is more interested in the blocks than me. He transforms into a little boy. He reaches out and hugs me with tears in his eyes. As I hold him he grows into a man. The man is wounded and cannot walk. I carry him to my home and put him to bed. I feed him soup and wipe his fevered head. He grows strong and healthy. He holds me again and now my body is filled with the powerful force of love that I felt as a child in the movie theater when I was five. Then the figure changes into my father. We weep together and I forgive him for everything. Then my father changes into the crippled Superman, Christopher Reeves. His skin begins to glow as he rises from the bed. He shows me that now he can stand on his own. He takes a few steps and we rejoice that he can walk again! The wounded masculine creature that used to terrorize me has now become my devoted Superman. He promises to serve and protect me. The terrorist's fearful energy in me has transformed into a powerful force of love. This is what is possible not only for my inner world, but for our world, for wherever there is terror, there is also the potential for love to transform everything.

As my body vibrates with this new reconciliation and healing, I hold this truth in the hologram of life: the people we see as terrorists can shift into our most powerful allies. This is what love does. It gathers the broken hearts and bodies of humanity and mends us into the fabric of a love that never dies, it simply changes forms.

As within, so without. As above, so below. And so it is, as it was in the beginning, is now, and shall be forever more. Blessed be.

~

The ultimate task humanity faces today is to stop killing our enemies and simply learn to love them.

"Teacher, which is the greatest commandment in the Law?" Jesus replied: "'Love the Lord your God with all your heart and with all your soul and with all your mind.' This is the first and greatest commandment. And the second is like it: 'Love your neighbor as yourself.' All the Law and the Prophets hang on these two commandments."

-Matthew 22:36-40

Then teachers of the law asked Jesus: but who is my neighbor? Jesus responded by telling the story of the Good Samaritan. In ancient Judea, Samaria was the land of the outcasts, the lost tribes of Israel. They were feared and seen as unclean. Jesus said: this is your neighbor. Those you deem your enemy are in fact your neighbor. Love them.

~

I dream I am watching a powerful woman ride a motorcycle. She falls, but she gets back up. She walks over to me and I can see clearly: she is me. I remember the timid girl who fell off the moped all those years ago. I realize: I have finally become a woman. I am becoming the powerful woman that I dreamed of when I was fourteen. I have learned to love the girl I wanted to lock away forever. I am a sacred woman. I am a sacred mother. I am a sacred priestess.

I am the whore and the holy woman.
-Sophia

My dog Thor starts having seizures. My sister and I are in denial. We come to visit. We both watch him suffer and shake. He goes completely blind.

"It's time to say goodbye, Jessie."

My mother calls me to come home and visit him. I try to be strong enough to hold both the love and the loss. I bring him close to me and bury my face in his fur. I thank him for being my friend through everything. I know he will return to the place from which he came, to the Love who created him.

My parents drop him off at the vet after I return home. They can't bear to watch him die. I would have stayed with him to the very end. But I know he is with me. Sometimes Cupcake visits me in my dreams too. They remind me that love is stronger than death, and that death is just another beginning.

~

After the Great Chicago Fire in 1871, much of the city is rebuilt with trees from the forests in North Eastern Arkansas, including the trees cut down in Blytheville.

~

One cold dark night in advent, I am sitting at my dining room table with wool socks pulled up to my knees, a long gray sweater draped over my pajamas and a lump of clay in my hand. Upstairs my son and husband are fast asleep. One cat curls around my leg, the other knocks ornaments off the Christmas tree. I can hear the wind outside, the chimes ringing. Blasts of cold Chicago air fly into the hundred year old house through the rotting windowpanes and creaky wooden doors.

There is an image burning in my mind: an image of a mother and child. It has been with me for weeks, appearing in my dreams, feeding me energy, excitement and hope. I want to honor her, to remember her presence, to give her some kind of material body.

I warm the gray clay with my hands and begin to push my fingers into the spine of her back. I meditate on the hard work I have been doing of drawing boundaries and facing other people's anger (and my own) rather than shrinking away from the things I fear. I have been working on speaking my truth when staying silent would be easier.

I leave generous mounds around her hips and thighs, she is kneeling, her head tilts up to the sky, her hair flows wildly down her back, and her mouth hung open in either a song or a scream or pure ecstasy. She must hold so much. She needs to be big. She kneels so that more of her body can connect with the ground. She opens her face to the heavens with a smile of pure delight. Her breasts fling wide, full of nourishment. Her stomach holds memories of pregnancy, still round and spacious. I take a small piece of clay and shape a little body, tiny feet tangled together, arms reaching out to touch, rolls of flesh so sweet I can almost smell the scent of a newborn. Skin to skin I place the child in the mother's arms and work the clay until the two become one. It's a girl, I think. A baby girl. I set the piece on the table to dry overnight and slip my cold body under the covers close to my husband.

Together we bring three children into the world. When I am delivering our babies and in the weeks that follow, my body is filled with the power of divine feminine energy. Experiencing this is like reuniting with an old friend. As the lochia flows from my body, the air is filled with the scents of salt water and freshly baked bread. I will not let myself dishonor the Goddess by turning a terrorist's eye to my swollen and stretched body. This body is holy, I remind myself. This skin is sacred.

Each of my births is a healing and empowering experience. I fear most repeating the rape trauma by having others do things to my body that harm me or my child. I want to finally trust my body's instincts and heal that long broken relationship. I study all about birth and how with each medical intervention the risk of C-section increases. I do not want to be cut open. I understand there are emergency situations. Still, I cannot believe that most births in America are an emergency. Too many mommas and babies are unnecessarily traumatized at birth. I have had enough trauma and I am ready to birth in ecstasy.

I read a lot and practice yoga and eat super healthy. I find my strength and practice setting fierce boundaries with the medical staff who have not experienced natural births. Some shun me, make fun of me, tell me I don't have to prove anything. But I don't care. I stick to my instincts and each of my births are the most amazing experiences I have ever had in my life. When I teach prenatal yoga now I tell the mommas—I did a lot of drugs and I can assure you that the high you get in a natural birth is better way better than them all. It's believed that DMT is released from the brain during a natural birth, the God particle that creates wondrous states as people enter the earth plane and also as they leave, if we can remember how to honor our nature again.

This is the flesh that was once objectified, feared, and raped. This is the flesh that I once easily gave away, that risked disease, teen pregnancy, and total abandonment. I have been resurrected. This same flesh has become fertile ground capable of holding and bearing life. And not only children, but creative work too. The emptiness dissolves as I expand full of nourishing energy. Now offering my body is holy work. I offer my body to that which needs to be born in me, to that which asks to come into the world through the doors of my heart. My flesh is food indeed. This is my body given for you.

My mother sits next to me in the car while I drive. My daughter takes her morning nap behind us in her car seat. Her name is Ela—an old Hebrew word for Tree, for the Tree of Life, the one found in the beginning of the Bible, in the garden, and the one at the end, the one that grows in the heavenly city and heals the nations' wounds with its leaves. Her birth is auspicious; I read on some random astrology chart that her birth day and time signifies the emergence of the Divine Feminine. I don't understand all that stuff, but that is exactly the sort of lineage I am planning on passing on to my daughter, so I'm going with it.

I am nervous to ask my mother questions about our past. But I want to understand what made her rebel against her Lutheran roots. Why she and Dad were drawn to charismatic fundamentalism when I was little. We drive away from our family's cabin, down old Wisconsin roads, near where I was born. In the early light my mother is even more beautiful. Her face sparkles like diamonds have been brushed across it, which holds more wrinkles than I remember.

It frightens me to see her aging, to know that the gods do fall from heaven. I can see her humanity now. I can see her with more compassion. I always imagine her younger than she is, safe inside her perfect skin. The new lines do not diminish her beauty; to me they only frame it like a memory around an old picture you don't ever want to forget. Her face is inviting, each feature accentuates the others. It's hard to look away sometimes. It's hard to believe that I thought I was ugly as a child, like my own resemblance to my mother was hidden from me for years. Like there could only be one fairest in the land. My mother keeps her hair cut short now, dyed blonde and spiky. She and Dad just bought a red motorcycle, leather clothes, and black riding boots. Seems they have a bit of a rebellious streak too.

~

I used to love looking at the old photographs of my father. In the Polaroid's he looks like a 60s rock star to me, one that belongs in a band like Led Zeppelin or The Who. His hair is dark and wavy, it hangs to his shoulders. He is shirtless, his abs are tight, his arms are muscular. He looks cool smoking a cigarette in his bellbottom blue jeans. He smiles easily back then, more freely than I remember growing up. His gaze is penetrating, his cheekbones are chiseled, his chin square. I can see this man more clearly now that I am older than he is in the picture. I can see what as a child I could not, that he is a wildly passionate man, sensual, even seductive. I can see that was a lot to contain inside a military uniform.

My father grew up on the south side of Chicago in Evergreen Park, Illinois. He was the captain of his high school basketball team, the head of his fraternity house, the big man on campus. I can see him, retelling the latest jokes, expanding them, enjoying the crowd hanging on his every word. I can see him, hung over, throwing broken records like Frisbees into Lake Michigan.

I can see him, a confident senior walking up to my mother, a timid freshman, the one who played her guitar and sang at the campus talent show, the one who brought an awed hush to the auditorium where people couldn't decide if it was her or her voice that was more beautiful. My mother's thick blonde hair hangs down to her elbows, parted in the middle, she is ethereal, otherworldly. She sings like an angel.

~

"So how did you and Dad end up in Madison after you got married?"

For some reason my mother keeps a thick veil over her past, even now that I'm all grown up with kids of my own, she won't let me know who she really was. I still feel unearthed when I am near her, like her solid disposition necessitates my breaking apart.

My mother takes a deep breath and looks out the window like she is collecting her memories out of the clear sky.

"It was a dark time," she says calmly.

She clicks through the story, like she's told it many times before. She tells me how she married my father just after the Vietnam War was over. My father wanted to be a pilot in the Air Force just like his older brother, but when they got back from their honeymoon they discovered two things that would set the course for the rest of their lives: my mother was pregnant with me and my father received a letter of rejection from the military saying that they were not admitting new pilots at this time.

My mother tells me that my father went to work for his father's employer, the Singer Company which sold vacuum cleaners and sewing machines. They offered him a job in Madison as the manager of a new store that rented out a small space in the mall. I remember going to visit my father at the Singer store. One day he presents me with a green blanket that he sewed for me himself. The edges are soft, chiffon; I roll them up into a point and run it across my lips and my nose. I call it my Fia and carry it with me everywhere. On really bad days, I pull it out of my dresser and I imagine that my Fia was really just a short name for the Divine Sophia who has comforted me since the very beginning.

The sun is still shining, making the white snow so bright it hurts your eyes to look at. My mother tells me she cleaned houses for extra cash, bringing me and my younger brother along with her and a few other kids that she babysat at the same time. We'd follow her around, messing up what she just cleaned, breaking things that weren't ours. My father was away all the time, working six or seven days a week from five in the morning until ten at night.

"I told him I wanted a divorce. I was crazy; I don't know how that would have fixed anything," she puts her index finger to her lips. "I was hanging out with the wrong crowd. My best friend was cheating on her husband," her hand falls back into her lap. She holds her purse, "It was a bad situation."

I fill in details of *bad situation*. I remember they smoked cigarettes—until I was at least five. Maybe there were also drugs. It was the 70s after all. I wish I knew their story. It would help me understand my own.

Miles of farmland surrounds us on both sides. Yellow crumpled corn stalks hide under the snow.

"I remember I woke up and found you at the foot of my bed one night," she returns her finger to her lips, and talks with her usual certainty. "You were just staring at me at three in the morning. You must have been two years old. That's when I remember my panic attacks began."

She dots the air with her manicured nails and I imagine my little girl-self standing strong, looking urgently in the dark for her mother.

"Why do you think I scared you?"

"I don't know. Maybe you just needed so much of me. And I didn't know who I was. We hit rock bottom when your father came home one day and said he quit his job with Singer. Said that they were closing all the stores, that they were going to reorganize the whole company. They wanted your father to sign a contract to work with the company through the transition. He wouldn't sign, so he had to quit on the spot. Oh my God. Imagine that. An unemployed husband and two kids."

She rubs her hands over the wrinkles on her forehead. "What a nightmare. He took a few odd jobs—like selling cars for a while so we could pay the bills. Finally, relief came when he got into the military—then we got a reliable income. We finally had some stability. We moved in with Grandma and Grandpa shortly after that and stayed with them for six months while your dad went off to boot camp."

~

When I was in high school our whole family went to counseling once. There seemed to be a small platoon of military personnel flitting around us with charts, bulging eyes and constant saluting of my very embarrassed father. I think our military counselor was a lower rank than my father which only increased the already small chance that this could possibly turn out well. Or maybe there were darker forces watching and taking close notes. I only remember my sister Emily talking and drawing pictures of her feelings while the rest of us sat with our arms crossed. Later I learned that those counseling records go on our father's military file. That he looks bad if we have issues. That our mental health would affect his career. We never go back.

~

"How did you make it through?"

We take the exit ramp right onto route 30. I have to pay closer attention to the details of the road now, the stoplights, the signs as the city reaches out to greet us.

"I met this woman—she talked like she knew God personally, like he was her best friend. I never heard of such a thing before. After I met her I knew that I wanted to know God like that too. I started hanging out with this woman and doing Bible studies with her and making new friends. I would put on Christian radio and watch the 700 Club and it would comfort me. It was the only thing that helped with the panic attacks."

I suspect my mother is also sensitive, and maybe her panic attacks were related to what she knew deep inside, what we both knew, but feared to consciously know.

"Growing up Lutheran, we didn't talk about God like that. This was a whole new world to me."

I think about this hunger for intimacy with the divine. This longing for the sacred to touch our everyday lives, to meet us in our suffering, to be as close as our mother's hug when we need it.

"How did your family talk about God?"

"It never made sense to me," she shakes her head. "I just didn't buy it—like I didn't buy their politics, this humanistic stuff. I knew that people were inherently bad. That I was bad. I would do the wrong thing just to see what would happen. We are all born in original sin, so we can't be trusted to do the right thing. There is nothing good in us," her eyes are piercing, I try to avoid them.

Her theology hits a deep nerve within me.

"Children are proof of original sin," my mother would say. "Just watch them; they are so selfish…You were so selfish."

I heard it my whole life. But now that I am older, I sense there is something more to her dark theology, maybe some unconscious self-hatred? As a child I saw myself as only bad. I struggled to gain confidence and a healthy self-esteem. Now I gravitate toward theologies that focus on the goodness of creation.

God saw everything that he had made, and indeed, it was very good.
-Genesis 1:31

"It sounds like you never felt like your parents understood you."

I step away from the constellation of emotions that are triggered in me. I watch my mother's face open, her eyebrows rise. Is it grief I see?

"I am the black sheep of the family." My mother shrinks in size and then she builds a fire. "They talked about social justice, but they were so elitist they couldn't even see it in themselves. Women were supposed to build their careers first then have a family. But I fell in love with your father. Madly in love. I quit school and got married so I wouldn't become an unwed mother. Heck, two of you were conceived on birth control. What was I supposed to do?" She is red and certain. "I know I was a huge disappointment to them." Her eyes are watery. "I know my father was disappointed in how I chose to practice my faith."

I never saw her parent's disappointment in her. I saw them beam at her with pride. Maybe what is harder is to face is her own disappointment in herself.

The real trap, however, is self-rejection...self-rejection is the greatest enemy of the spiritual life because it contradicts the sacred voice that calls us the "Beloved." Being the Beloved constitutes the core truth of our existence."

- Henri J.M. Nouwen

I ask my mother's family why she might feel like the black sheep. They don't understand why she sees herself this way. They tell me they always thought my mother was brilliant, beautiful, and popular. My Grandmother even tells me that she and Grandpa thought my mother might go to the seminary and become a Lutheran pastor.

"My folks loved the intellectual stuff. Heady theology and classical music. They didn't get rock music. They didn't get my emotions. They encouraged me to become a music teacher, to carry on the classics. Geesh. I just wanted to sing the music that moved me."

She dabs a Kleenex across her forehead. Suddenly my heart floods with compassion for her and I understand more why it was difficult for parents to see me growing intellectually at college.

The legacy of the wounded feminine is a long history that affects all of our families. Women have had to betray women through the age of patriarchy. When women's temples were taken over by patriarchal gods and the priestess temples and oracle centers were closed, divine feminine wisdom fell, like Sophia from heaven, and our crowns were broken like hers. Instead of crowns, many of us wore Medusa's mad snakes as we accumulated trauma upon trauma. Mothers betrayed daughters, sisters betrayed sisters in order to survive. We had to betray ourselves in order to get our basic needs met in a culture that had declared our innate wisdom heretical, taboo, illegal, unscientific, and passé, for over two thousand years.

Nothing exerts a stronger psychic effect upon the environment, and especially upon children, than the unlived life of the parents.
-Carl Jung

My Grandmother's friends call her Tulla. Or Ruth. I love the wedding photograph where she is running with red lips, flowers in her hands, her dress lifted, chasing her beloved, Erling. They were a team building Lutheran churches. He'd preach powerful sermons and had a knack at resolving conflict peacefully. She'd challenge high school kids in games of ping pong. If they lost they had to join her choir.

The towns had never seen choirs so grand.

I remember my Grandmother telling me about the last time she was depressed—right after my mother's older sister was born, Auntie Jo. They knocked her out to take the baby, which was normal in those days. It had been a difficult delivery; men in white coats stood around her invading her body while she lay unconscious. During her recovery she fell into a deep depression. She moved in with her parents. She couldn't shake the sadness. Her milk dried up before she figured out how to breastfeed the baby or any of her other children. While she was recovering, my grandmother overheard her mother say to her father, "I don't know how long we can continue to take care of her and the baby." My grandmother told me in that moment she simply chose to be happy. Whenever future troubles came, she learned to giggle.

And this has worked for her. Though I am aware of my own tendency of "spiritual bypassing" and the ability to glide right over the pain that is too difficult to bear. I am learning I need to make small, sometimes big descents, to go down into my depths and have compassion on the suffering I find there, that more of She may rise with me.

My grandmother's light and laughter give me so much hope. But I am afraid of the silences in my family too. The things we choose not to think of, not to speak of. Just three generations ago my ancestors left their homeland and worked to survive the harsh winters of the South Dakota plains. When my great-grandfather's father left the family for several months to find work, his first words upon his return were, "Is everyone still alive?" This was a time when neighbors were found dead in the fields in the spring after the snow had finally melted. My people lived by clinging to all the hope they had. Rumination was a luxury. It is a gift and a work they have passed down to me.

~

It is still difficult for my family to speak about the darkness. We haven't learned quite how. Living around other Lutheran Norwegian descendants now, I see that many of us struggle with this. I am still learning. I mean really, I had to write a whole book just to begin the conversation.

~

The word Wisconsin comes from the Indian language, from the tribes who live here for nearly 12,000 years before the whites fought them off the land. The settlers can't say it right. They spell it lots of different ways until it finally morphs into Wisconsin. The meaning is disputed. It has something to do with water. Some say it means, "this stream meanders through something red."

By the time Christopher Columbus reached the Caribbean in 1492, historians estimate that there were 10 million indigenous peoples living in U.S. territory. But by 1900, the number had reduced to less than 300,000.

-United to End Genocide

How can I not think of blood when I gaze at the crimson rocks jetting out from the earth around me? So much innocent blood has spilled on this land. How can we still be blind to the consequences? I can feel how the land cries out for redemption in my bones. I sense the nature spirits and the ancient sacred guardians of earth awakening and returning to bring us to consciousness or to judgement.

To fully comprehend U.S. policy toward Indians it is important to realize that policy was grounded in the nation's fundamental commitment to territorial expansion. This commitment arose not just from the aggregation of individual settlers' and speculators' pursuit of wealth, but also from the premise—central to Americans' republican political philosophy—that liberty depended on widespread ownership of private property. To build what Thomas Jefferson described as an "empire for liberty," then, mandated obtaining Indian lands. How would this be done? Policymakers envisioned an ideal scenario in which Indians would willingly sign treaties ceding their lands in exchange for assistance in becoming civilized. But what if Indians refused to cede their lands? What if they rejected the "gift" of civilization? At that point, U.S. policymakers consistently stated, Indians would be subject to war—not the limited warfare that European legal theorists had agreed was acceptable between civilized nations but a war of extermination. In 1790 Secretary of War Henry Knox sanctioned such a war when he ordered the U.S. Army to "extirpate, utterly, if possible" a confederacy of Indians centered in Ohio that had rejected U.S. demands for a land cession. Facing similar opposition seventeen years later, President Jefferson sent word to Indians near Detroit that "if ever we are constrained to lift the hatchet against any tribe, we will never lay it down till that tribe is exterminated, or driven beyond the Mississippi," adding that should Indians go to war, "they will kill some of us; we shall destroy all of them." Genocidal war, then, was not just an option, it was necessary in situations of Native resistance.

- Jeffrey Ostler, Genocide and American Indian History

I turn left on West Gorham Street, then left on Wisconsin Ave and pull into the parking lot of Bethel Lutheran church—the place I was baptized. In the Bible, Bethel is the place where Jacob rests when he is running away from his twin brother Esau who wants to kill him because he stole his birthright. Jacob falls asleep on a rock and dreams of a ladder connecting the cold stone to heaven, of angels descending and ascending upon it. God looks down from the top of the ladder and promises Jacob—the trickster, the liar, the thief—God promises Jacob the land of Canaan. When Jacob awakes he anoints the stone with oil and names the place Bethel which in Hebrew means 'house of El' or house of God. This is the place I was baptized into our family's faith: the dreaming place, the place of the trickster, and ladders that span from earth to heaven.

"The night I brought you home from the hospital Grandma Zdenek told me to put you in your crib and let you cry it out. She said you need to teach the baby when they are young that they cannot control you. I held my legs all night and tried not to cry as I listened to you wail. I was such a young mother. I didn't know what I was doing."

The church seems small from the outside, but we walk into the narthex to discover otherwise. Large windows throw the light around the white walls of the entryway. The sanctuary is dark when we walk in. The only light illuminating the space is filtered in through the stain glass windows which are everywhere. The hair on my arms stands up. The air is thicker in here, but not stale; no, it is moving, alive, mysterious. Some churches feel dead on the inside. You can taste the bitter words that have been spoken, smell the despair that weighs people down. This space feels different. It feels like the prayers of the congregation are still lingering around the pews, like whatever source of strength they fed on came in large quantities and there are leftovers for us.

"We used to sit right here," my mother points to an overflow area in the back left corner. I spot a picture of Our Lady of Guadalupe upon the wall nearby; underneath her is a small table that holds candles and matches for prayers. I love that she is here, the divine mother, pregnant with hope looking over those in despair, the young woman who appeared on the hills of Tepeyac and commanded her presence known to the bishop—to the world. Many thought she was an apocalyptic image from Revelation, her belt a symbol of pregnancy, her sash holding the cosmos. The beginning and the end held together inside the contours of her image. "Hold us together in love," I pray to her.

I walk down the center aisle up to the altar, taking my time, taking it all in, the beams in the ceiling, the dark wood of the pews, the light through the stain glass windows. My mother snaps a photo of me by the baptismal font which is up front by the altar. But something is not right. In the pictures of my baptism, we stand against white walls, not in the illuminated shadows of the sanctuary.

In the 1970s, while researching in the Library of Congress, I found an obscure history of religious architecture that assumed a fact as if it were common knowledge: the traditional design of most patriarchal buildings of worship imitates the female body. Thus, there is an outer and inner entrance, labia majora and labia minora; a central vaginal aisle towards the altar; two curved ovarian structures on either side; and then in the sacred center, the altar of the womb, where the miracle takes place—where males give birth.

-Gloria Steinem

"Mom, is there another chapel in the church?"

"I don't know," she says. "I don't remember much about this place."

We walk around the hallways until we find a sign that says, *The Good Shepherd Chapel*. The Good Shepherd story is one that I love teaching to children. It's a feminine image of God as a mother, rounding up her sheep, protecting them, searching desperately for them when they are lost. We stand outside the closed wooden door and look up at the skylight at least two stories above us. The sun illuminates one giant painting on the wall. Thick strokes of browns and pinks muddy the canvass like watered earth. Tucked in the shadows and mire, a small white sphere emerges, fragile yet forceful. Is it the pearl of great price? Is it new life itself? It reminds me of a photograph I saw recently taken inside of the womb just after the egg has been fertilized. I am haunted at the sight: before limbs or head or a body can be seen, we are all cliffs and valleys, we are desert. All of us are Adam, *Adama*, which in Hebrew simply means "earth creature."

My mother is fascinated with a different picture, a smaller one in the corner—one of the empty tomb. It is colored in the blackest black, shiny, and thick oil. A single ray of light points to white linen cloth, a missing person.

I remember my mother telling me that she gave up her dreams of the opera stage for us. I was a honeymoon surprise. My mother was twenty years old when she had me. She reminds me frequently that her labor lasted thirty eight hours, a problem child even before I was born. I was suck, sunny-side up. She begged doctors to cut her open and take me out. But a large nurse works with my father to turn my mother over and I flip. I am born in meconium with my fist entering the world first. She tears a lot. My mother said she knew I was going to be a fighter from day one. Maybe I will also be a writer.

I am raised to believe that life is about sacrifice. But I rebel. I pursue my dreams. I want life to be about joy too. I think while my mother rejoices with my successes, they also cause her pain. They remind her of all the things she lost as a young woman— dreams that died and were never resurrected, dreams that were never even born into the world. Things I think she'd rather forget about, because the pain is too great. Maybe she fears it's too late for her dreams. But it never really is. We can begin dreaming again today.

We enter the small chapel.

"Yes, this is it," she says. I take a picture of the font—a colorful ceramic bowl atop a square blond wooden stem.

"This is style is totally 70s," I remember the photograph well. My grandfather is holding me. I am in a long white dress, only a few weeks old. He is wearing a mustard colored shirt with his clerical collar and a beige blazer with elbow pads. My mother's siblings stand around me: Auntie Jo, Uncle Tim, Aunt Pam, and Aunt Mary Kay. They are all young kids dressed in wide collars, paisley prints donning dark horned rimmed glasses.

I hold my daughter as my mother and I reach to touch the font. Here we stand, three generations of women around the sacred waters.

The central ceremony of patriarchal religions is one in which men take over the yoni-power [the sacred feminine energy] *of creation by giving birth symbolically. No wonder male religious leaders so often say that humans were born in sin—because we were born to female creatures. Only by obeying the rules of the patriarchy can we be reborn through men. No wonder priests and ministers in skirts sprinkle imitation birth fluid over our heads, give us new names, and promise rebirth into everlasting life. No wonder the male priesthood tries to keep women away from the altar, just as women are kept away from control of our own powers of reproduction. Symbolic or real, it's all devoted to controlling the power that resides in the female body.*

-Gloria Steinem

I am cutting ties with any spirituality that would put a male authority over my body. I am being reborn in the image of Her, as I am a unique expression of the divine feminine. From Her womb we are all born sacred. We are breathed upon earth creatures made of star dust knit together in the desert of our sacred mother's womb—which is the cosmos itself. Each of us a miracle, a wondrous miracle.

We are spiritual beings planted in soil of flesh and bone. Come to life on a tiny planet in a remote part of the Milky Way galaxy. Some of us were birthed from Gaia herself. Others descended from the stars to populate this unique diverse garden planet that is struggling to regain its ecological equilibrium. Many of us came here to assist the planet at this time. We passed through the horns of angels and rode the backs of sacred cows. We were knit together on the loom of our Star Mothers. We are the descendants of dying suns, held together by darkness and light. We are warmed by an aging star as we circle around a mysterious black hole. We are an infinitesimally small dot in the cosmic web of life. So precious. So profound. So powerful. So fragile. So momentary. So fleeting. So everlasting. We are like the seed that falls to the ground and cracks open and though the seed dies the life within the seed does not. We are the fruit of creation's ancient journey. We are made of the same elements that formed the planets. And we are so good. We are not born in original sin. We are born of the sacred womb of all creation, burrowed deep in Her sacred earth. Deep in the desert of Her body, we came forth like water from Her rock. We bloomed like green blades from the buried grain. And we each reflect Her presence, as all of her creation does. She is all around She is rising up within us. And She is fierce. And She is good, She is very good indeed.

~

Our spirituality needs a cosmic upgrade. It's time to move away from the tipping point of destroying the earth and open to receive the divine feminine wisdom as the Yin that moves in balance with the Yang. It is not enough to simply allow women a place at the altar (which many denominations still do not allow). It is long past time for images of the Divine Feminine to be welcomed into our collective consciousness again. I would ask the church that I have served for ten years and others in places of spiritual leadership to consider my story and see if we open our imaginations to the sacred feminine for the sake of our collective healing in this time. For as long as the images of God remain strictly male in our religion, half of the divine will continue to be stripped of her sacred essence and devalued also in ourselves.

Our sacred texts call her Shekinah. Shakti. Sophia. I want to pray to Her. Because I am a girl. Because we are women, sisters, daughters, mothers, and grandmothers. Because the Bible says, "Let us create humanity in **OUR** image," but the majority of Christians only worship the He part. Because Jesus stood up for women, but the early church fathers and 2000 years of Christian tradition have deified and canonized men's voices, while highlighting the Roman kingly virtues of strength, power, perfection, rule, victory, and might. Because trying to be perfect and victorious is not good for me or my community or the planet. Because I used to think that woman was the source of evil, because many people still think she is. Because Eve has been blamed for too long, because eating from the Tree of Knowledge has many benefits, as does curiosity. Because the female body is no less holy than the male. Because Jesus told us to take his body, but it is our bodies that have been taken. Because when I nursed my children I knew what Jesus meant when he said my flesh is food indeed. Because everyday sexism still exists, because some interpretations of the Bible actually encourage it, because my seminary still discussed whether or not women should be ordained. Because Mary's virginity was never the point. Because it still sounds weird to say, "Dear Mother," or "In Her name we pray," because I want to pray to Her with others until it sounds completely natural, completely knee-jerk, until She's not just an idea, but an incarnation. Because we are neither whole nor holy without Her.

I am learning how to be a good enough mother to myself now. I am discovering how pain can be transformed into power. I am claiming my anger. Learning how to direct it, to heat up the cold spaces I inhabit, use it to write, to sing, to preach. To move from the place of the victim to a place of empowerment.

One night, at a dark coffee shop in room full of friends I gather all my courage to use my voice to create new life. I birth my creation into the world. My body shakes. These are the signs of labor. I sit at my keyboard and share my story publically for the first time in a song:

Thirteen when he had me on the concrete as I said please,
I hope they like me now.
They were sixteen and seventeen the skaters the strangers and me
The new girl in town.

Take my flesh an take my blood
I needed so much love
So I gave my flesh and I gave my blood
My Rock Baby

High fives all around the room after she cried in the bathroom cause the blood scared her so, "you popped her cherry, boy—way to go!"

Take her flesh and take her blood
You needed so much love
So you took her flesh and you took her blood

Your Rock Baby
Rumors gathered steam
She fucked the whole football team
Now every guy wants a piece of me

She's been under our covers
Under our skin
Under all this hate we keep her in
She's our miracle in the making

Our Rock Baby

And even if you can't hear her,
When he enters the city,
When he opens the gate,
You will hear the rocks say:
Prepare the way! Prepare the way! Prepare the way!
I will speak
Today.

I am greeted by a room full of friendly faces. They clap their hands and hug me with tears in their eyes.

"See?" I tell my demons. "You were wrong."

And when I say this their angry masks fall to the ground and all the wounded children come out and celebrate with me. And we remember what was said long ago: the wise ones build their houses upon the rocks.

~

Some Native Americans have been given names that tell of their brave stories and triumphs. I feel I need a new name. Maybe: The Land that was Conquered has been Redeemed. I am revealing to you the trauma I am working to heal, not for anyone to feel sorry for me, that's not the point. I'm not the point. I'm just playing a role, just as you are, in a story that is much bigger than ourselves. I'm sharing my story so that we can remember our mission in the grand scheme of things.

My great grandfather was a circuit rider preacher. He rode his horse around to minister to the early settlers in the plains of the Dakotas. In one visit (sometimes annually) he would marry, bury, baptize, and absolve the whole community. He also served in Mayville, North Dakota where my grandmother grew up. My ancestors had a homestead near Estoria, South Dakota. Like many around these parts, my ancestors inherited Native land in the Homestead Act. They received the land as "a gift from God" thanks to some crafty theological work called: The Doctrine of Discovery which contained the harmful ideas of Manifest Destiny. This doctrine basically declared white Europeans more holy than the earth based indigenous people, and gave settlers divine permission to dominate and assimilate the Native Americans, their children, their way of life, stealing their lands like the Hebrew people stole Canaan, doing evil in the name of God.

See how these larger traumas echo throughout time.

~

When I was thirteen, I quickly learned how the tender feminine was grounds for seizing and dispensing. I felt used and thrown away like all the other plastic containers that are tossed into landfills. We are taught that we are valued for what we produce, not for who we are. At a young age I learned that my inner world was not valuable to the dominant culture. I learned my role was to be object, not subject. What my culture did and continues to do to the Natives, it also does to me and to you, for conformity is its own kind of rape. It denies the beautiful diverse expressions of humanity. It trades the depths and dimensions of our souls for a 3D concrete reality that insists that the highest law in all of creation is not love but: power. We each must choose which law to obey, Cosmic Law or the ruling powers of this world which are presently bent on destroying creation.

The spirituality I inherited from my ancestors was lofty and intellectual and disconnected from the body and from the earth. It had to be, for it bore the karmic consequences of the dominating and assimilating culture. My spiritual stories tell of being kicked out of the garden. The Natives do not, for they are the original caretakers of the garden.

As ministers, my ancestors gave absolution to the settlers for their sins against the Natives. But the wounds of generational trauma still squirm under our stoic Scandinavian codes of silence. Wishing the problem would just go away does not make it go away. I know that the word repentance means "to turn around" and that true forgiveness restores and reconciles us with one another. True forgiveness heals.

It is strange how life works, always circling us around the past, giving us more opportunities to learn our lessons and grow. Life has brought me to live on this same land where my ancestors lived long ago. I am presently just an hour away from where my great grandfather ministered and my grandmother grew up. Life tested me again as my fourteen year marriage fell apart shortly after I moved here for my former husband's job. I had to dig deep to apply all that I had been learning. The dramatic trial triggered the trauma of 8th grade and more: I also felt the long history of trauma experienced by mothers who had their personhood put on trial, who've had their children taken from them, as complete strangers happily stepped forward to offer their testimonies against me. The court was very interested in my personal (including sexual) history (and not his). Behind the High School, my 8th grade gesture of suicide, and my drug use in college were all brought up in court as evidence to why at 38 with all my professional work with children, graduate studies, ten years of personal therapy, and years of loving my kids like crazy and doing my best to raise them in a healthy, peaceful home, I still ought to be considered an unfit mother. I went deep into those ancient roots of pain and it was a tremendous initiation. I had to stare down any remaining self-hatred in order to make it. I had this irrational fear of losing my children and the urge to cry all day long which pushed me to truly learn how to witness with compassion whatever was arising within. With so much on the line, I was forced to practice self-love in the very depths of my being and discover that I could be alone in the world without a man to protect me, as terrifying as that felt, it was the only way. I saved myself with daily yoga and meditation and built my own business.

November 3, 2016: I am wearing my Grandfather's alb and my Grandmother's ancestral jewelry. My hair moves like the golden prairie in the wind. My eyes reflect the cornflower blue sky which canopies wide over these Dakota plains. I am intrinsically connected to the land. No one can separate us. We are born connected. What is done to the land is done to me. The Natives have suffered for these sacred truths for many generations.

I am at the sacred fire of Standing Rock with over five hundred spiritual leaders from around the world. I am here to make amends for myself and all who wish to join me. For many generations we have been able to deny our connection to our bodies and to the land. In this generation we cannot. The time we are going to rise.

I watch as the clergy present to the Native American Elders the Doctrine of Discovery to burn.

"We were wrong," we declare. My body quakes like it did years ago when I finally shared my story with Steve. Something big is opening within us all. Never before have so many people of different ancestral and religious backgrounds gathered together in peace, in prayer, unified in cause and love for one another and the land.

Young and old Native women speak on behalf of their community, for it was the women that called this community together to protect the water and it is the heart of a woman that has the power to stand against an army with a feather.

"We have been waiting for you all to come for a very long time. Seeing you all here, this heals us. We are so happy that you are here. We forgive you."

On that day I received absolution for myself and my people from the Native women. Their tears washed the black snake of disconnection from my body as they affirmed something that has been difficult for me to hold onto: if the land is sacred, then so are we. So many years the slick toxins of self-hate and shame polluted my body and kept me severed from my instincts. I am a conquered land no more. I am redeemed. As I receive their forgiveness I am invited to return to the Garden, to return to my body, and to return to my soul. And so are you.

My story is but an echo of a much larger rape that is happening to the earth, and maybe this is why we as individuals are supposed to stay silent, lest we wake up and see that the rape of the earth is connected to the rape of the dignity of our humanity. For what we do to the earth and to others, we ultimately do to ourselves and to our children and to our children's children. The sins of the father are passed down to the next generation. But look: a time of rebirth is at hand as the prophets have said from times of old. For more than a new theology, we need our sacred girls, women, and mothers to return to the center of our consciousness, to make their way again to the garden cities of earth, to be for us pillars and stones and way-showers again.

Part IV
THE HEALING LEAVES

In the end
what has been done in secret
will be shouted from the rooftops.
We shall see face to face
and be known fully as we are fully known.
And all shall come
from every tribe
and every nation
to the city of light
to gather around the tree of life
to be healed.
And there will be no more crying
and no more tears
and we will tell
of the things we always knew
but had forgotten.

> *You will love again the stranger who was your self.*
> *Give wine. Give bread. Give back your heart*
> *to itself, to the stranger who has loved you*
>   -Derek Walcott

INCARNATION

I have a dream. I see a great field, a colorful quilt of patchwork squares. The harvest has come. A vibrant old woman rises from the ground. As she walks toward me I notice that her body is covered in a dress made of the fields of the earth. She has my eyes and she reaches out to touch my head with the palm of her hand. I hear her speak,

"Remember me."

But she is not me. She is a more beautiful image of wholeness than I am today. She wears my history on her body; she also wears all of human history on her body. She is Sophia-Jesus. She is the Cosmic Mother.

I look closer. I see punctured wounds that are still bleeding and others filled with wildflowers. I see green fields, rolling hills, and wide oceans. I see dark woods, lost children, and dangerous cliffs. In her dress, all my distant memories are sewn together.

"Come home," she says, "Tell your story and come home."

I finish the first chapter. I write about the land on which I have lived. I write to redeem it. I am digging up the fallow ground and I am planting something new. I write and reveal what is truly naked and eternally beautiful: my vulnerability, my voice and my heart.

I hear a new sound. The vibrations lift me to a land of my own, to the heavenly castle honed of flesh and bone. God's breath moves through the mended flute. This is my home, the place I belong. It is fluid and ever changing, like the wind.

~

I am flying over Lake Michigan in a small airplane. The sun is warm against my arm; I put my face to the window. It has been a long winter. I peer at our little lives below, our little houses on our little squares of land. Usually I find the scenery comforting. But today, the squares are taunting, too tame and dominated. I find relief in the wild rivers, in the lakes and their curves—their unpredictable moves, round and womanly.

I look down at my little girl sleeping in my arms.

The sun is more beautiful in the water's reflection, sparkling and dancing. The trees are wild too—those that have been left alone—they cluster near the water, roots deep in the earth. I am disturbed by the neon green squares of water cut into the ground, holding toxins, holding the waste of us all. The illusion is control. But the truth is wild.

~

The land beneath me is changing. No longer perfect squares, but roads that meander and twist. The land is older. Not built on a grid, but on the hills of the past. When the buildings and streets crop up they look arbitrary, spontaneous, as if they too have been planted out of scattered seed.

I rent a car and drive over the rolling hills to Rome, New York. The air is different up here. I watch a paper moon rise in a purple sky. And I know she is here, the spirit of five year old me and all her joy.

~

In the early 1800s people from all over the area flock to Rome, New York to see for themselves this revival that breaks out when Charles Finney speaks. Upon entering the town, many confess feeling the presence of God. People are slain in the spirit when he proclaims the gospel.

Finney preaches three times one Sunday on Romans 8:7, "The mind set on the flesh is hostile toward God." These words reflect the dualism of Platonic and Greek thought. They are not good news to me. For how can God be removed from the flesh? How can the drop of water in the Eucharistic wine become separated again? But at the time of Finney's preaching they still hold power. Heads lower, people weep with deep conviction. For many days after local leaders gather in people's homes with Mr. Finney to inquire about all that is happening. At each meeting, the crowd grows larger. People are overcome with emotion. Finney urges them to keep composed to go quietly to their homes to pray. But loud wailings erupt; people are slain in the spirit and fall down on the floor where they had just been standing. Eventually Finney needs to find a larger space to conduct meetings. In the twenty days he spends preaching in Rome there are over 500 conversions in the town.

During the conversions, apparently three local skeptics are drinking at the bar and ridiculing all the happenings around them. When they get up to walk home one suddenly falls down dead. From that point on, any doubt that is left in the minds of the locals quickly dissipates. Soon inhabitants of Rome can't go anywhere without seeing people praying, reading their Bibles, weeping or laid out cold in the Spirit.

When Sheriff Bryant of Utica comes to Rome on business, he is cynical about the revival happening in the sister city. In fact, he and his friends have a great many laughs about it. Riding into Rome on his one-horse sleigh he crosses the old canal about a mile from town. As soon as he crosses the canal, a strange feeling comes over him; awe, wonder, sorrow, something totally unexplainable. The closer he gets to town the stronger the sensations grow until he has to admit that the presence of God saturates the air around the city. I wonder, is it some kind of advanced technology that creates these experiences? Is it the Holy Spirit? If Jesus is an alien, I guess that explains how he got beamed backed up to heaven at his ascension.

~

In the late 70s something of a revival breaks out in Rome, New York again. Keith Green—a passionate folk singer with a wild John the Baptist flavor, challenges his peers to kick drugs, new age spirituality and the free love values of the time to live authentic lives committed to Jesus instead. Keith is deeply moved by the religious history of Rome, New York and with his rising fame he brings new attention to this spiritual place in some writing he does on Charles Finney with his wife. My parents, along with other post-long haired hippies, join the group when my father is stationed at Griffiss Air Force Base on his first assignment. After finishing up his Master's degree at Texas A&M, my father is now employed by the US government as a weatherman.

~

I remember the story of my father driving to work one afternoon in 1982. He and my mother have just had an argument about God.

I wonder what sort of mysteries float on the wind up here. I imagine the clouds turn red above as my father questions, "How do I know you are even real?" Then, maybe the light becomes blinding. Whatever happens in those moments, my father pulls the car over to the side of the road and invites Jesus into his heart. I always thought that's why the Air Force built a weather base in Rome, New York. Forecast today: "Seventy percent chance of the Holy Spirit descending this morning. Drive carefully."

Now my father freely shares with me his stories of divine encounters with God. As he talks his eyes fill with tears. His lips shake. I have seen him wipe his face when he stands silently in front of the CD player as a choir sings about God coming to visit one's cottage door, or when the moon is shining full above his home, or when he prays. When he retires from the military, it's like the hard shell around him retires too. Who would have thought that underneath that blue uniform my father was hiding a sensitive mystic?

~

I can feel my stomach leaping, my heart pounding. My thoughts are racing. This is crazy! Why am I here? What if they tell me that I'm going to burn in hell? That I'm a lapsed Christian who's been dragged into the hands of the devil through Episcopal liturgy, feminism, and witchcraft? What if they all want to lay hands on me and pray the devil out of me?

I make a few rules for myself: I'm not going to tell them that I've worked in the church for the past seven years. In fact, I'm not going to tell them much at all. I'm just going to listen and try to understand where they are coming from. I am curious about my spiritual experiences I had as a child. Is this the foundation of my faith or is it all just some kind of charismatic TBN craziness?

I pull out of the hotel parking lot and make my way north on Wright Drive towards the flags. I drive straight through where the military gate used to be, past the street I used to live on which is no longer there. I pass the runway, the weather station where my father used to work, the historical B52 Bomber on display between a few evergreen trees. I drive through the land that once was Griffiss Air Force Base, and into the business district of Rome, New York.

The streets are decorated with restaurants and gas stations, schools and banks and tacky old streamers that hang over the car dealerships and bars. I turn right on Turin Road. The church is up ahead, less than a mile, on the left. I can hardly breathe. I drive slowly and practice pranayama to calm my nerves. *Be courageous. You can do this.*

I'm an introvert by nature. It takes a lot of energy for me to be in public. Add modern day prophets and questionable theology to the mix and you have a recipe for…an encounter with the Holy Spirit? I laugh out loud. I remind myself of Karl Barth. That finding God is like reaching out to the stranger and leaping into the void, going to those places that are unknown and uncomfortable. Here I go again.

I see it in the distance. A small little brick church with a big sign out front: Rome Christian Center Welcomes You! An older man is standing in the equally small parking lot, wearing a tight orange jacket that leaves his large middle exposed. His gray hair is longer and curling beneath his matching orange baseball cap. He points an orange colored flashlight at me and directs me to one of the many open spaces. Their website boasts that this church will be the site of End Times revival. They are ready.

It's ten 'til and I doubt they are going to get the turnout they've hoped for today. I put the car in park, turn off the engine and take a few more deep breaths. My daughter, Ela is already asleep. I wrap the pink paisley sling around my shoulders and tuck her in gently. A few more cars pull in after me, old minivans rusting around the edges, cars at least fifteen years old. One woman emerges from the teal car next to me, hair sprayed up tall on top of her head, she's dressed in tight stonewashed jeans, her face is wrinkled with sadness, make-up, and regret. She crushes her smoldering cigarette butt into the ground with her black motorcycle boots. She reminds me in some way of another dimension of myself.

I stand up straight and put on my best churchy face.

An uncomfortable looking young man greets me at the entrance. When I shake his hand and smile at him he looks sheepishly away. I walk straight into the Narthex, which is set up with four long tables and a buffet of breakfast food and coffee. Light beams in from the long windows that run along the back wall. I find the coat rack and hang up my winter jacket. I recognize Pastor Ned immediately. He has kind brown eyes and a narrow face. The top of his head is shiny and bald. Black hair wraps around his ears. He's dressed in gray suit pants, a tie, and a white collared shirt.

"Julie?" He smiles.

"Jessica, her daughter," I put my hand out to shake his.

"Oh my gosh. You look just like I remember your mother. And who is this little angel?"

"This is Ela."

"She's a doll. Boy do I have a thing for younger women." I bite my lip and hope he didn't mean that how it sounded.

"Have you been in ministry this whole time?" I sway to keep Ela asleep.

"Well, I had a rough patch a while ago. I took three years off cause things just weren't working out. We had merged with another congregation and it didn't go well and we lost everything. But after three years I realized that this is what I do—it's all I know how to do. So four years ago, we purchased this building and God has been blessing us ever since." It happens to be an old Lutheran Church.

"Wow. That's great," I smile.

"How old were you when you were here?" Ned scratches his head.

"Five, six," I say as I scan the crowd. There are about thirty folks chatting around the room.

"I can't wait for you to hear this prophet. Man, we had an amazing night last night. He prophesied over people until 10:30!"

He points to a man in the back of the room who looks like I imagine the biblical character of Abraham in a light blue 1970's suit.

"Tell me about your folks. What are they up to these days?"

"My folks are living in the St. Louis area where Mom works as a worship leader at their church."

At the height of his career, the Air Force offered my father a top weather job at the Pentagon. When he turned down the offer because he felt deeply that it wouldn't be in the best interests of his children to live in D.C. they wanted to send him to Greenland for a year without mom. So he retired.

"So they're both still believers?" His eyes widen.

"Yup. They've always been involved in churches my whole life."

"Wow. You know there's not too many folks I know like that. I've watched so many people fall away. It's so good to know they're still keeping the faith!"

I smile and let the complexities of my thoughts pass through my mind.

I find my way into the nursery to give Ela a quick diaper change so we're both ready for whatever is going to happen next. I find a friendly young woman, about my age with a toddler wrapped around her leg. "I guess we used to be friends," she reaches out and gives me a hug.

"Really?"

"Ned's my Dad. We used to play together when we were kids. I'm Sheri."

She smiles beautifully showing her dimples that punctuate a kind face framed by bouncy black curls. My spirit rushes forward inside, an instant recognition.

"I'd like to thank everyone for coming this morning," Pastor Ned's voice fills the room. "You are not going to regret it. Those of you who were here last night can testify to the power of the Holy Spirit that was in the room. We heard so many words from God. People received answers to prayer and the blessings of the Lord. Lives were changed. Hearts were healed. We are so blessed to have a modern day prophet with us today. I know you'll help me give him a warm welcome."

Everyone claps their hands.

"In just a few more minutes we are going to make our way into the sanctuary so gather your things and head on in so we can begin to invite the presence of the Lord into our midst."

There is no stage up front—no piano. Not even a musician. They plug in a small speaker and blast praise music through it. People run to the front of the church, they lift up their hands and wave colorful flags around that say, "Jesus Saves" and "My Redeemer Lives." They sing in their prayer languages. I watch little children dance in the back of the church, a smile spreads wide on the face of a young girl. I wonder what she will think of all of this when she grows up.

As the congregation prays, the room grows warm. Several people fall down on the floor in front of the altar. I watch their bodies shake. My memory is affirmed.

The prophet makes his way to the front of the church. As he preaches a charismatic and impassioned sermon, I size up the patriarchy, intellectually dismiss the theology, and cringe at the emotionalism. I'm not yet schooled on the deep spiritual tradition of using altered and trance states. They didn't teach us that at seminary.

I am afraid when the prophet looks at me. He begins to move toward the congregation. He places his hands on the head of a young woman. He speaks in tongues. She screams and falls to the floor.

"Someone needs to help that young lady," he says. "She's filled with lots of dangerous temptations and her life is about to become a big mess if someone doesn't help her."

He moves onto her husband. He lays his hands on his head and speaks in tongues.

"Son—you've got some changes to make in your life—you gotta drink less, you gotta treat your wife better."

The man begins to weep. He continues to move like this throughout the crowd, touching each on the head, delivering scathing rebukes and haunting prophesies. He's at the end of my row now. My heart begins to race. I won't survive this. I quietly leave the sanctuary and join Ela in the nursery. My body is trembling. I can still hear the prophet's voice coming through the sound system. A hushed silence fills the air and I think he is finally finished. And then I hear Pastor Ned's voice.

"Jessica? Where is Jessica?"

He tells the prophet that there is one more woman he must prophesy over.

"They're calling for you," Sheri smiles at me. My heart falls into my feet. I pick up Ela and drag myself into the sanctuary.

"Come on up here," Pastor Ned says. "This young woman came to our church when she was five. Her parents used to play the music.

Her mother began our first praise band. She had the most beautiful voice. Jessica—come hear what the Lord has to say to you this morning."

It's Palm Sunday. In most churches I'd be waving a palm frond and shaping it into a cross. The worst thing that can happen is that I will be humiliated in front of everyone, I think. Whatever happens, I will write about it, and that gives me a feeling of protection. I take a deep breath and walk up to the front of the church.

I stand a foot taller than the prophet.

"Sit down," he says. "I don't like women who are taller than me."

What an insecure jerk, I think. I prepare for my public reprimand on the evils of feminism and the wide way of liberal Christianity, but when the prophet places his hands on my head I feel it again, as strong as it has ever been, the love in this moment in time, in this strange place, with these strange people, in this strange flesh that had once been rebuked as a whore and since become a woman, a mother, and a minister.

"The Lord is pleased with you, child," he whispers. "You have overcome much in your young life. It hasn't been easy. But you have persevered." He says many things to me that deeply resonate and guide me through the next phases of my life.

He takes my hand and pulls me up to stand. I forgive him for being a jerk.

"Dance with me," he says.

He twirls me in a circle as he sings a strange melody about the daughters of God. As he sings a little out of key and his voice cracks, it dawns on me: one day, when the wind blows the dust back to where it came, I shall remain there and finally see the face of the One who put this wondrous love inside me.

~

As I drive home over the hills my eyes grow wide, my lips push back to my ears and I laugh like Daisy Mae. I had come to refute my religious background. To prove that the Divine Feminine is above all of this nonsense. But I am learning that She thrives in the imagination. One tradition tells that as Sophia fell from heaven and she lost her crown that the imaginal realms of earth were taken over and used to imagine evil. A part of our healing is to reclaim our imaginal spaces for the greatest good of all beings.

We have wept the blood of countless ages as each of us raised high the lance of hate...Now let us dry our tears and learn the dance and chant the life cycle tomorrow dances behind the sun in sacred promise of things to come for children not yet born, for ours is the potential of truly lasting beauty born of hope and shaped by deed. Now let us lay the lance of hate upon this soil.
-Peter Blue Cloud

I finish writing my story. I train to become a yoga instructor. I declare my body and space sacred and sovereign. I create liturgies of movement and song. I honor the cycles of the moon and my menses. I weave together the spiritual threads of Jesus' message, the wisdom of sacred women who have gone before me. I embrace my intuitive skills and begin to do readings and practice healing people. I attend church in the sanctuary of my own body (and every so often at the local Episcopal church too). I am creating my own sacred community in the snowy tundra of Northern Minnesota, as a pioneer of a different kind.

Because religion has such a compelling hold on the deep psyches of so many people, feminists cannot afford to leave it in the hands of the fathers. Even people who no longer "believe in God" or participate in the institutional structure of patriarchal religion still may not be free of the power of the symbolism of God the Father... religion fulfills deep psychic needs by providing symbols and rituals that enable people to cope with limit situations in life (death, evil, suffering) and to pass through life's important transitions (birth, sexuality, death).
-Carol P. Christ

When Inanna rises from the dead in the underworld, she passes through each of the seven gates as she makes her way back to heaven. At each portal, which may also represent one of the seven chakras, a piece of her queenly adornment is returned to her. She has literally been to hell and back. She has witnessed the suffering of her sister Ereshkigal and she was judged and killed. The life force returns to her as the pain and terror of the Dark Mother are witnessed with compassion. Like the two snakes climbing the pole on the caduceus, our life force flows with power when we have attended to our deep roots of suffering, then the light can activate and restore our crown.

On her return to heaven, Inanna chooses to look upon her beloved Demuzi, a shepherd god, the good son who she meets as an equal. She does not sit on a pedestal as a beautiful earth goddess, for as she rises she still has underworld demons around her and she is still raging with the force of new life. This powerful woman must be met as equal for the life cycle to continue. Patriarchy's narcissists and grand inquisitors squirm in her presence, for many are still unwilling to descend into their own pain or to find a right relationship with the sacred feminine or to face and forgive themselves for the pain they have caused; they are the ones who will be burned at the end of the age in the transformation of the world or they can choose to descend and find compassion for all their pain.

Variants say Demuzi begged his sister to go in his place instead or that he transformed into a snake to make the descent—much like Shiva, or Christ, the sacred masculine is willing to sacrifice earthly comforts, worldly power, disembodied over-intellectualization, overly sentimental "too good" and too disconnected ideas about his relationship to the earth and the feminine in order to discover his true noble heart revealed in the fires of transformation. Each of us gets to decide if we will go consciously to the underworld, or if we will wait unconsciously for the resurrected ones to gaze upon us with judgement.

Whatever you do to the least of these, you do to me.

-Jesus

Today Native American Indians in the US are twice as likely to live in poverty. Life expectancy is the lowest among all people and infant mortality is the highest. Native Americans are violently victimized at twice the rate as African Americans. They are more likely to die of an accident, suicide, or alcohol related causes. The American Psychological Association has written that their current mental and psychological conditions are directly related to their history of trauma.

We each have a job to do. The descendants of the colonists need to acknowledge the atrocity, and indigenous people, we have a job to do too: it is to forgive.
 -Lyla June, Diné (Navajo) musician, poet, youth activist

Finally, the United States officially apologized to the Native American people. The apology is buried in The Defense Appropriate Act of 2010, H.R. 3326 on page 45 between detailed paragraphs outlining military spending. It was quietly signed on December 19, 2009.

American Indians were twice as likely to experience a rape/sexual assault compared to all races.
 -U.S. Bureau of Justice Statistics

According to RAINN, the Rape, Abuse & Incest, National, Network: sexual assaults happen every two minutes in the U.S. 44% of victims are under the age of 18. 80% are under the age of 30. 38% of rapists are friends of the victim. 97% of rapists will never spend a day in jail. 99% of rapes are committed by men.

When feminine energy is no longer feared but honored and returned to her rightful place at the center of community life these numbers will go down. When dominance and assertion of power is no longer the solution to conflict, but the solution is love then we will heal the planet.

- *The crime rate against women in the United States is significantly higher than in other developed countries—the United States has a rape rate that is 13 times higher than*

> *England's, nearly four times higher than Germany's, and more than 20 times higher than Japan's.*
> - *There were more women injured by rapists in 1989 than Marines wounded by the enemy in all of World War II.*
>
> -Senate Judiciary Committee July 31, 1990

Many of us are experiencing an awakening of the Divine Feminine as her consciousness is rising within us again after thousands of years of repression. We are having a variety of responses from denial to confusion to celebration. As we begin to open our eyes and deepen our awareness of the centuries of violence experienced and perpetuated upon humanity we may cower in the face of so much primal wounding and rage—or we may not yet be able to face it.

Change is coming so that the fire that once burned 'witches' in the town square becomes the fire for awakening spiritual transformation. The key is to see how we are both killer and wounded. Yes I am victim, but I am also Queen of Heaven. I am Earth Goddess and also Kali wielding knives dripping with blood ready to kill illusions. I am all facets of the fragmented life force. I am fully capable of both good and evil. I have wounded so many in my path to consciousness. When my core wounds were triggered, I did to others as was done to me: when I discovered my ex with another woman, I vengefully posted a nude photograph of him and his mistress on his social media. It took me about two years to really see what I had done, to face that I had acted to wound him just as I had been wounded, even though I knew the depths of that pain and I would not wish it on another—in a flash of rage, I did! I have publicly humiliated others (even in writing this book) just as I have been publicly humiliated. I am no different from my abuser. I must practice compassion. It is the only way.

I am both my shadow and my light. That is the power of the knowledge of good and evil. It's knowing fully our capacity to be both saint and sinner and to learn the ancient art of integration as the infinite dance of opposites creates sacred symmetry throughout the entire cosmos. This is our time of initiation into unity consciousness—an invitation to share in the mind of Christ-Sophia. And it's a bumpy awakening! Our work is to refrain from demonizing or worshipping the opposites in ourselves or others and hold onto the love at our center of our being. We cannot hide from our shadows, nor can we hide our light under a bushel any longer. As we dissolve the ancient "gotcha" culture that exploits humanity—echoes from our past crucifixions, inquisitions, and witch burnings, we create instead a culture of compassion. As soon as a shadow rears its head, we invite the daemon home like the prodigal sons and daughters, and then we throw a party.

As we allow all parts of self to be witnessed and healed, we transform our inner and outer terrorists who have kept us living in systems of fear and trauma. It is clear that ancient sacred feminine wisdom has been left out of most of our spiritual awareness and practice in the West. It is She who has the potential to bring down the systems of power that no longer serve our highest good, to transform terror and mother the wounded lovers and children as she holds all of our fragments under the great expanse of her wide wings.

Just as Enki sent agents of healing to tend Inanna's dead body when she was reduced to nothing but a rotting piece of meat writhing on a pole in the underworld, so do we today, open our hearts to receive healing from the Eternal River of Life that can reach our collective wounds as deep as they go. For when we receive compassionate witnessing upon all our suffering, we will release new life like Ereshkigal releases her sister to rise again. When we face the truth of the suffering we have caused, when we are nailed to the truth of what we are capable of, then we find a way where before there was none: we find consciousness, compassion, forgiveness and grace. For those who humble themselves shall be exalted. Then we will do what Christ told us we could always do: heal the sick, raise the dead and be born again in the image of our divine mothers and fathers.

Let the whole world see and know that things which were cast down are being raised up and things which had grown old are being made new.

-The Episcopal Book of Common Prayer

I am She.

I am Sophia.

I am She who has fallen from the heights of heaven into the depths of the abyss and been put under the rule of the tyrants of this world for an age that an even greater glory may come.

I am She.

I am She who has seen, She who knows, She of the night owls and She of the wolves.

I am She.

I am She who entered into the deepest bowels of the beast.
I am She who has the keys to unlock the light from the deepest deep.
I am She who is the inmost interior of all holy and sacred things.

I am She.

I am She who agrees to leave the splendor of the light of all mysteries, She who removed my crown and my royal robes to descend into the deep.

I am She who beholds all suffering.

I am She.
I am She who agreed to break into ten thousand pieces that my seeds of light would one day spring.

I am She.

I am She who proclaims from inside the groaning earth: Sing!
I am She who makes the rocks sing.

I am She who pleads to Jesus, She who sings when he sends his light
to me from the heights of heaven into the deepest deep.

I am She who sees behind all masks into the true nature of things.
I am She who brings life through your lips,
She who parses all double tongues.
I am She who is Terror.
She whom women scorn for their men look to me for salvation.
I am She the destroyer of all illusions.
She who is Whore, She who loves all of creation,
She the sacred woman.

I am She the keeper of women's blood and birth mysteries,
She who has known the betrayal of women as they fell under
patriarchal rule,
She the chalice,
She who bore the teachings that nursed King Jesus.

I am She who is Eve, the Mother of all Creation.
She who says: take and eat.
She who frees from the shame that consciousness brings.
She of the very beginning.
She of the deep now,
She of eternity and life beyond the grave.

I am She the ever-changing one,
She who is Life herself.

I am She who is Shelter, She your most tender lover.

Come now shake off your grave clothes and rise with the Spring,
for I am She, the one who was lost but is found again.

I am Sophia, Queen of Heaven, She the consort of God,
She who unlocks true love from the stoniest hearts,
She the light that breaks through the darkest seed,

She who cries out from the deep,
She who sings, until all creation is redeemed.

May Her songs rise in us.

AFTERWARD

It is November 24, 2012 just after midnight. My family is recovering from turkey and stuffing, dishes and fussy babies who are now quietly asleep. My mother opens another bottle of wine and my father fills all of our glasses. I have just finished the rough draft of my memoir and I am giving it to my parents to read.

"Jessica—there are some things in life that should never be talked about!"

My mother flattens the wrinkles out of her forehead.

"Our Norwegian ancestors knew the art of silence—they knew that certain things were forbidden from being spoken. It's for the good of the community that we honor and keep that silence. We sacrifice our voice and our selfishness so that there is peace and harmony for others."

All those strange Bible verses start flooding my mind, the ones commanding women to remain silent so that order can prevail in the churches.

My sister, my former husband and my father all look to me and await my reply.

"Like your mother does," my father interjects. "She gives so much for you—she's a saint."

"I know Dad. She is."

Both of them have been wonderful grandparents to my children.

"But Mom—you can talk about things—it's good to talk about stuff—it's healing," Emily gently presses her. My sister has spent the past ten years in therapy too. Both of us are learning to be whole.

"I'm not reading it, Jessica. No way," my mother insists. "I don't want to know. Those were some of the hardest years of my life and I don't want to ever relive them again. I can't. You were Beelzebub!"

"Mom! They were hard for me too." My eyes begin to water.

"Maybe if you knew the whole story, you would understand."

"What are you so afraid of?" Emily raises the wine glass to her lips.

"I'm afraid that you won't understand me," she says.

"Mom—I still don't understand you!" I chuckle. "And I want you to understand me too."

"I think you'll be surprised," my ex says (this was before our marriage fell apart). "It's not like that—it's her personal journey."

"I know more than you think I do about those years," she pours herself another glass of wine. In the evenings she becomes another woman. Lately she drinks and speaks more freely.

"I'm sure you do—but we never have talked about any of it," I watch the red legs drip down my wine glass.

"Jessica—I know you were raped," she says. "And I think I know the guy who did it."

Everything inside of me curls up. My body begins to shake.

"It was that colonel's son wasn't it? That one day, at that party with Marissa? His mother always hated me. All those bitchy colonel's wives—they were so mean to me. God I hated Blytheville."

"What? No—Mom. No. Not a colonel's son."

I put my head in my hands.

"Oh my God," my mother puts her hands over her mouth.

"I didn't mean to bring anything up. I am so sorry I said anything."

"You knew I was raped?"

My sister and I lock eyes. Her face is as white as mine.

"I remember. You came home one day. And you curled up on the couch."

"How could we not know?" My father says. "We aren't as dumb as you always thought."

"But—if you knew why didn't you ever say anything to me?"

I thought once I finally told them—I thought things would make sense for us all. I thought they would maybe find a way to have compassion on all those years. But they already knew? All along? I watch my happy ending unravel before me.

"How are we supposed to help you if you don't talk to us? Can you tell me how we can teach kids to tell their parents when they are hurting? You rejected me, Jessica. You pushed me away. How was I supposed to reach you?"

My head hurts. I thought our family values were to stay silent? That's what I did. I did what was expected.

"I'm sorry Mom—I was just a kid. I thought you would reject me."

My father sniffles and hands me a tissue. My mother comes running over to me and wraps her arms around me.

"How could I ever reject you," she says. "You are my precious Jessica. I am so sorry honey. I didn't know what to do. I just didn't know what to do."

My father embraces us both.

"You know what's the best pot to smoke?"

I laugh, "Are we finally going to share our secrets, Dad?"

"No," my Mother says. "You won't respect us."

"Mom—there is nothing you can do to lose my love. I love you no matter what."

"That's not true—if you knew…"

"Mom!" Emily snaps. "We respect you more when you're real with us."

"No," she says. "No you won't."

Her shame is palpable. She dabs her eyes, "Jessica—you need to think really hard about this. If you publish this you could ruin your career. How can you ever work in the church—or ever become successful with your music, or writing?"

"I don't know how it will turn out, Mom. And I'm okay with that. Won't you please read my story Mom?"

She sniffles and rubs her forehead.

"Ok, Jess. I'll read it."

~

A few months later she e-mails me her initial response. It is worse than I imagined it could possibly be. She sends me several long pages of bullet pointed complaints. She is angry. She is defensive. She thinks I got the story all wrong. That I made things up. She doesn't mention the sexual abuse at all. I feel like an unreliable witness of my own life. A bad girl. I am crushed. An ancient pain returns to my body. My mind becomes cloudy. I am floating in space again. The self-hatred returns.

But I have acquired some new skills for self-caring now. I practice deep breathing. I hold the old photograph my father took of me days after I was raped behind the high school. No matter what anyone else thinks of me, I must behold this girl now. I must see her pain. Her loneliness. And her broken heart. I can embody the Mother Goddess now. At least this is my practice, to see how Persephone and Demeter are essentially opposite ends of the same pole of energy within us all.

I realize I have to stop asking my parents to take care of this girl (like I had always hoped they or some guy would). I know they are proud of me. But still, sharing my story is the ultimate act of defiance. The family system—well basically my whole life functioned if I kept silent, if I remained the bad girl and held the projections of other people's shadows and secrets.

"I'm going to take care of you," I promise.

I tuck the picture between the pages of my book of poetry and music. I know this girl wants to share her voice. She wants me to tell her story. And I have to live with the consequences of speaking. The truth will set me free, even as it breaks all of our illusions of safety. But I must be free. Free to live not as a victim, not as some sealed off fantasy, but as a complicated human being capable of bearing love and pain.

I spend time in meditation and prayer focusing on my heart center and feeling affection for my mother, who I realize is deeply hurting too.

And then my mother totally surprises me.

My dearest Jessica,
First I need to apologize for my initial reaction to your story. It wasn't the proper one, nor the one you needed. A dear friend has helped me process through the initial shock and helped me see better. Everyone should have a friend like her.

I don't have words to say how sorry I am for being so naïve, and without a clue. My heart breaks for the 13 year old child who had her life stripped away from her so viciously. Had I had any idea what you were going through I would have done anything to save you from it.

I can't imagine the horror and the hell you went through. There was no way a child of that age could have navigated through the events of that summer. You were ruined. Your childhood was stolen from you. It's miraculous that you stayed alive. I thank God you were strong enough to fight your way through, even if it cost you nearly everything to do so.

I've racked my brain trying to think of why we didn't try to get some psychological help at the time. I don't have the answer to that. It was 24 years ago and I don't think that was the first avenue people took. I was so clueless to the real reason for your behavior that I think I just thought it was the way 13 year old girls behaved when they were trying to spread their wings. I'm so sorry. We really didn't know what to do.

I now see that you were traumatized, and as humans deal with trauma, they don't think rationally. You were doing whatever you could to make sense of your situation and to hold on. I see why, I think I'm beginning to understand.

I can see why we were crazy in your eyes...to not see through to your soul. We would have rescued you. God, I wish we had that time back. I would give my life to give you those years back to you. You deserved a happy childhood. You, someone so full of promise and depth, had best part of your life cut away from you in a violent manner. I mourn for your lost years and lost opportunities.

I don't blame you for any of it. Your reactions were understandable. You were in survival mode without any compass with which to navigate. I wish there would have been some adult who would have seen what was happening, someone who would have protected you, or helped us see what was going on. We thought you were just being difficult. We didn't know you were fighting for your life.

We held on to any ray of light we saw in you.

I can't believe you've carried this horrific burden for 24 years. And how powerful is God's love in you that you continued to carry it with grace these past 14 years, as God has been working to make you whole again, to give you back your life, and to redeem the years that were stripped from you.

I can't undo my ignorance of the past 24 years, but I will try. I am sorrier than you will ever know. I love you more than my own life.

Mom

At thirty seven years old, one year after I asked my parents to read my memoir, my mother invites me to sit down and work through our past with her new Jungian analyst. We meet upstairs in the church where we held my grandpa's funeral and my wedding. This place has held so much sorrow. And so much joy.

POSTSCRIPT

Christian Roberts has no public record of sexual perpetration. Jason found him on Facebook and I reached out to him and told him I had written a book about what happened in Gosnell. On February 22, 2013 he sent me the following note:

> *I am so sorry if I hurt you. I was a broken kid who was abused and, as you can imagine, also confused. I came to Christ in my late teens and my life totally changed. Please rest assured, since I have come to Christ, I have changed. I would never hurt anyone. I have been married for over 18 years to a wonderful Christian woman who has helped me in my healing process. My wife and I are praying God will heal you from your pain and give you His peace that surpasses all understanding.*

After all the years I spent searching for my voice, I decided there was only one word that could adequately sum up all that I was feeling in this moment. I simply replied, "Wow." He was slick as ever. I hoped for the best, but I am no longer naïve.

A few years later I found out that my message was a pivotal moment for Christian Robert's former wife, now ex. She said his face was white as a ghost when he read it and after one too many strange accusations, she finally began to wake up. She has since been in contact with me and several other parents who have children in his care who seem to be displaying signs of sexual abuse. They have all asked me to tell my story so that they can gain legal protection for their children. The state of Arkansas has lifted the statutes of limitations and I have been in contact with an old friend from Blytheville who grew up to become a lawyer who has assured me that Christian Roberts broke the law and I would have a case.

In my conversations with the former wife of Christian Roberts I learn that they met shortly after he moved away from Gosnell in a very similar way that we met: she was the new girl, and he appeared connected and popular and he took her under his wings. According to her and what she has pieced together over the years, Christian Roberts was put into some kind of a counseling program at a military base in Colorado Springs around the same time I went to live with my aunt and uncle just an hour north of him in Denver. Her understanding was that his family discovered he molested a younger cousin when he was twelve, similarly to how his uncle had molested him as a child. According to her, he had had some kind of previous treatments by the government "to fix" this issue. His family did not disclose this information to his ex-wife until many years after they were married. She too is awakening from a web of lies that began to draw her family into contact with dark agencies.

It all begs the question: if a military psychological facility in Colorado knew Christian Robert's history of childhood sexual perpetration upon a young child, then why would he be able to gain employment at another military facility in Gosnell, AR, at a youth center no less, with access to other young children? Why would he be allowed to work as a mentor and coach and given hours of unsupervised access to hundreds of vulnerable military children? Who was opening the doors for him and for what purpose? Are there secret military programs running out of Colorado Springs and Bellevue, Nebraska that used Christian Roberts, and many others, as pawns to abuse children or commit other acts of violence or spread religious propaganda? Is our government abusing its own citizens without our awareness or consent? And for what purpose? Why are so many sexual abuse scandals swept under the rug by well-orchestrated powers that be? Why have such extreme social taboos been put in place to keep victims silent and questioning our own experiences of reality? Who is benefiting from all this secrecy?

Ultimately I am not interested in punitive consequences for Christian Roberts. I want all of our children to be protected and given safe spaces to thrive in a healthy environment and I hope for all of us healing—even him. As I write this now, news of elite pedophilia rings in politics, religion, entertainment, law, virtually all of the top power sectors in our society are coming to our awareness around the world. This is not just an individual problem; this is a collective problem that our human awakening will have to heal and restore as it roots out the black goo. We will have to stop being naïve and we will have to be brave and move in accord with the highest laws of love. Sophia is now awakening the knights of old. It's time to restore the grail.

~

My father has never told me any classified information. He has insisted that he could, but he would have to kill me. I recall him telling me that he personally believes UFOs may be related to weather and man-made secret government projects. Some of the top secret work he did on satellites has now been declassified. Much of what I sense, I have gathered from my own dreams, memories, intuitions and research as I continue to connect my piece of the puzzle to our grand cosmic history.

~

I do look again for Jesus in the sky and I pray that he and our Sacred Mothers will come soon and lead us into a new era where the Prince of Peace rules in love. I do not look for a savior outside of myself though. I had to learn the hard way that our bodies are sanctuaries, houses of light for the Christ-Sophia presence on earth. I had to learn to love myself.

May we find ourselves awake in the dream, may we take courage as we work to transform our terrors into to joy, and may we find the ways to heal our collective wounds so that we may remember how to live together in divine love and cosmic unity.

~

In the legend of Standing Rock, a Dakota man married an Arikara woman and shortly after his bride bore them a child, he took another wife for himself. The tribe tore down their tepees to move on to another location, but the despondent new mother sat down on the land and refused to leave. The tribe left her behind, but after a few days the husband sent his brother's to retrieve his first wife, for he was concerned she may kill herself in anguish. The brothers returned and found the mother and child had turned to stone. From that day forth the tribe carried the stone of the woman who chose to become one with the earth rather than betray her own soul. Her people placed her stone in the center of their community as a reminder of her wisdom. The stone has since been returned to where this woman first took her stand against patriarchy. You can visit her stone in front of the Standing Rock Indian Agency in North Dakota.

GRATITUDE

It has taken a village of compassionate witnesses to raise me. I am most grateful to my family who despite our challenges (and my uncomfortable oversharing) continue to turn to the message of Jesus and his gospel of love as we make our way towards Jerusalem our happy home together. Thank you for the life-saving support you gave me through my divorce when all my old wounds were triggered again; we have healed so much. Thank you for your patience and your willingness to change and grow with me. Thank you for forgiving me for those times I lashed out at you from my own core wounds, for all the times I was unable to show you the face of love that you truly are.

Deep bows to my tender therapists, Debbie and Steve, for their time and loving kindness toward me, for their rays of hope and guidance down many difficult roads: yes some are no longer an option, and I'm so glad I to have turned many, many pages.

Thank you, Episcopal Church for welcoming me, for extending deep hospitality to me, for inviting me to use my gifts of creativity and music to share the message of Jesus's deep love with so many people.

To all the youth group kids I had the honor of walking along side of, kids who have had to navigate their own set of formidable challenges, you amaze me and inspire me. Leg kick! To my babysitter, Caroline Carani who wanted to share the first draft of this book with her high school friends and encouraged me to get this story out there for her generation, I cannot thank you enough for all the love and joy you brought into our lives.

Thank you to my dear friend and amazing mother, Siobhan who flew me to women's spirituality conferences and gave me the keys to her cabin so I could write the first draft of this book.

Thank you to my former agent, Maryann Karinch for believing in me and in this book and putting the fire under my feet to keep at it.

To all the sacred women who have walked along side me and taught me to straighten my back and lift my head a little higher, especially my grandmothers, my aunts, my mother, my cousins and my sister. To the new spiritual pioneers of the Divine Feminine, women like Meggan Watterson and Marguerite Rigoglioso and Kaia Ra, women who make my heart leap with some profound recognition; as I see the living Goddess in you, it helps awaken Her in me. We are remembering the ancient ways. To all my sisters at Seven Sisters Mystery School who provide safe sacred space to explore our feminine essence and remember the mystery teachings of old, blessed be.

To all the yogis who come to my classes, to those who are willing to go on adventures in wellness, thank you for opening your hearts and imaginations and co-creating sacred space with me for us all to heal.

I want to thank David, my ex-husband, for walking a hard road with me, for his help in editing the first drafts of this manuscript, for three beautiful children. May you continue to become the tall tree of your destiny. I regret we couldn't keep growing together in marriage, but I am so glad that we get to keep growing.

Oh Jason. Thank you for letting me dig up our past, and for holding me through a nightmare with all your love.

Aaron, I never thought our paths would cross again after all these years, but you knew we would and so here we are. You have become quite the magical shaman and dear friend. Thank you for your support as I faced so many old fears, and for opening doors for me to heal and grow in ways I never imagined.

Grant, for your laughter and leveling up skills, for your tender compassionate presence and embodied sacred masculine essence, for your amazing dadding, and your digital shaman skills that worked much magic during the final editing of this book. Thanks for being weird with me.

And my dear children, may your eyes be shielded from this book until divine timing allows it to unlock, if ever. This or better for the greatest good of all. You three have been my greatest teachers. I love you all more than I can bear. May I not ever be an obstacle for your soul's growth. May you find healing for any trauma I have inadvertently passed on to you. And may you always listen to your heart, may you care for yourselves and creation as truly beloved (and clean up after yourselves). I know I have struggled at times to balance being mommy and paying the bills and it pains me that I have not always been able to give you my full presence. I hope one day mothers everywhere won't ever have to choose between being present for their children and working, desperately at times, for our family's survival. May love find a way. May She help fill in our gaps and bring us all home to the sacred garden one day. And may you be free to discover the answers that make the most sense to you!

For all you dear readers who descend into these depths with me, I am eternally grateful for your compassionate witnessing. May you find your life more enriched for this journey to the underworld and back.

Before this book ends, may our eyes be blessed now. May the scales fall. May the veils part. May we from this day forward look upon ourselves and others with the sort of fierce compassion that will raise the dead and redeem the planet.

And remember, it's all about love.

END NOTES

PROLOGUE-TRANSCENDENCE

p.7 **"Our lives begin to end"**: Martin Luther King Jr., "I Have a Dream" (speech, Washington, DC, August 28, 1963), American Rhetoric,
http://www.americanrhetoric.com/speeches/mlkihaveadream.htm.

p.8 **[Pat Robertson] talks about the end of the world**: YouTube, accessed November 20, 2013,
http://www.youtube.com/watch?v=uDT3krve9iE.

p.8 **He says the devil is using feminists**: YouTube, accessed November 20, 2013,
http://www.youtube.com/watch?v=Um42nBDx3tA.

p.8 **Images of flames and scary faces haunt our living room**: YouTube, accessed November 20, 2013,
http://www.youtube.com/watch?v=_cVGwIhMIV8.

p.11 **O Lord, You have seduced me, and I am seduced; you have raped me and I am overcome:**. Translation by A. Heschel, *The Prophets Harper Perennial Modern Classics*; 1st Perennial classics edition (October 16, 2001) 144. Heschel argues that the words used by Jeremiah to describe God's impact upon his life are same words used for seduction and rape in the legal terminology of the Bible and that most translations of the text soften the original language.

p.11 **The name of the private school is Maranatha! —a word found in Corinthians, which is neither Greek nor Hebrew, but a transliteration of an Aramaic phrase that means, "our Lord has come" or "our Lord is coming!" or "our Lord, come!"**: Walla Walla College Newsletter of the School of Theology and the Institute of Bible, Church & Culture, 3 no. 2, (Autumn 2003): accessed November 20, 2013,
http://www.wallawalla.edu/academics/departments/theology/ibcc/newsletters/0302/index.html?a=13.

CHAPTER 1-WHORE

p.23 **"What appears to be a catastrophe"**: Rachel Naomi Remen, "Listening Generously" on the radio program *Speaking of Faith with Krista Tippet*, (July 29, 2010). Accessed November 20, 2013,
http://www.onbeing.org/program/listening-generously/124.

p.23 **"You shall not oppress a resident alien":** *The New Revised Standard Version*, copyright 1989, 1995 by the Division of Christian Education of the National Council of the Churches of Christ in the United States of America. Subsequent scripture passages also quoted from same source unless otherwise noted.

p.27 **"Religions centered on the worship of a male God":** "Why Women Need the Goddess" was presented by Carol P. Christ in the keynote address to an audience of over 500 at the "Great Goddess Re-emerging" conference at the University of Santa Cruz in the spring of 1978. It was first published in *Heresies: The Great Goddess Issue* (1978), 8-13, and reprinted in Carol P. Christ and Judith Plaskow, eds., *Womanspirit Rising: A Feminist Reader on Religion* (San Francisco: Harper & Row, 1979), 273-287, as well as in Carol P. Christ, *Laughter of Aphrodite: Reflections on a Journey to the Goddess* (San Francisco: Harper & Row, 1987) 117-132.

p.28 **Chickasawba, the old road named after an Indian Chief:** The USGen Web Project, *Mississippi County, AR History*, Submitted by: Michael Brown, September 1998. Use with permission only. Brown cites: *Biographical and Historical Memoirs of Eastern Arkansas.* Chicago: Goodspeed Publishers, 1890. Accessed November 20, 2013, http://files.usgwarchives.net/ar/mississippi/history/goodspd.txt.

p.29 **Native Americans asked De Soto to pray to his God for rain:** Ibid.

p.37 **You have taken our land and made us outcasts:** *The World of the American Indian*, (National Geographic Society, 1974) p. 384.

p.42 **Victims of Sexual Assault are:** World Health Organization, "The World Report on Sexuality and Violence," 2002. Accessed November 20, 2013, http://www.ncadv.org/files/SexualAssault.pdf.

p.42 **If childhood sexual abuse is not treated:** U.S. Department of Veterans Affairs, P.T.S.D: National Center for PTSD, Child Sexual Abuse. Accessed November 20, 2013,
http://www.ptsd.va.gov/public/pages/child-sexual-abuse.asp.

CHAPTER 2-DAUGHTER

p.47 **"I decided that it is better to scream":** Nadezhda Mandelstam and Max Hayward, *Hope Against Hope.* (New York: Modern Library, 1999), 43.

p.48 **The Iroquois tribe lived in New York between Niagara Falls and the Adirondack Mountains:** *Iroquois History*, Accessed November 20,

2013, http://www.tolatsga.org/iro.html & *Indians.org*, Accessed November 20, 2013, http://www.indians.org/articles/the-mohawk-tribe.html.

p.48 **The tribes were matrilineal:** *Iroquois Women* © 1 October 2001, Portland State University. Accessed November 20, 2013, http://www.iroquoisdemocracy.pdx.edu/html/iroquoiswoman.htm.

p.48 **Ft. Stanwix:** *City of Rome, Our History*, Accessed November 20, 2013, http://www.romenewyork.com/index.asp?org=71.

p.48 **Others fled their homeland when trouble erupted and followed the Ohio River west:** *Intertribal Monitoring Association of Indian Trust Funds*, Accessed November 20, 2013,
http://www.itmatrustfunds.org/Tribes_folder/Quapaw.htm.

p.48 **The Umahan, or Omaha:** *Quapah Origins, retold by Richard L. Dieterle.* Accessed November 20, 2013,
http://www.hotcakencyclopedia.com/ho.QuapahOrigins.html.

p.48 **Ugakhpa:** *Arkansas Secretary of State* © 2011, Accessed November 20, 2013,
http://www.sos.arkansas.gov/educational/students/abstractArkansas/Pages/nativePeople.aspx.

p.50 **The law mandated profane prostitutes:** Nancy Qualls-Corbett, *The Sacred Prostitute, Eternal Aspect of the Feminine* (Inner City Books, Toronto, 1988) p.38.

p.51 **Traditional developmental narratives describe coming of age as a gradual solidifying and strengthening of the subject—the dawning realization of the self:** White, Emily. Fast Girls: Teenage Tribes and the Myth of the Slut (Berkley Trade, 2003) p.109-111.

p.52 **This land was once covered in forests**: *History of Blytheville, Arkansas.* CommunityLink © 1996–2013. All rights reserved. Accessed December 3, 2013, http://communitylink.com/blytheville-arkansas/2011/09/19/history/.

p.56 **The artifacts found nearby have been dated back to prehistoric times:** *The History of Mississippi Country*, Accessed December 3, 2013, http://www.argenweb.net/mississippi/history.htm. Mapping the Chickasawba Mound, Accessed December 3, 2013, http://www.academia.edu/3210337/Mapping_Chickasawba_Mound.

p.57 **Inanna, an ancient Sumerian Goddess, possibly a precursor of Sophia, Mary Queen of Heaven, and Persephone, must pass through seven gates:** Perera, Sylvia Brinton. *Descent to the Goddess, A Way of Initiation for Women.* (Airlift Book Company, 1982).

p.59   **People who suffer from Post-Traumatic Stress disorder:** Kalsched, Donald E. *The Inner World of Trauma, Archetypal Defenses of the Personal Spirit.* (Routledge, 1996).

p.68   **Some Native American tribes placed the newly dead high in trees:** Tree and Scaffold Burial, Introductory Study to the Morturary Customs among the North American Indians © 2000-2005 by Na.Nations.com, Accessed December 12, 2013. http://www.nanations.com/burialcustoms/scaffold_burial.htm.

p.68   **In some tribes, the warrior's horse is killed and placed beneath the scaffold to accompany his spirit into the afterlife:** Historical Records and Accounts of Native American Indian Tribes and their culture, art and symbols. Posted July 31, 2011. Accessed December 12, 2013.   http://americanindianshistory.blogspot.com/2011/07/native-american-burials-trees-and.html

p.68   **I read the Pawnees would tie an unmarried girl they had captured from another tribe upon the scaffold:** Internet Archive LIBRARY OF THE UNIVERSITY OF ILLINOIS AT URBANA-CHAMPAIGN. Full text of "The sacrifice to the morning star by the Skidi Pawnees" by Ralf Linton Assistant Curator of North American Ethnology Field Museum of Natural History Department of Anthropology © 1922. Accessed December 12, 2013. http://archive.org/stream/sacrificetomorni06lint/sacrificetomorni06lint_djvu.txt.

p.78   **Dead Ringers**, VHS, directed by David Cronenberg (1988; USA: 20th Century Fox, 1988).

p.87   **"At the core of that father-lover complex is the father-god whom she worships and at the same time hates because..."** Marion Woodman in: Kalsched, Donald E. *The Inner World of Trauma, Archetypal Defenses of the Personal Spirit.* (Routledge, 1996).

CHAPTER 3-PUELLA AETERNA

p.90   **"Women with disabilities are raped and abused at twice the rate of the general population."** U.S. Bureau of Justice Statistics. 2000 Sexual Assault of Young Children as Reported to Law Enforcement, 2000 (Sobsey 1994).

p.94   **Premenstrual Dysphoric Disorder:** *Trauma and PTSD – An overlooked pathogenic pathway for Premenstrual Dysphoric Disorder?* H.-U. Wittchen, A. Perkonigg, and H. Pfister, Technical University of Dresden, Institute of Clinical Psychology and Psychotherapy, Dresden,

Germany and Max Planck Institute of Psychiatry, Munich, Germany. Arch Women's Ment Health (2003). Accessed December 14, 2013. http://www.qucosa.de/fileadmin/data/qucosa/documents/10532/678_PP.pdf.

p.99 **De Soto convinces the indigenous people that he is a sun god:** Hudson, Charles M. (1997). *Knights of Spain, Warriors of the Sun.* "Death of de Soto". University of Georgia Press. P. 349-52. Accessed on December 14, http://en.wikipedia.org/wiki/Hernando_de_Soto#cite_note-Hudson_Death-of-de-Soto:349-52-30.

p.100 **The Goddess was once worshiped in temples, on hills and high places:** see 1 Kings 11:5, 2 Kings 23:4-14, Song of Solomon.

p.102 **"Knee-hi-miah!" my brother screams. "No! Bildad the Shoe-height!":** This is a reference to the book of Nehemiah and Bildad the Shuhite in Job 18.

p.104 **"You know what time it is…"** Romans 13:11-14.

p.108 **In some Native American burial rites, the women gathered around the corpse cutting their bodies and pouring their blood over the dead to…** Historical Records and Accounts of Native American Indian Tribes and their culture, art and symbols. Figure 20 represents scarification as a form of grief-expression for the dead. Posted July 31, 2011. Accessed December 12, 2013.
http://americanindianshistory.blogspot.com/2011/07/native-american-burials-trees-and.html.

CHAPTER 4-NEW GIRL

p.115 **"Leaving behind nights of terror and fear, I rise…"** Angelou, Maya. "Still I Rise." Black Sister: Poetry by Black American Women, 1746-1980. Ed. Erlene Stetson. Bloomington, IN: Indiana Univ. Press, 1981. 265.

p.118 **Richard S. Little:** Littleton, Colorado, Anything But Little, Government Historical Pages, Accessed on December 29, 2013, http://www.littletongov.org/index.aspx?page=182.

p.132 **"Stir up in ___ the gift of your Holy Spirit: the spirit of wisdom and understanding, the spirit of counsel and might, the spirit of knowledge and the fear of the Lord, the spirit of joy in your presence, both now and forever."** The Lutheran Book of Worship, Confirmation Service Rite, 1978.

CHAPTER 5-CHEERLEADER

p.137 **"Sexuality and spirituality are pairs of opposites that need each other..."** Jung in Kalsched.

p.139 **I learn about all the characteristics of a child predator:** See, How We Can Spot a Child Molester on PsycholoyToday.com, Accessed December 29, 2013 http://www.psychologytoday.com/blog/shadow-boxing/201206/how-can-we-spot-child-molester.

p.155 **"Many young people engage in sexually risky behaviors..."** Centers for Disease Control and Prevention, Sexual Risk Behavior: HIV, STD, & Teen Pregnancy Prevention, Accessed on December 29, 2013, http://www.cdc.gov/HealthyYouth/sexualbehaviors/.

p.175 **Bluebeard:** A French fairy tale by Charles Perault. See also Fitcher's Bird by the Brother's Grimm.

p.178 **In the red room:** See Kalsched.

p.183 **Confucius**: via Thomas a Kempis, *The Imitation of Christ*.

CHAPTER 6-HIGH PRIESTESS

p.189 **Jung saw a transformation chamber in which the traumatized ego was broken down:** Kalsched.

p.189 **The name Nebraska comes from an Indian word meaning flat water:** Nevada Department of Tourism and Cultural Affairs, Accessed December 30, 2013,
http://nevadaculture.org/index.php?option=com_content&task=view&id=1099&Itemid=27.

p.189 **Glaciers used to cover this land that once was an inland sea bed:** Nebraska During the Cenozoic Era, Accessed December 30, 2013, http://eas.unl.edu/~tfrank/History%20on%20the%20Rocks/Nebraska%20Geology/Cenozoic/cenozoic%20web/2.2/Nebraska%20in%20the%20Cenozoic%20Era.html.

p.191 **Colonel Peter Sarpy is a French Creole:** City History of Bellevue, Accessed December 30, 2013, http://www.bellevue.net/CityInformation/HistoryofBellevue.aspx.

p.196 **The Lakota word for Thunderbird means "sacred" and "wings":** Thunderbird Mythology, Accessed December 30, 2013, http://www.princeton.edu/~achaney/tmve/wiki100k/docs/Thunderbird_(mythology).html.

p.197 **A common theme in Native American spirituality is a fascination with the circle and unity:** Eds: Nerburn, K &

Menglekoch, L. *Native American Wisdom.* Classical Wisdom Collection, New World Library: San Rafael California © 1991.

p.192 **When I grew up I learned that Offutt was rumored to house an MKUltra program:** Silver, Timothy. *Lifting the Veil,* Accessed December 10, 2016, http://freepdfhosting.com/28a68f3405.pdf. My father worked for a top secret program at Offutt for six years, during my 5-7th grades and Junior-Freshman year in high school.

p.199 **The Native American peace pipe ceremony creates a sacred relationship between the Creator and the people of the land:** Native American's Online, Native American Pipe Ceremony, Accessed December 30, 2013, http://www.native-americans-online.com/native-american-pipe-ceremony.html.

p.200 **In one myth of the corn woman:** Myths Encyclopedia, Myths and Legends of the World, Accessed December 30, 2013, http://www.mythencyclopedia.com/Ca-Cr/Corn.html.

p.212 **…baptism the priest took the Paschal candle above his head:** Johnson, Maxwell, *Images of Baptism,* Liturgy Training Publications © 2001, p 59.

p.216 **The Peyote religion:** Ethnobotanical Leaflets, Peyote and Native American Culture, Accessed December 30, 2013, http://www.ethnoleaflets.com/leaflets/peyote.htm.

p.218 **"…young drivers with A.D.H.D. are two to four times as likely as those without the condition to have an accident…":** *Learning to Drive with A.D.H.D.* by John O'Neil published in the New York Times on March 23, 2006. Accessed December 30, 2013:
http://www.nytimes.com/2012/03/27/health/add-and-adhd-challenge-those-seeking-drivers-license.html?pagewanted=all&_r=0

p.231 **Settlers have difficulty staying off the sacred sites of the Pottawatomi:** Reminiscences of Nodaway County and the Platte Purchase by Nathaniel Sisson, Accessed December 30, 2013, http://www.mogenweb.org/nodaway/earlyhist/1911.htm.

p.232 **Nodaway County has a violent past:** Northwest Missouri State B.D. Owen's Library, Colter-Gunn Incident Bibliography (December 1930 - January 1931) Accessed December 30, 2013, http://www.nwmissouri.edu/library/courses/history/COLTERGUNN.HTM.

p.239 **The risk of sexual re-victimization, according to the Center for Disease Control:** Multiple Revictimization of Rapes, What is the

Explanation? Rape Crisis Website, Accessed December 30, 2013, http://www.ibiblio.org/rcip/mvrv.html.

CHAPTER 7-PADAWAN

p.253 **"The woman who is a virgin, one in herself, does what she does not for power or out of the desire to please, but because what she does is true.":** Harding, Esther, Women's Mysteries, qtd. In Marion Woodman, Addiction to Perfection: The Still Unravished Bride (Toronto: Inner City Books, 1982) 83.

p.254 **"Let those who fear the LORD say: 'His love endures forever.'":** Psalm 118.

p.255 **...ancient fertility goddess:** Religious Tolerance .Org, Ontario Consultants on Religious Tolerance, Christian symbols: Fish (Ichthus), cross and crucifix, Accessed on December 30, 2013, http://www.religioustolerance.org/chr_symb.htm.

p.256 **"The mind abhors a vacuum. Symbol systems cannot simply be rejected, they must be replaced":** Ibid. Christ, Carol.

p.263 **Shortly after the Dakotas are fought off the land:** Visiting Northfield, Accessed on December 30, 2013, http://www.visitingnorthfield.com/history.html.

p.266 **In 1862 desperate hurting Natives begin to band together against the settlers:** The Dakota Conflict Trials, by Douglas O. Linder, Accessed on December 30, 2013,
http://law2.umkc.edu/faculty/projects/ftrials/dakota/Dak_account.html.

CHAPTER 8-VIRGIN

p.277 **"As I understand the virgin archetype, it is that aspect of the feminine, in man or in woman, that has the courage to Be and the flexibility to be always Becoming...":** Woodman, Marion. *The Pregnant Virgin.* p 80?

p.292 **Indian artifacts found in the western hills of North Carolina:** Asheville, North Carolina, Cherokee, North Carolina, Accessed on December 31, 2013,
http://www.ashevillenc.com/area_info/cherokee_nc.

p. 293 **In 1830 Congress passes the Indian Removal Act:** PBS, Indian Country Diaries, Accessed December 31, 2013,
http://www.pbs.org/indiancountry/history/trail.html.

p. 295 **"Over the years, I have come to realize that the greatest trap in our life is not success, popularity, or power, but self-rejection..."**

Nouwen, Henri J.M. *Life of the Beloved, Spiritual Living in a Secular World,* The Crossroads Publishing Company © 2002, p.27.

p.300 **"Hope is the thing with feathers that perches in the soul":** Dickinson, Emily. "Hope is the thing with feathers." Poetry X. Ed. Jough Dempsey. 25 Aug 2004. 31 Dec. 2013, Accessed December 31, 2013, http://poetry.poetryx.com/poems/2396/.

CHAPTER 9-MOTHER

p.305 **If you bring forth what is within you, what you bring forth will save you:** Translated by Meyer, Martin, *The Gospel of Thomas,* Saying 70, Harper One Second Revised Edition: April 2004 p.53.

p.338 **"...the traditional design of most patriarchal buildings of worship imitates the female body...":** Steinem, Gloria in the forward of Ensler, Eve. *The Vagina Monologues,* V-Day Edition. Random House © 2007 p xxxv.

p. 340 **"The central ceremony of patriarchal religions is on in which men take over the yoni-power...":** Steinem, Ibid.

p.313 **Figure 1. Ego Self Axis,** Edinger, E. F. (1992). *Ego and Archetype: Individuation and the Religious function of the Psyche,* p. 5. Boston: Shambala Publications, Inc.

p.316 **Snakes are symbols of renewal and resurrection:** Chevalier, Jean, Gheerbrant, Alain, & Buchanan-Brown, John (Translator) *The Penguin Dictionary of Symbols,* Penguin Books 1997. p 844-847. See also, The Symbol Dictionary.Net, Accessed December 31, 2013, http://symboldictionary.net/?p=1933.

p.318 **"Lord God, heavenly King, almighty God and Father, we worship you, we give you thanks, we praise you for your glory":** The Book of Common Prayer, Rite II Eucharist.

p.319 The International Consultation on English Texts has proved the translation for the Episcopal Book of Common Prayer and the Lutheran Book of Worship which translates the Holy Spirit as a "He" even though in the Greek the article is neuter and not gender specific. The English Language Liturgical Commission's translation more accurately captures the original Greek by using the word "who." The updated Roman Missal in 2011 changed their translation to "who."

p.319 **It has been suggested that the earliest form of the Holy Trinity was derived from the Gnostics: Father (The Creator), Mother (Sophia/Wisdom) and Son (Christ):** See the Gospel of Philip.

p.321　Bolen, Jean Shinoda. *Goddesses in Everywoman, Powerful Archetypes in Women's Lives the Twentieth Anniversary Edition*. Quill, 2004., Johnson, Elizabeth A. She *Who Is, The Mystery of God in Feminist Theological Discourse*. Crossroad Herde, 1992.

p.325　**"I am the whore and the holy woman":** Translation by, George W. MacRae, Thunder Perfect Mind, The Gnostic Society Library, The Nag Hammadi Library, accessed on April 9, 2017, http://gnosis.org/naghamm/thunder.html.

p.335　**By the time Christopher Columbus reached the Caribbean in 1492, historians estimate that there were 10 million indigenous peoples living in U.S. territory. But by 1900, the number had reduced to less than 300,000:** United to End Genocide, accessed on April 9, 2017, http://endgenocide.org/learn/past-genocides/native-americans/.

p. 336　**"To fully comprehend U.S. policy toward Indians it is important to realize that policy was grounded in the nation's fundamental commitment to territorial expansion":** American History Oxford Research Encyclopedias, accessed on April 9, 2017, http://americanhistory.oxfordre.com/view/10.1093/acrefore/9780199329175.001.0001/acrefore-9780199329175-e-3#acrefore-9780199329175-e-3-div1-5.

p.326　**After the Great Chicago Fire in 1871, much of the city is rebuilt with trees from the forests in North Eastern Arkansas, including the trees cut down in Blytheville:** Greater Blytheville Area, Chamber of Commerce, Accessed on December 31, 2013, http://www.greaterblytheville.com/live_and_work/history.aspx.

p.333　**the greatest trap in our life is not success, popularity, or power, but self-rejection..."** Nouwen, Henri J.M. Ibid.

CHAPTER 10-INCARNATION

p.353　**"You will love again the stranger who was your self":** "Love After Love" is a poem by Derek Walcott, part of *Collected Poems, 1948-1984* (1986). Steven Gould Axelrod (ed.) (2012). *The New Anthology of American Poetry: Vol. III: Postmodernisms 1950-Present*. Rutgers University Press. p. 257.

p.353 **God's breath moves through the mended flute**: I must nod to the Sufi poet Hafiz whose poetry I love and who also writes, " I am the hole on the flute that Gods breath flows through."

p.354 **In the early 1800s people from all over the area flock to Rome, New York to see for themselves this revival that breaks out when Charles Finney speak:** Memoirs of Charles Finney, from the website, The Gospel Truth, Accessed on December 31, 2013, http://www.gospeltruth.net/1868Memoirs/mem13.htm. See also the website of Last Days Ministry, and the writing of Keith and Melody Green, Accessed December 31, 2013 http://www.lastdaysministries.org/Groups/1000087751/Last_Days_Ministries/Articles/By_Charles_G/God_Comes_To/God_Comes_To.aspx. See also The Christian History Institute, https://www.christianhistoryinstitute.org/magazine/article/charles-grandison-finney/.

p.357 **Their website boasts that this church will be the sight of End Times revival:** About Rome Christian Center, Accessed December 31, 2013m http://romechristiancenter.org/About_RCC.html.

p.363 **Whatever you do to the least of these, you do to me:** Mathew 25:40.

p.362 **We have wept the blood of countless ages:** *The World of the American Indian*, (National Geographic Society, 1974) p. 384.

p.362 **"Because religion has such a compelling hold on the deep psyches of so many people, feminists cannot afford to leave it in the hands of the fathers…":** Christ, Carol Ibid.

p.363 **Today Native American Indians in the US are twice as likely to live in poverty … See:** http://en.wikibooks.org/wiki/American_Indians_Today/Current_problems Mental Health Disparity Fact Sheet, by the American Psychological Association, Accessed December 31, 2013, http://www.psychiatry.org/File%20Library/Practice/Diversity%20OMNA/Diversity%20Resources/Fact-Sheet---Native-Americans.pdf.

p.364 **The apology is buried in The Defense Appropriate Act of 2010:** Native News Network, Connecting Native American Voices, http://www.nativenewsnetwork.com/apology-to-american-indians-unacceptable.html.

p.364 **"We each have a job to do. The descendants of the colonists need to acknowledge the atrocity, and indigenous people, we have a job to do too: it is to forgive":** Speech by Lyla June, Diné (Navajo) musician, poet, youth activist presented to over 500 clergy at Standing Rock in Cannon Ball, ND on November 3, 2016.

p.364 **American Indians were twice as likely to experience a rape/sexual assault compared to all races:** RAINN Rape, Abuse, & Incest National Network, Accessed December 31, 2013, http://www.rainn.org/get-information/statistics/sexual-assault-victims.

p.364 **According to RAINN, the Rape, Abuse & Incest, National Network Sexual: sexual assaults happen every two minutes in the U.S,** See above link.

p.364 **The crime rate against women in the United States is significantly higher than in other country…:** Kansas State University, Accessed December 31, 2013,
http://www.k-state.edu/media/webzine/Didyouhearyes/stats.html.

p.366 **Let the whole world see and know that things which were cast down are being raised up and things which had grown old are being made new:** The Episcopal Book of Common Prayer, Ordination Service.

Select Bibliography

Birkerts, Sven. *The Art of Time in Memoir, Then, Again.* Graywolf Press, 2008.

Christ, Carol P. "Why Women Need the Goddess: Phenomenological, Psychological, and Political Reflections." *Women and Values Readings in Recent Feminist Philosophy.* Wadsworth Publishing, 1986.

Cohen, Kerry. *Loose Girl, A Memoir of Promiscuity.* Hyperion, 2008.

Eliade, Mircea. Rites *and Symbols of Initiation, the Mystery of Birth and Rebirth.* Spring Publications; Reprint edition, 2009.

Griffin, Susan. *A Chorus of Stones, the Private Life of War.* Anchor Books, 1992.

Griffin, Susan. *Rape, the Politics of Consciousness.* Harper & Row, 1979.

Griffin, Susan. *The Eros of Everyday Life, Essays on Ecology, Gender and Society.* Doubleday, 1995.

Johnson, Elizabeth A. She *Who Is, The Mystery of God in Feminist Theological Discourse.* Crossroad Herde, 1992.

Kalsched, Donald E. *The Inner World of Trauma, Archetypal Defenses of the Personal Spirit.* Routledge, 1996.

McKee, Robert. *Story.* Harper Collins Publishing, 1997.

Myers, Linda Joy. *The Power of Memoir, How to Write Your Healing Story.* Jossey-Bass, 2010.

Perera, Sylvia Brinton. *Descent to the Goddess, A Way of Initiation for Women.* Airlift Book Company, 1982.

Pinkola Estes, Clarissa. *Women Who Run With the Wolves, Myths and Stories of the Wild Woman Archetype.* Ballantine Books, 1992.

Ramshaw, Gail. *Under the Tree of Life, the Religion of a Feminist Christian.* Continuum Publishing, 1998.

Rigoglioso, Marguerite. *The Cult of Divine Birth in Ancient Greece.* Palgrave Macmillan, 2009.

Silverberg, Robert. *The Mound Builders.* Ohio University Press, 1968.

Qualls-Corbett, Nancy. *The Sacred Prostitute, Eternal Aspects of the Feminine.* Inner City Books, 1988.

TePaske, Bradley A. *Rape and Ritual, A Psychological Study.* Inner City Books, 1982.

White, Emily. *Fast Girls, Teenage Tribes and the Myth of the Slut.* Berkley Books, 2002.

Woodman, Marion. *The Pregnant Virgin.* Inner City Books, 1985. (p. 78).

Woolger, Jennifer & Roger. *The Goddess Within, a Guide to the Eternal Myths that Shape Women's Lives.* Fawcett Columbine, 1987.

Websites

http://www.native-americans-online.com/
http://www.bellevue.net/CityInformation/HistoryofBellevue.aspx
http://www.uark.edu/campus-resources/archinfo/blytheaker.html
http://communitylink.com/blytheville-arkansas/2011/09/19/history/
http://www.argenweb.net/mississippi/history.htm
http://files.usgwarchives.net/ar/mississippi/history/goodspd.txt
http://www.nanations.com/burialcustoms/scaffold_burial.htm
http://americanindianshistory.blogspot.com/2011/07/native-american-burials-trees-and.html
http://archive.org/stream/sacrificetomorni06lint/sacrificetomorni06lint_djvu.txt
http://www.romenewyork.com/organization.asp?orgid=73
http://romechristiancenter.org/
http://www.lastdaysministries.org/Groups/1000087751/Last_Days_Ministries/Articles/By_Charles_G/God_Comes_To/God_Comes_To.aspx
http://www.pbs.org/indiancountry/history/trail.html
http://www.ashevillenc.com/area_info/cherokee_nc
http://www.wresfm.com/avl_black_history.php
http://www.ethnoleaflets.com/leaflets/peyote.htm
http://www.geoman.com/jim/ancientmystery.html
http://www.nwmissouri.edu/library/courses/history/COLTERGUNN.HTM
http://www.mogenweb.org/nodaway/earlyhist/1911.htm
http://www.visitingnorthfield.com/history.html
http://www.hotcakencyclopedia.com/ho.QuapahOrigins.html
http://www.rainn.org/get-information/statistics/sexual-assault-victims
http://www.k-state.edu/media/webzine/Didyouhearyes/stats.html
http://www.ibiblio.org/rcip/mvrv.html
http://www.thesongsofhafiz.com/hafiz-and-madness.htm
http://aktalakota.stjo.org/site/News2?page=NewsArticle&id=8818
http://divinecosmos.com

TARALOMA
EARTH TEMPLE

VISIT TARALOMA EARTH TEMPLE
Come home to your sacred body.

www.taraloma.com

Jessica Zdenek, Dove Oracle Priestess

ALSO BY JESSICA ZDENEK

Paper Cranes: A Collection of Poems by Jessica Zdenek

Available on Amazon.com

Made in the USA
Lexington, KY
05 October 2018